Reading Architecture
A Visual Lexicon SECOND EDITION

Owen Hopkins

Laurence King Publishing

Introduction

What makes a work of architecture? In his seminal *An Outline of European Architecture*, first published in 1943, the great architectural historian Nikolaus Pevsner made a now famous comparison: 'A bicycle shed is a building; Lincoln Cathedral is a piece of architecture.' 'Nearly everything', he continued, 'that encloses space on a scale sufficient for a human being to move in is a building; the term architecture applies only to buildings designed with a view to aesthetic appeal.'

Few would disagree that a building's appearance is among an architect's chief concerns. However, the insistence that something as subjective as 'aesthetic appeal' be the defining characteristic of a work of architecture is more contentious. Beauty is in the eye of the beholder, and even if a building is 'designed with a view to aesthetic appeal', there is no reason why those who view it would necessarily find it appealing.

In reality, people's responses to architecture are individual, often inconsistent and are constantly changing. A dramatic case in point is the Brutalist architecture of 1960s and 1970s Britain, which polarized opinion when first built and continues to do so today. Yet despite the divergence in opinion, few would doubt its claim to be architecture. Furthermore, the distinction Pevsner draws between a building – which he implicitly characterizes as being purely functional, its form and materials solely determined by its intended function – and a work of architecture is too stark in reality. Even buildings whose architects proclaim to be following entirely functionalist philosophies – crystallized in the dictum 'form follows function' – are designed so that they communicate the function they are intended to fulfil through their appearance.

All modes of architecture have the power to transmit ideas and emotions irrespective of whether a building is designed to elicit 'aesthetic appeal'. I would suggest that what makes a building architecture is its ability to communicate and to transmit meaning; indeed, we might say that architecture is 'building with meaning'. Far from a literal art, the ways in which meaning in architecture are encoded and transmitted are unique and quite different to, say, how one might 'read' a painting. Architectural meaning can be constructed in many different ways: through form, materials, scale, ornamentation or, most explicitly, signage. Thus, the meanings that a building can hold inevitably tend to be abstract: for example, the demonstration of a patron's social and cultural status through building in the latest fashionable style; the memories and associations activated by reviving an older architectural style; or the display of wealth and power in a building's scale and the use of expensive materials and ostentatious ornamentation. At its core, a work of architecture is a representation of its builders or patron – and in varying extents, its architect too – their ideas, aspirations and motivations, as well as the social, economic, political and environmental contexts in which they are formed. This book, therefore, is about how meaning is constructed in architecture.

The origins of the architectural dictionary or glossary – for although this book does not conform to those types, it has its roots in those precursors – lie in the seventeenth and eighteenth centuries when the architectural interests of professionals and amateurs alike saw a slew of publications meeting that demand. Sometimes an architectural dictionary or glossary was included as a kind of appendix to a longer work, and this is often still the case today. Even when existing as independent works, most architectural dictionaries or glossaries are, from the very earliest examples, arranged alphabetically, with illustrations a secondary consideration, if present at all.

Some works have tried to give more priority to the visual, most notably Jill Lever and John Harris's *Illustrated Dictionary of Architecture, 800–1914* (1991; first published in 1969 as *Illustrated Glossary of Architecture, 850–1830*). However, even in a work such as this, for someone faced with an unfamiliar architectural element in a building or drawing, it still remains very difficult to find out its name and description. As with a web search engine, you need to know what you are looking for before you can find it.

In addition, as with Lever and Harris's book, few such works cover twentieth- and twenty-first-century architecture or, if they do, hardly at all. The reasons for this deficiency are not hard to understand. While Classical and Gothic architecture, with their relatively coherent repertoires of architectural detail, lend themselves to such classificatory expositions, much modern and contemporary architecture, whose descriptive terms are in any case still in comparative flux, does not employ such readily assimilable stylistic languages. While inevitably heavily indebted to existing works, this book aims to go beyond their limitations both in its structure and extent.

Encompassing Western architecture, from Classical Greece right up to the present day, this book is intended to act as a visual guide to the various ways in which a building can be articulated: from wall renderings and roof structures, to column types and decorative mouldings. It is heavily illustrated so that almost every element is represented in annotated photographs or line drawings. From the start, the intention behind the book has been to transcend the problems inherent in traditional architectural dictionaries or glossaries arranged alphabetically. Consequently, the book prioritizes buildings themselves through photographs and annotations and, in its structure, breaks architecture down to its fundamental ideas and components.

The book consists of four heavily cross-referenced chapters. The first chapter focuses on ten Building Types. Although the examples of each type vary in time and place, they have been chosen because they embody certain characteristics integral to that particular type. Other building groupings included in this chapter have been made in accordance to forms or morphologies which have been deemed enduring over time and been influential on many different building types. In this way, the chapter is intended to act as the reader's 'first port of call', so that when confronted with, say, a public building, one can turn to that section and find the example with the most closely matching architectural characteristics. From there, one can follow the various 'signposts' to chapters 2 and 3, which deal with particular elements in more detail.

The second chapter, Structures, stems from the premise that almost all architectural languages are in some way derived from the basic articulation of a building's structure. As such, it transcends particular architectural styles to focus on several basic structural elements – Columns and Piers and Arches – as well as the structures enabled by and which are characteristic to widely used building materials: Timber, Concrete and Steel. This chapter functions similarly to the first in 'signposting' to other chapters but also, because of its greater detail on particular elements, acts as a final destination in its own right.

Chapter 3 focuses on Architectural Elements – key components present in all buildings irrespective of style, scale or form. These are Walls and Surfaces, Windows and Doors, Roofs, and Stairs and Lifts. Along with a building's overall form and scale, the way in which particular architectural elements are used is one of the chief means by which a building can be made to convey meaning. Consequently, the articulation of these elements, such as in the rendering of a wall, the spacing and particular style of windows or choice of roof cladding material, can vary dramatically and the chapter aims to chart as many of these as possible.

The fourth and final chapter consists of a standard glossary which includes cross-references to where each term is illustrated in the rest of the book. The glossary comprises only elements mentioned in the first three chapters, and, like the book itself, while comprehensive, it is not encyclopaedic. With the book's main focus being on visible elements and features, many components pertaining to usually obscured building structures are not represented. Also, some overly archaic terms are omitted for the sake of clarity and space. It is also important to note that the book concentrates on the Western architectural tradition; although as architecture has become globalized in the second half of the twentieth century, some more recent examples are included from outside Europe and its spheres of influence. Readers dealing with non-Western buildings can refer to more specialized works.

'Architecture aims at eternity', remarked Christopher Wren, the great architect of seventeenth- and early-eighteenth-century London. Fittingly, this observance is vividly acted out by his very own St Paul's Cathedral, which stands as an enduring emblem of the city and nation. Few buildings are constructed with the same grand aspirations and ostentation as St Paul's. Yet from the grandest monument to the lowliest shack, all buildings have the potential to offer powerful insights into both the societies that created them and those that see and use the building today. Thus, the ability to read a building and to decode its meanings offers not simply a greater understanding of that particular building but of how society and the world around us is constituted – and is one which this book hopes to make easier.

The Classical Temple

The Renaissance Church

The Baroque Church

Fortified Buildings

The Medieval Cathedral

Country Houses and Villas

Street-Facing Buildings

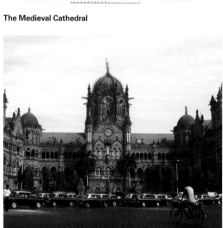

Public Buildings

The Modern Block

High-Rise Buildings

Contemporary Buildings

CHAPTER 1 Building Types

The notion of building type is a fundamental component of the practice, theory and study of architecture. Building types have existed as long as two separate buildings have been built to carry out the same function – and could thus be grouped according to that common function. Types range from the very broad, such as houses or churches, to the comparatively narrow – for example, science laboratories or observatories. Furthermore, within particular typologies there are whole series of subtypologies: for example, while buildings used for human habitation are classed as houses, there are, of course, many different types of house.

Although typologies can permeate through the centuries, building types are not immutable but are dependent on the political, economic, religious and social conditions of a particular period or location. For example, as the ecclesiastical examples included in the medieval cathedral, the Renaissance church and the Baroque church illustrate, changes in religious practice and theory have at various times over history induced the evolution or, indeed, formation of new cathedral and church typologies. Moreover, deep-seated changes in societies have precipitated the creation of new building types. The advent of the modern age saw the rise of new and often revolutionary – both in structure and aesthetics – building types related to industrial means of production. Yet the formation of new building types in this way has not necessarily precluded adaptation and appropriation from existing typologies. A notable example of this was the erection in the eighteenth and nineteenth centuries of great public buildings which invariably drew from a host of ancient Roman sources and typologies.

Several building types – the **Classical Temple**, the **Medieval Cathedral**, the **Renaissance Church** and the **Baroque Church** – have been selected for this chapter because they stand as fundamental models in the history of architecture. Other 'metatypes', such as **Country Houses and Villas** and **Public Buildings**, have been chosen because, while there is wide variety within these broad groupings, there exist certain fundamental characteristics that transcend style and are more to do with siting and function, which those types of building inescapably embody.

As buildings' functions have increased, diversified and become more specialized, so existing building types have been superseded and, as noted above, others have emerged. While type remains central to the study of a building in its historical context, the various types and subtypes are too numerous for it to be an entirely effective means of categorization and identification. Thus, in this chapter several categories have been introduced, alongside standard building typologies, which group and distinguish buildings at a level of abstraction above that of type: that is, according to archetypal forms or morphologies that have endured over time. In these sections, buildings are grouped according to fundamental shapes or features: the **Modern Block** considers buildings whose cuboidal form derives from the particular structural properties of modern materials; **High-Rise Buildings** similarly groups buildings according to common formal characteristics; **Street-Facing Buildings** transcends particular time periods to encompass buildings responding to the fundamental constraints of a street-facing site; and **Contemporary Buildings** considers the key trends and forms that define architecture today.

These categories and examples do, inevitably, prioritize exterior elevations over interior spaces. While some interior elements have been included in some examples, in others there exists too much disparity for any particular building to act as a broad-ranging example. Rather than being wholly comprehensive, these key groupings are intended to help elucidate the elements of the particular types that fall under them as well as acting as signposts to later sections, focused on their various architectural components.

The Classical Temple › The Temple Front

A much emulated type in the history of architecture, the colonnaded Greek temple, from which the Roman variety derived, is thought to have emerged between the tenth and seventh centuries BC. Early temples were constructed from mud-bricks to which were later added wooden columns and superstructures, thus forming the familiar but highly adaptable prototype. Between the sixth and fourth centuries – during the height of Classical civilization – stone became the material of choice and was used for the great many temples that were built throughout the Greek peninsula.

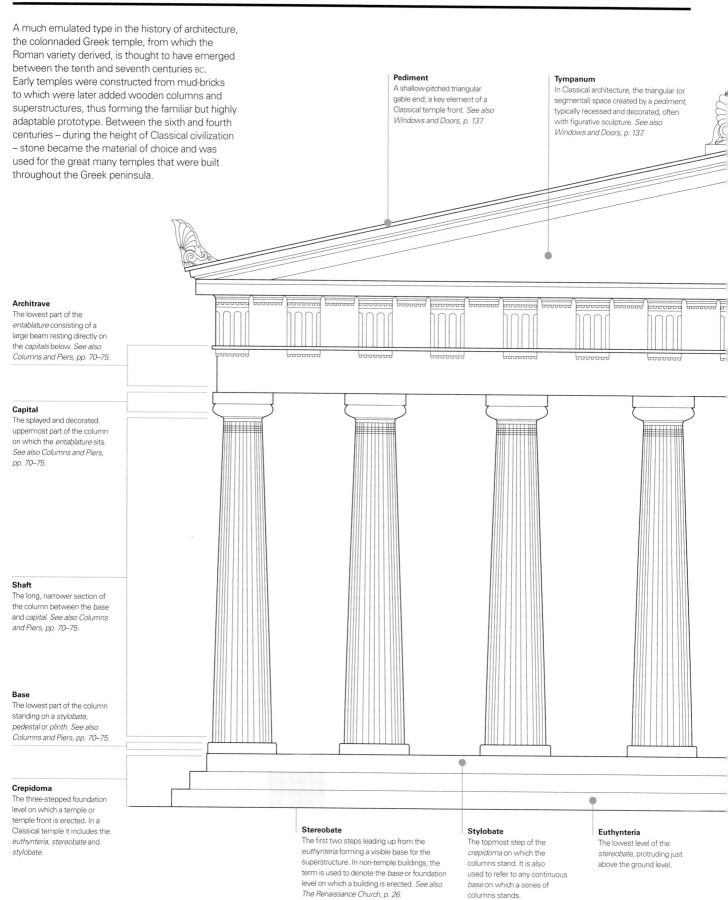

Pediment
A shallow-pitched triangular gable end; a key element of a Classical temple front. *See also Windows and Doors, p. 137.*

Tympanum
In Classical architecture, the triangular (or segmental) space created by a *pediment*, typically recessed and decorated, often with figurative sculpture. *See also Windows and Doors, p. 137.*

Architrave
The lowest part of the *entablature* consisting of a large beam resting directly on the *capitals* below. *See also Columns and Piers, pp. 70–75.*

Capital
The splayed and decorated uppermost part of the column on which the *entablature* sits. *See also Columns and Piers, pp. 70–75.*

Shaft
The long, narrower section of the column between the *base* and *capital. See also Columns and Piers, pp. 70–75.*

Base
The lowest part of the column standing on a *stylobate*, *pedestal* or *plinth. See also Columns and Piers, pp. 70–75.*

Crepidoma
The three-stepped foundation level on which a temple or temple front is erected. In a Classical temple it includes the *euthynteria, stereobate* and *stylobate.*

Stereobate
The first two steps leading up from the *euthynteria* forming a visible base for the superstructure. In non-temple buildings, the term is used to denote the *base* or foundation level on which a building is erected. *See also The Renaissance Church, p. 26.*

Stylobate
The topmost step of the *crepidoma* on which the columns stand. It is also used to refer to any continuous *base* on which a series of columns stands.

Euthynteria
The lowest level of the *stereobate*, protruding just above the ground level.

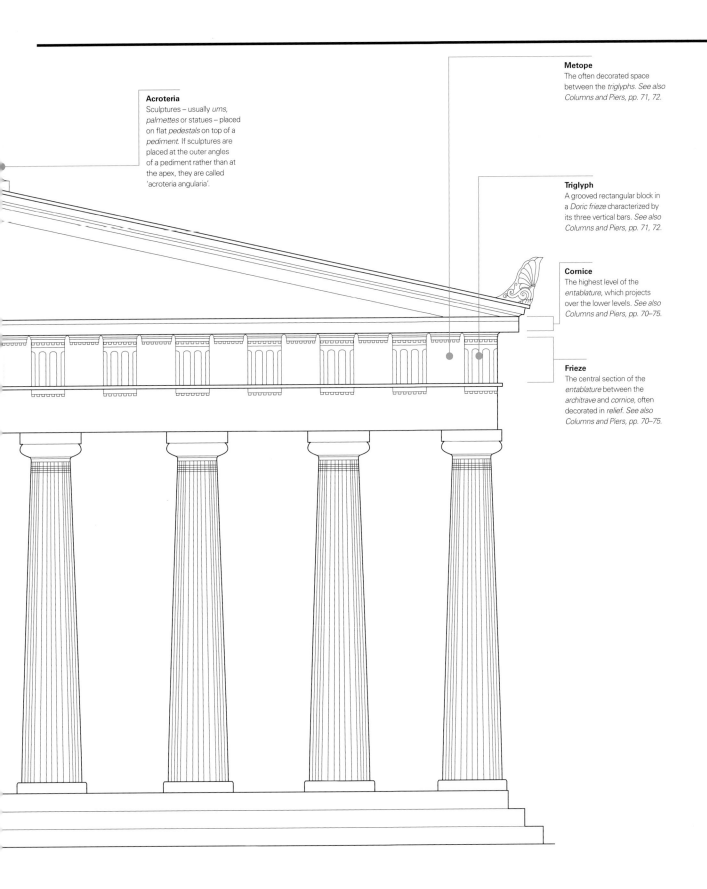

Acroteria
Sculptures – usually *urns*, *palmettes* or statues – placed on flat *pedestals* on top of a *pediment*. If sculptures are placed at the outer angles of a pediment rather than at the apex, they are called 'acroteria angularia'.

Metope
The often decorated space between the *triglyphs*. See also *Columns and Piers, pp. 71, 72*.

Triglyph
A grooved rectangular block in a *Doric frieze* characterized by its three vertical bars. See also *Columns and Piers, pp. 71, 72*.

Cornice
The highest level of the *entablature*, which projects over the lower levels. See also *Columns and Piers, pp. 70–75*.

Frieze
The central section of the *entablature* between the *architrave* and *cornice*, often decorated in *relief*. See also *Columns and Piers, pp. 70–75*.

The Classical Temple › Temple Front Widths

As well as in the particular Classical order employed, temple fronts can differ according to the number of columns used and the distance between them (called 'intercolumniation'). Temple fronts with two, four, six, eight or ten columns can be found in many periods of architecture and, thanks to their inherent adaptability, on a wide variety of building types. In a Classically correct building, only even numbers of columns are used so as to ensure a void (as opposed to a solid column) at the centre of the composition.

Distyle ›
A temple front composed of two columns (or *pilasters*). *See also Public Buildings, pp. 47, 50.* (South doorway, Palace of Charles V, Alhambra, Granada, Spain.)

Tetrastyle ››
Four columns. *See also Public Buildings, p. 47.* (Thomas Jefferson's Monticello, Virginia, USA.)

Hexastyle ››
Six columns. *See also Country Houses and Villas, p. 35; Public Buildings, p. 50.* (Maison Carrée, Nîmes, France.)

Octastyle ›
Eight columns. (Pantheon, Rome, Italy.)

Decastyle ›
Ten columns. (University College, London, UK.)

Cyclostyle ››
Circular range of columns (without a *naos* or core). *See also (peripteral) tholos, p. 12.* (Rotunda, Stowe, UK.)

The Classical Temple › Intercolumniation

The distance between two adjacent Classical columns – 'intercolumniation' – is dependent not only on the prescriptions of the particular Classical order but also on the parameters of a strict proportional system. These were defined most famously by the Roman architect Vitruvius in the first century BC and were subsequently taken up by a whole host of Renaissance theorists.

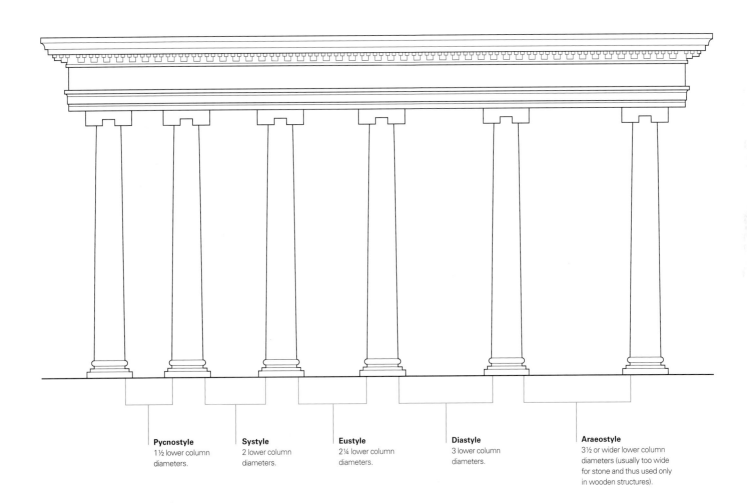

Pycnostyle
1½ lower column diameters.

Systyle
2 lower column diameters.

Eustyle
2¼ lower column diameters.

Diastyle
3 lower column diameters.

Araeostyle
3½ or wider lower column diameters (usually too wide for stone and thus used only in wooden structures).

The Classical Temple › Types

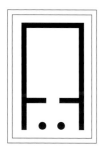

Temple in antis
The simplest temple form. It has no *peristasis*, and the fronts of the protruding walls of the *cella* – called *antae* – and two columns of the *pronaos* provide the frontal emphasis.

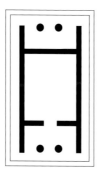

Double temple in antis
A temple in antis with the addition of an *opisthodomos*.

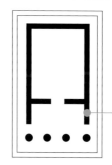

Prostyle
When the *pronaos* is fronted by *free-standing columns* (usually four or six).

Antae
The fronts of the two protruding walls of the *cella* that make up the *pronaos* (or the *opisthodomos*), often articulated with a *pilaster* or applied half-column.

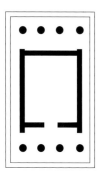

Amphiprostyle
A *prostyle* arrangement is repeated for the *opisthodomos* as well as for the *pronaos*.

Peripteral
A temple surrounded by *colonnades* on all four sides.

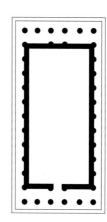

Pseudoperipteral
The sides of the temple are articulated with *engaged columns* or *pilasters* rather than *free-standing columns*.

(Peripteral) tholos
A circular range of columns surrounding a circular *cella*. *See also Cyclostyle, p. 10.*

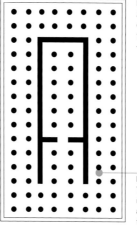

Dipteral
A temple surrounded on all four sides by two rows of columns – a double *peristasis*.

Peristasis
The single or double row of columns forming an envelope around a temple and providing structural support.

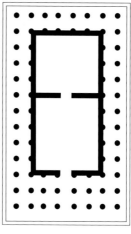

Pseudodipteral
A temple in which the *pronaos* is articulated by a double row of *free-standing columns*, the sides and rear having a single colonnade (which may be matched by *engaged columns* or *pilasters* on the *naos*).

The Classical Temple › Internal Spaces

Greek temples were constructed to house sacred cult statues of deities, the most famous being Phidias's long-lost monumental gold statue of Athena in the Parthenon. Temple plans were fairly consistent, born from a discrete number of spatial elements. Although the plan emerged in accordance with the specific functions of the type, the tight integration of plan and elevation means that buildings based on the type, even if their functions are different (for example, a nineteenth-century public building) often maintain vestigial planning components derived from the temple typology.

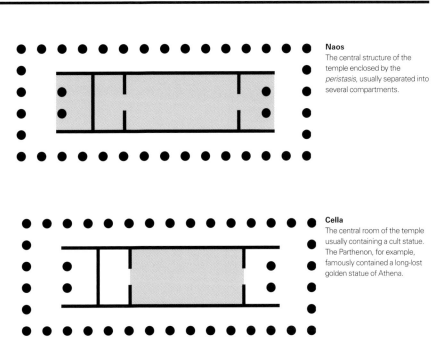

Naos
The central structure of the temple enclosed by the *peristasis*, usually separated into several compartments.

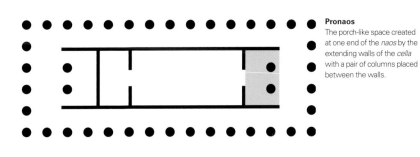

Cella
The central room of the temple usually containing a cult statue. The Parthenon, for example, famously contained a long-lost golden statue of Athena.

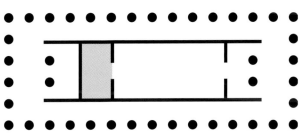

Pronaos
The porch-like space created at one end of the *naos* by the extending walls of the *cella* with a pair of columns placed between the walls.

Adyton
A rarely included room at the far end of the *cella* which, if present, is used instead of the cella to hold the cult object.

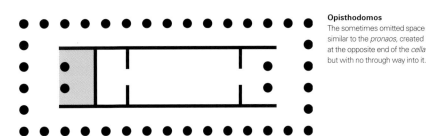

Opisthodomos
The sometimes omitted space similar to the *pronaos*, created at the opposite end of the *cella* but with no through way into it.

BACK　　　　　　　　　　　**FRONT**

The Medieval Cathedral › West-End Portal

Intended to impress and inspire, the medieval cathedral's west and transept arm fronts were usually composed around a tri-partite series of openings whose large surrounds were often heavily decorated.

The cathedral at Chartres, illustrated here, is considered to be one of the finest examples of a Gothic cathedral. Its west front and south tower date from the mid twelfth century, while the taller and more flamboyant north tower was added in the sixteenth century. The south portal with its profusion of decorative sculpture was completed in the early thirteenth century.

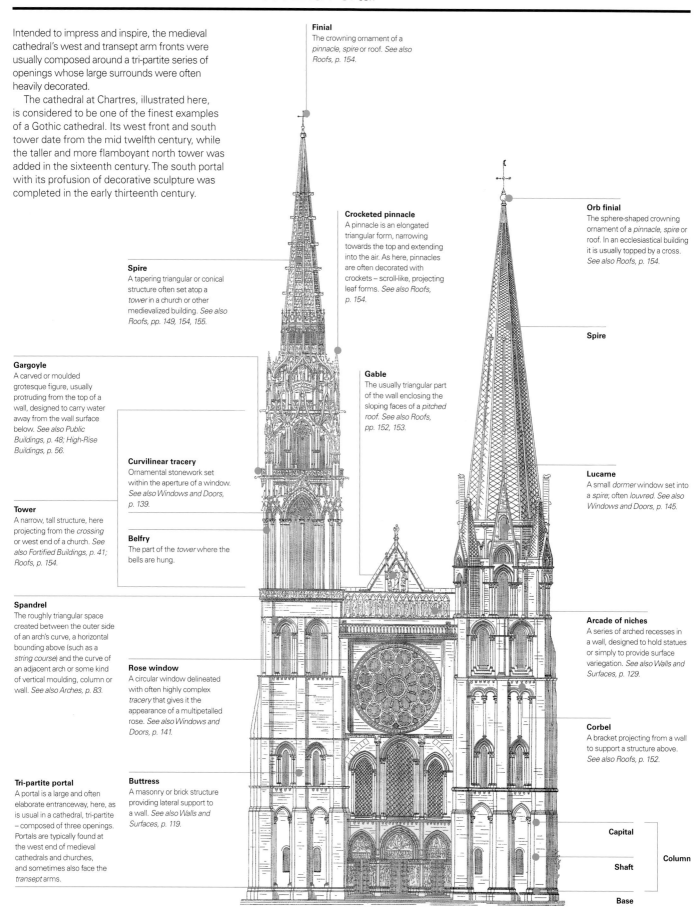

Finial
The crowning ornament of a *pinnacle, spire* or roof. *See also Roofs, p. 154.*

Crocketed pinnacle
A pinnacle is an elongated triangular form, narrowing towards the top and extending into the air. As here, pinnacles are often decorated with crockets – scroll-like, projecting leaf forms. *See also Roofs, p. 154.*

Spire
A tapering triangular or conical structure often set atop a *tower* in a church or other medievalized building. *See also Roofs, pp. 149, 154, 155.*

Gable
The usually triangular part of the wall enclosing the sloping faces of a *pitched roof. See also Roofs, pp. 152, 153.*

Orb finial
The sphere-shaped crowning ornament of a *pinnacle, spire* or roof. In an ecclesiastical building it is usually topped by a cross. *See also Roofs, p. 154.*

Spire

Lucarne
A small *dormer* window set into a *spire;* often *louvred. See also Windows and Doors, p. 145.*

Gargoyle
A carved or moulded grotesque figure, usually protruding from the top of a wall, designed to carry water away from the wall surface below. *See also Public Buildings, p. 48; High-Rise Buildings, p. 56.*

Curvilinear tracery
Ornamental stonework set within the aperture of a window. *See also Windows and Doors, p. 139.*

Tower
A narrow, tall structure, here projecting from the *crossing* or west end of a church. *See also Fortified Buildings, p. 41; Roofs, p. 154.*

Belfry
The part of the *tower* where the bells are hung.

Spandrel
The roughly triangular space created between the outer side of an arch's curve, a horizontal bounding above (such as a *string course*) and the curve of an adjacent arch or some kind of vertical moulding, column or wall. *See also Arches, p. 83.*

Rose window
A circular window delineated with often highly complex *tracery* that gives it the appearance of a multipetalled rose. *See also Windows and Doors, p. 141.*

Arcade of niches
A series of arched recesses in a wall, designed to hold statues or simply to provide surface variegation. *See also Walls and Surfaces, p. 129.*

Corbel
A bracket projecting from a wall to support a structure above. *See also Roofs, p. 152.*

Tri-partite portal
A portal is a large and often elaborate entranceway, here, as is usual in a cathedral, tri-partite – composed of three openings. Portals are typically found at the west end of medieval cathedrals and churches, and sometimes also face the *transept* arms.

Buttress
A masonry or brick structure providing lateral support to a wall. *See also Walls and Surfaces, p. 119.*

Capital

Shaft

Base

Column

The Medieval Cathedral › South Transept Portal

Pinnacle
An elongated triangular form, narrowing towards the top and extending into the air. See also Roofs, p. 154.

Clustered column
A column composed of several shafts. See also Columns and Piers, p. 69.

Parapet
A low protective wall or balustrade running along the edge of a roof, balcony or bridge. See also Roofs, p. 152.

Gable
The usually triangular part of the wall enclosing the sloping faces of a pitched or gabled roof. See also Roofs, pp. 152, 153.

Buttress
A masonry or brick structure providing lateral support to a wall. See also Walls and Surfaces, p. 119.

Pitched or gabled roof
A single-ridged roof with two sloping sides and gables at the two ends. The term pitched roof is sometimes used to refer to any sloping roof. See also Roofs, pp. 148, 152.

Gablet
A small gable used to top a buttress. See also Roofs, p. 153.

Octofoil window
A window shape formed by tracery using eight foils – the curved space formed between two cusps. See Windows and Doors, p. 138.

Clerestory window
A window piercing the upper storey of the nave, transepts or choir and looking out over the aisle roof.

Niche with statue
A statue set in an arched recess in a wall surface. See also Walls and Surfaces, p. 129.

Curvilinear or flowing tracery
Tracery – ornamental stonework set within the aperture of a window – formed from series of continuously curving and intersecting bars. See also Windows and Doors, p. 139.

Undercroft window
A window giving light to the crypt.

Perron
An exterior set of steps leading to a grand entranceway or portal.

Tri-partite portal
A portal is a large and often elaborate entranceway, here, as is usual in a cathedral, tri-partite – composed of three openings. Portals are typically found at the west end of medieval cathedrals and churches, and sometimes also face the transept arms.

Aisle window
Window piercing the outer walls of the aisles – spaces on either side of the nave behind the main arcades.

The Medieval Cathedral › Plan

The medieval cathedral plan was based on the Latin cross, with a long nave, transept arms protruding from either side and the chancel beyond. While conforming to this overall schema, there are countless variations – almost as many as there are cathedrals – which differ in accordance to particular liturgical and practical requirements. Variations include second transept arms, double aisles, further entrances along the nave, extra chapels at the east end, and the addition of a whole host of subsidiary structures like chapter houses and cloisters outside the cathedral itself.

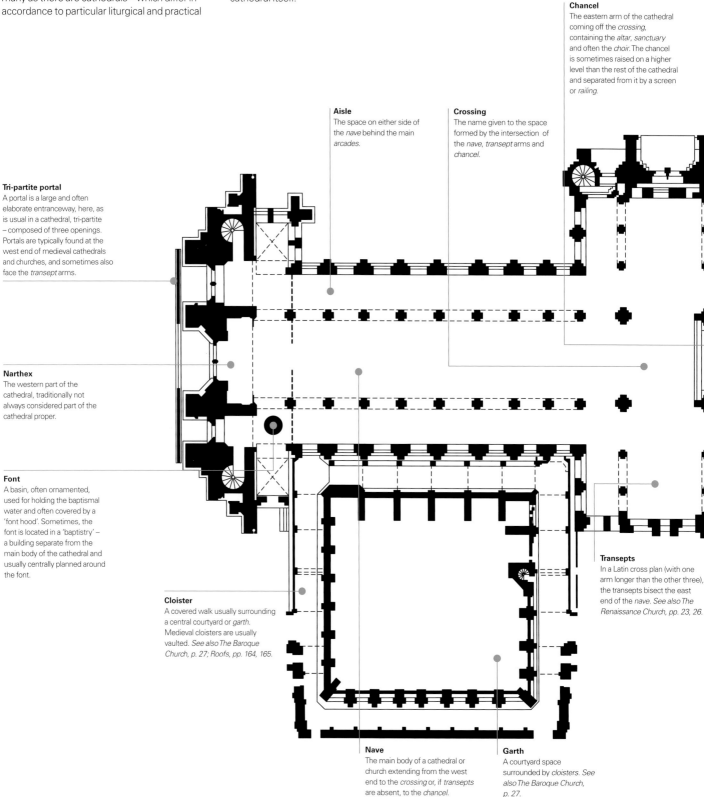

Chancel
The eastern arm of the cathedral coming off the *crossing*, containing the *altar*, *sanctuary* and often the *choir*. The chancel is sometimes raised on a higher level than the rest of the cathedral and separated from it by a screen or *railing*.

Aisle
The space on either side of the *nave* behind the main *arcades*.

Crossing
The name given to the space formed by the intersection of the *nave*, *transept* arms and *chancel*.

Tri-partite portal
A portal is a large and often elaborate entranceway, here, as is usual in a cathedral, tri-partite – composed of three openings. Portals are typically found at the west end of medieval cathedrals and churches, and sometimes also face the *transept* arms.

Narthex
The western part of the cathedral, traditionally not always considered part of the cathedral proper.

Font
A basin, often ornamented, used for holding the baptismal water and often covered by a 'font hood'. Sometimes, the font is located in a 'baptistry' – a building separate from the main body of the cathedral and usually centrally planned around the font.

Cloister
A covered walk usually surrounding a central courtyard or *garth*. Medieval cloisters are usually vaulted. *See also The Baroque Church, p. 27; Roofs, pp. 164, 165.*

Transepts
In a Latin cross plan (with one arm longer than the other three), the transepts bisect the east end of the *nave*. *See also The Renaissance Church, pp. 23, 26.*

Nave
The main body of a cathedral or church extending from the west end to the *crossing* or, if *transepts* are absent, to the *chancel*.

Garth
A courtyard space surrounded by *cloisters*. *See also The Baroque Church, p. 27.*

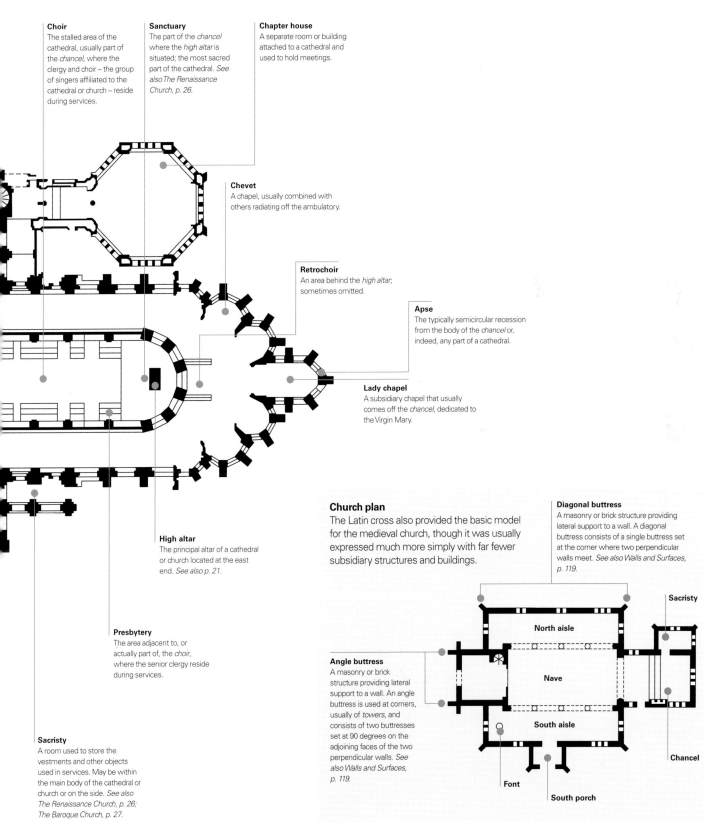

Choir
The stalled area of the cathedral, usually part of the *chancel*, where the clergy and choir – the group of singers affiliated to the cathedral or church – reside during services.

Sanctuary
The part of the *chancel* where the *high altar* is situated; the most sacred part of the cathedral. *See also The Renaissance Church, p. 26.*

Chapter house
A separate room or building attached to a cathedral and used to hold meetings.

Chevet
A chapel, usually combined with others radiating off the ambulatory.

Retrochoir
An area behind the *high altar*, sometimes omitted.

Apse
The typically semicircular recession from the body of the *chancel* or, indeed, any part of a cathedral.

Lady chapel
A subsidiary chapel that usually comes off the *chancel*, dedicated to the Virgin Mary.

High altar
The principal altar of a cathedral or church located at the east end. *See also p. 21.*

Presbytery
The area adjacent to, or actually part of, the *choir*, where the senior clergy reside during services.

Sacristy
A room used to store the vestments and other objects used in services. May be within the main body of the cathedral or church or on the side. *See also The Renaissance Church, p. 26; The Baroque Church, p. 27.*

Church plan

The Latin cross also provided the basic model for the medieval church, though it was usually expressed much more simply with far fewer subsidiary structures and buildings.

Diagonal buttress
A masonry or brick structure providing lateral support to a wall. A diagonal buttress consists of a single buttress set at the corner where two perpendicular walls meet. *See also Walls and Surfaces, p. 119.*

Angle buttress
A masonry or brick structure providing lateral support to a wall. An angle buttress is used at corners, usually of *towers*, and consists of two buttresses set at 90 degrees on the adjoining faces of the two perpendicular walls. *See also Walls and Surfaces, p. 119.*

North aisle

Nave

South aisle

Sacristy

Chancel

Font

South porch

The Medieval Cathedral › Section

The repeating arch is the integral structural as well as aesthetic component of a cathedral's interior. The round-headed arch supported by thick piers and walls is characteristic of Romanesque architecture. The structural possibilities of the pointed Gothic arch, which emerged in the twelfth century, allowed masons to build higher and with thinner supports. The advent of the flying buttress allowed the creation of large clerestory windows, which admitted much more light and, importantly, became frames for ornamental tracery and stained glass.

ROMANESQUE

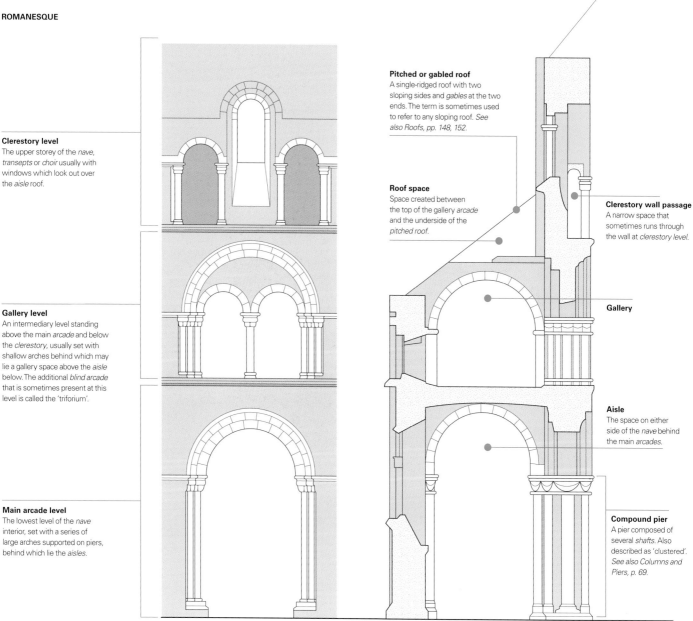

Clerestory level
The upper storey of the *nave*, *transepts* or *choir* usually with windows which look out over the *aisle* roof.

Gallery level
An intermediary level standing above the main *arcade* and below the *clerestory*, usually set with shallow arches behind which may lie a gallery space above the *aisle* below. The additional *blind arcade* that is sometimes present at this level is called the 'triforium'.

Main arcade level
The lowest level of the *nave* interior, set with a series of large arches supported on piers, behind which lie the *aisles*.

Pitched or gabled roof
A single-ridged roof with two sloping sides and *gables* at the two ends. The term is sometimes used to refer to any sloping roof. *See also Roofs, pp. 148, 152.*

Roof space
Space created between the top of the gallery *arcade* and the underside of the *pitched roof*.

Clerestory wall passage
A narrow space that sometimes runs through the wall at *clerestory level*.

Gallery

Aisle
The space on either side of the *nave* behind the main *arcades*.

Compound pier
A pier composed of several *shafts*. Also described as 'clustered'. *See also Columns and Piers, p. 69.*

Elevation

Section

EARLY ENGLISH

Flying buttress
A buttress is a masonry or brick structure that provides lateral support to a wall. Flying buttresses are typical in cathedrals and consist of 'flying' half-arches that help to carry down the thrust of the nave's high *vault* or roof. *See also Walls and Surfaces, p. 119.*

Lancet window
A tall and narrow pointed window, often grouped in threes; named after its resemblance to a lancet. *See also Windows and Doors, p. 141.*

Pitched or gabled roof
A single-ridged roof with two sloping sides and *gables* at the two ends. The term is sometimes used to refer to any sloping roof. *See also Roofs, pp. 148, 152.*

Rib
A projecting strip of masonry or brick that provides the structural support to a *vault. See also Roofs, p. 157.*

Web
The infilled surface between *ribs* in a *rib vault. See also Roofs, p. 161.*

Tympanum
In medieval architecture, the often decorated infilled space above the *imposts* of an arch supported by two smaller arches. *See also Windows and Doors, p. 137.*

Trumeau
The central *mullion* in an arched window or doorway, supporting a *tympanum* above two smaller arches. *See also Windows and Doors, p. 138.*

String course
A thin, horizontal moulded banding running across a wall. When a string course is continued over a column, it is called a 'shaft ring'. *See also Walls and Surfaces, p. 120.*

Spandrel
The roughly triangular space created between the outer side of an arch's curve, a horizontal bounding above (such as a *string course*) and the curve of an adjacent arch or some kind of vertical moulding, column or wall. *See also Arches, p. 82.*

Shaft
The long, narrower section of the column between the *base* and *capital. See also Columns and Piers, pp. 70–75.*

Capital
The splayed and decorated uppermost part of the column on which the entablature sits. *See also Columns and Piers, pp. 70–75.*

Base
The lowest part of the column standing on a *stylobate, pedestal* or *plinth. See also Columns and Piers, pp. 70, 71, 73, 74, 75.*

Equilateral arch
An arch formed from two intersecting curves, the centres of which are at the opposing *imposts.* The chords of each curve are equal to the arch *span. See also Arches, p. 80.*

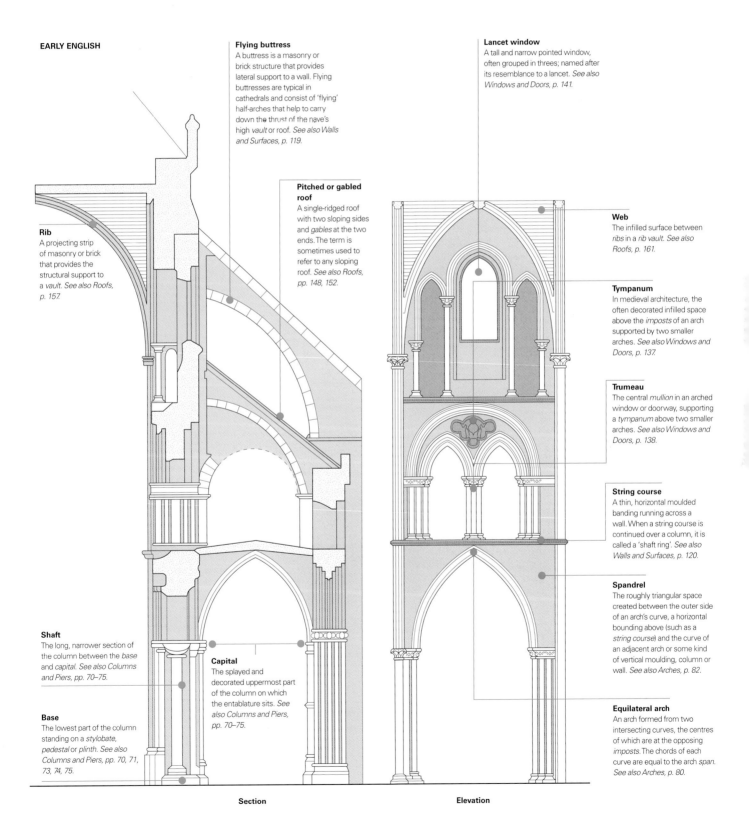

Section

Elevation

The Medieval Cathedral › Furnishings

Font ›
A basin, often ornamented, used for holding the baptismal water; sometimes covered by a 'font hood'. (Blagdon Church, Blagdon, Somerset, UK.)

Stoup ››
A small basin filled with holy water usually placed on the wall near the cathedral or church entrance. Some congregation members, especially in Roman Catholic churches, dip their fingers in this water and make the sign of the cross upon entering and leaving.

Rood/chancel screen ›
A screen separating the *choir* from the *crossing* or *nave*. The rood refers to the wooden sculptural representation of the Crucifixion surmounted on the rood loft above the rood beam. Sometimes a second screen called a 'pulpitum' is used to separate the choir from the crossing or nave, with the rood screen positioned further to the west. (Church of Our Lady, Bruges, Belgium.)

Pulpit ››
A raised and often ornamented platform from where a sermon is delivered. (Clonfert Cathedral, County Galway, Ireland.)

Tester/sounding board ›
The board suspended above the *altar* or *pulpit* to help project the voice of the priest or preacher. (Church of the Blessed Virgin Mary, Old Dilton, Wiltshire, UK.)

Baldacchino ››
A free-standing ceremonial *canopy* usually made of wood and often with cloth hangings. (St Peter's, Rome, Italy.)

Stalls ›
Rows of seats, usually in the *choir* but also elsewhere in the church, typically fixed with high sides and backs. (Church of San Giorgio Maggiore, Venice, Italy.)

Altar rails ››
A set of *railings* separating the *sanctuary* from the rest of the cathedral or church. *See also The Renaissance Church, pp. 26, 28.* (St Andrew's Church, Lyddington, Rutland, UK.)

Altar ›

The structure or table located in the sanctuary at the east end of the cathedral or church where Communion takes place. In a Protestant church, a table instead of a fixed altar is usually used for the preparation of Communion.

Predella ›

The step (here, steps) on which the *altar* stands above the rest of the *chancel*. The term can also refer to the paintings or sculptures at the bottom of an *altarpiece* or *reredos*. *See also The Renaissance Church, p. 28; The Baroque Church, p. 29.* (Basilica of El Escorial, Madrid, Spain.)

Ciborium ›

A *canopy*, usually supported by four columns, which covers the *altar*. (Euphrasian Basilica, Poreč, Croatia.)

Altarpiece ››

A painting or sculpture set behind the *altar*. *See also The Renaissance Church, p. 28; The Baroque Church, p. 29.* (Minorite Church of St Anthony of Padua, Eger, Hungary.)

Reredos ›

A usually wooden screen placed behind the *high altar*, often decorated with scenes depicting religious iconography or biblical events. (St George's Church, Bloomsbury, London, UK.)

Tabernacle ››

A box or container, often elaborately ornamented, in which the reserved sacrament is stored. (Jesuit church at Estancia Santa Catalina, Cordoba, Argentina.)

The Renaissance and Baroque Church › Exterior

The renewed appreciation of Classical architecture that emerged during the early fifteenth century in Italy was perhaps the most visibly enduring feature of the rebirth of Classical learning and culture that characterized the Renaissance. While the architecture of ancient Rome was now appreciated with a new vigour, the Romans had, of course, never constructed churches or cathedrals of a type that was now required. Therefore, few specific Classical models existed from which Renaissance architects could easily draw. Consequently, various architects reinterpreted the language of Classical architecture, abstracting its proportional systems and deploying its decorative elements for the requirements of their age.

Even in its still unfinished state, the Classical ideals of symmetry and harmony are notably apparent in the exterior of Giuliano da Sangallo the Elder's Santa Maria delle Carceri, Prato (1486–95). The building is a study of a rational approach to the theory and application of the elements of Classical architecture.

Giuliano da Sangallo the Elder, Santa Maria delle Carceri, Prato, Italy, 1486–95.

Cupola
The structure, usually circular or octagonal in plan, set atop a *dome*, heavily glazed so as to admit light into the space below. Also known as a 'lantern'. *See also Roofs, p. 157.*

Circular colonnade
A repeating series of columns supporting an *entablature*, here set in a circle.

Drum
The cylindrical structure on which the *dome* itself is raised. Also called a 'tambour'. *See also Roofs, p. 157.*

Pediment
A shallow-pitched triangular *gable* end; a key element of a Classical temple front. *See also Windows and Doors, p. 137.*

Tympanum oculus
A circular window set into the *tympanum* – the triangular space created by a *pediment*.

Ionic entablature
An entablature is the super-structure above the *capital* level composed of *architrave*, *frieze* and *cornice*. For the Ionic order, *see also Columns and Piers, p. 73.*

Coupled Ionic pilasters
Pilasters are flattened columns that project slightly from the face of a wall. When two are placed side by side they are said to be 'coupled'. For the Ionic order, *see also Columns and Piers, p. 73.*

Roman Doric entablature
The superstructure above the *capital* level, composed of *architrave*, *frieze* and *cornice*. For the Roman Doric order, *see also Columns and Piers, p. 71.*

Orb finial
The sphere-shaped crowning ornament of a *pinnacle, spire* or roof. In an ecclesiastical building it is usually topped by a cross. *See also Roofs, p. 154.*

Conical roof
A roof in the shape of a cone, usually sitting atop a *tower* or covering a *dome*. *See also Roofs, p. 149.*

Oculus
A simple circular window with no *tracery*. *See also Windows and Doors, p. 141; Roofs, pp. 157, 158.*

Pedimented doorway
A pediment is a shallow-pitched triangular *gable* end. It is a key element of a Classical temple front and is often used, as here, to top an aperture. *See also Windows and Doors, p. 137.*

Two-tone marble facing
See also Walls and Surfaces, p. 100.

Coupled Roman Doric pilasters
Pilasters are flattened columns that project slightly from the face of a wall. When two are placed side by side they are said to be 'coupled'. For the Roman Doric order, *see also Columns and Piers, p. 71.*

Transept
In a Greek cross plan, one of four projections from the church's central core. *See also The Medieval Cathedral, p. 16.*

The Renaissance and Baroque Church › Exterior

Built a century and a half after Santa Maria delle Carceri, the dramatic curving forms of Francesco Borromini's San Carlo alle Quattro Fontane, Rome (1638–41) illustrate a reinterpretation and reinvigoration of the Classical language. The church is a key example of the Baroque. A movement in architecture and art that favoured effects of drama and illusion, Baroque was, at root, bound up with seventeenth-century changes in church practices and politics, especially the Counter Reformation.

Francesco Borromini, San Carlo alle Quattro Fontane, Rome, 1638–41.

Corinthian entablature
The entablature is the superstructure above the *capital* level composed of *architrave, frieze* and *cornice*. For the Corinthian order, *see also Columns and Piers, p. 74.*

Coupled Greek Doric columns
Coupled columns are those placed side by side. For the Greek Doric order, *see also Columns and Piers, p. 72.*

Mask
A decorative motif, often a stylized human or animal face. *See also Walls and Surfaces, p. 128.*

Corinthian column
A typically cylindrical upright shaft or member composed of *base, shaft* and *capital*. For the Corinthian order, *see also Columns and Piers, p. 74.*

Broken-based pediment
A pediment whose horizontal base is broken in the centre. *See also Windows and Doors, p. 137.*

Column base panel
A panel is a rectangular recession or projection in a surface, here set into a column *base*.

Balustrade
A series of *balusters* that supports a *railing* or *coping*. *See also Windows and Doors, p. 144.*

Crossette
A corner of a rectangular moulding, especially one around a window or door, with small, vertical and horizontal off-sets or projections. *See also Walls and Surfaces, p. 126.*

Ionic entablature
The superstructure above the *capital* level composed of *architrave, frieze* and *cornice*. For the Ionic order, *see also Columns and Piers, p. 73.*

Ionic column
A typically cylindrical upright shaft or member composed of *base, shaft* and *capital*. For the Ionic order, *see also Columns and Piers, p. 73.*

Sculpture set within an arch

Concave temple front
A temple front which, rather than presenting a flat surface, recedes in the form of a curve.

Balustraded parapet
A parapet is a low protective wall running along the edge of a roof, *balcony* or bridge. A balustrade is a series of *balusters* that support a *railing* or *coping. See also Windows and Doors, p. 144; Roofs, p. 152.*

Medallion
A circular or oval decorative plaque, usually adorned with a sculptural or painted figure or scene. *See also Walls and Surfaces, p. 128.*

Corinthian entablature soffit
A soffit is the underside of a structure or surface, here the projection of a Corinthian *entablature.*

Orb finial
The sphere-shaped crowning ornament of a *pinnacle, spire* or roof. In an ecclesiastical building it is usually topped by a cross. *See also Roofs, p. 154.*

Cartouche
A typically oval tablet form, surrounded by scrolling and sometimes with a carved inscription. *See also Walls and Surfaces, p. 126.*

Convex aedicule
An aedicule is an architectural frame set into a wall, deployed to indicate a shrine in a sacred building, draw attention to a particular work of art or, as here, to provide additional surface variegation. *See also Walls and Surfaces, p. 119.*

Niche
An arched recess into a wall surface designed to hold a statue or simply to provide surface variegation. *See also Walls and Surfaces, p. 129.*

Niche with statue
A statue set in an arched recess into a wall surface. *See also Walls and Surfaces, p. 129.*

Term
A *pedestal* tapering towards the bottom and topped by a bust of a mythological figure or animal. The name 'term' derives from Terminus, the Roman god of boundaries. A variant is the 'herm' – when the head is a representation of Hermes/Mercury, the Greek/Roman messenger god. *See also Walls and Surfaces, p. 128.*

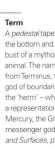

The Renaissance and Baroque Church › Plan

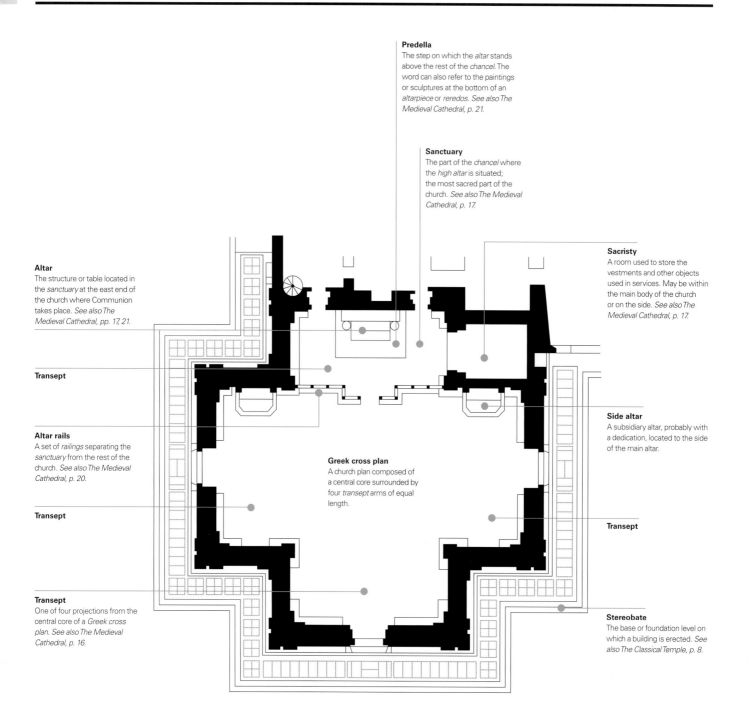

Predella
The step on which the *altar* stands above the rest of the *chancel*. The word can also refer to the paintings or sculptures at the bottom of an *altarpiece* or *reredos*. *See also The Medieval Cathedral, p. 21.*

Sanctuary
The part of the *chancel* where the *high altar* is situated; the most sacred part of the church. *See also The Medieval Cathedral, p. 17.*

Sacristy
A room used to store the vestments and other objects used in services. May be within the main body of the church or on the side. *See also The Medieval Cathedral, p. 17.*

Altar
The structure or table located in the *sanctuary* at the east end of the church where Communion takes place. *See also The Medieval Cathedral, pp. 17, 21.*

Transept

Altar rails
A set of *railings* separating the *sanctuary* from the rest of the church. *See also The Medieval Cathedral, p. 20.*

Transept

Side altar
A subsidiary altar, probably with a dedication, located to the side of the main altar.

Greek cross plan
A church plan composed of a central core surrounded by four *transept* arms of equal length.

Transept

Transept
One of four projections from the central core of a *Greek cross plan*. *See also The Medieval Cathedral, p. 16.*

Stereobate
The base or foundation level on which a building is erected. *See also The Classical Temple, p. 8.*

Sacristy
A room used to store the vestments and other objects used in services. Sometimes located within the main body cathedral or church or as a room to the side. *See also The Medieval Cathedral, p. 17.*

Altar
The structure or table located in the *sanctuary* at the east end of the church where Communion takes place. *See also The Medieval Cathedral, pp. 17, 21.*

Cloister
A covered walk, usually surrounding a central courtyard or *garth*. Medieval cloisters are usually vaulted. *See also The Medieval Cathedral, p. 16; Roofs, pp. 164, 165.*

Predella
The step on which the *altar* stands above the rest of the *chancel*. It can also refer to the paintings or sculptures at the bottom of an *altarpiece* or *reredos*. *See also The Medieval Cathedral, p. 21.*

Niche
An arched recess into a wall surface, designed to hold a statue or simply to provide surface variegation. *See also Walls and Surfaces, p. 129.*

Side altar

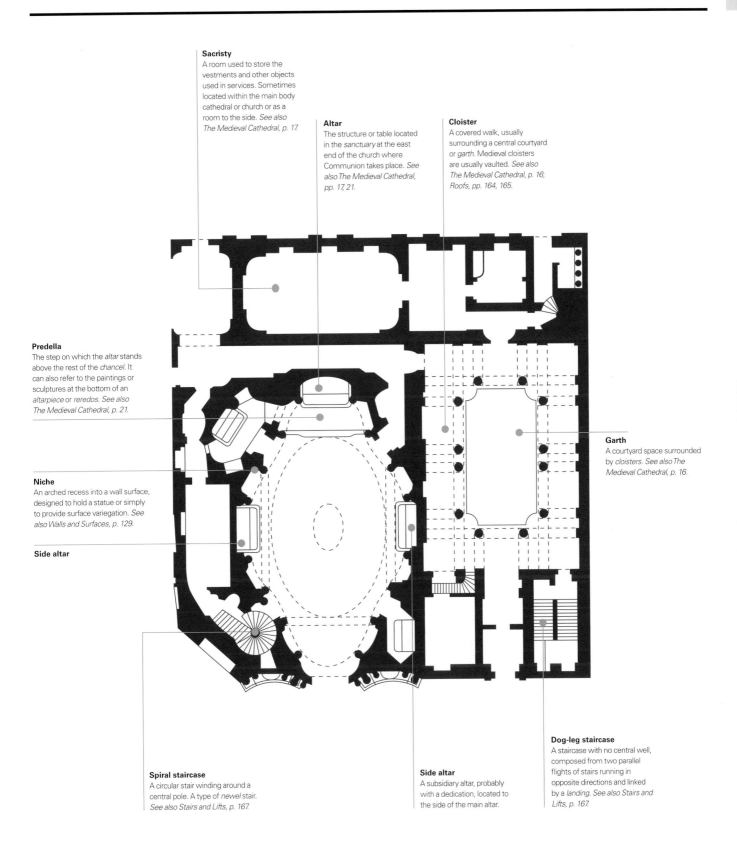

Garth
A courtyard space surrounded by *cloisters*. *See also The Medieval Cathedral, p. 16.*

Spiral staircase
A circular stair winding around a central pole. A type of *newel* stair. *See also Stairs and Lifts, p. 167.*

Side altar
A subsidiary altar, probably with a dedication, located to the side of the main altar.

Dog-leg staircase
A staircase with no central well, composed from two parallel flights of stairs running in opposite directions and linked by a *landing*. *See also Stairs and Lifts, p. 167.*

The Renaissance and Baroque Church › Interior

An integral element of the Renaissance church or cathedral was a strict proportional logic of space. While the Gothic building was an essentially modular design, the new ones were often constructed around a tightly integrated plan, usually with a centralized domed space (sometimes with a conventional nave attached). The frequently used cross plan with transept arms of even length is known as the Greek cross.

In Santa Maria delle Carceri, the interior space makes use of several key features of Roman architecture – the Classical orders, aedicules and, especially, the dome – to construct an elegant internal logic.

Corinthian cornice
A cornice is the highest level of the *entablature*, which projects over the lower levels. For the Corinthian order, *see also Columns and Piers, p. 74.*

Corinthian frieze
A frieze is the central section of the *entablature* between the *architrave* and *cornice*, often decorated in relief. For the Corinthian order, *see also Columns and Piers, p. 74.*

Corinthian architrave
The lowest part of the *entablature* consisting of a large beam resting directly on the *capitals* below. For the Corinthian order, *see also Columns and Piers, p. 74.*

Segmental pediment
Similar to a triangular pediment except that the triangle shape is replaced by a shallow curve. *See also Windows and Doors, p. 137.*

Altarpiece
A painting or sculpture set behind the *altar*. *See also The Medieval Cathedral, p. 21.*

Adjacent fluted Corinthian corner pilasters
Pilasters are flattened columns that project slightly from the face of a wall. Here they are shown with 'fluting' – the indentation of a column or pilaster with vertical recessed grooves. For fluted columns see *also p. 69;* for the Corinthian order *see also Columns and Piers, p. 74.*

Lectern
A stand from which to speak, with a sloping front to hold a book or notes. Used in some churches in place of a *pulpit*.

Balustraded altar rails
Altar rails are a set of *railings* separating the *sanctuary* from the rest of the church. Here they are supported by a series of *balusters* thus forming a *balustrade. See also The Medieval Cathedral, p. 20; Windows and Doors, p. 144.*

Altar
A structure or table located in the *sanctuary* at the east end of the church where Communion takes place. *See also The Medieval Cathedral, pp. 17, 21.*

The interior of Borromini's San Carlo is far more complex than that of Santa Maria delle Carceri, full of undulating curves and recesses, but is no less founded on the elements and proportional systems of Classical architecture.

Pendentive medallion
A pendentive is the curved triangular section formed by the intersection of a *dome* and its supporting arches. Here, the pendentive is set with a medallion – a circular or oval decorative plaque usually adorned with a sculptural or painted figure or scene. *See also Walls and Surfaces, p. 128; Roofs, p. 158.*

Putto
Figure of a small male child, usually unclothed and with wings; also sometimes called an 'amorino'. *See also Walls and Surfaces, p. 129.*

Coffered apse
An apse is the typically semicircular recession from the body of the *chancel* or, indeed, any part of a church. Here it is 'coffered' – inset with a series of sunken rectangular panels called *lacunaria*. *See also Roofs, p. 158.*

Composite entablature
The superstructure above the *capital* level composed of *architrave*, *frieze* and *cornice*. For the Composite order, *see Columns and Piers, p. 75.*

Concave pediment
A pediment in the form of a receding curve.

Engaged Composite column
A column is engaged when it is not *free-standing* but is built into a wall or surface. For the Composite order, *see Columns and Piers, p. 75.*

Niche
An arched recess into a wall surface, designed to hold a statue or simply to provide surface variegation. *See also Walks and Surfaces, p. 129.*

Altarpiece
A painting or sculpture set behind the *altar*. *See also The Medieval Cathedral, p. 21.*

Altar
A structure or table located in the sanctuary at the east end of the church from where Communion takes place. *See also The Medieval Cathedral, pp. 17, 21.*

Fortified Buildings › Keep Castle

As defensive structures, castles – the pre-eminent fortified buildings in the history of architecture – derived from hill forts, yet were in many ways quite different building types. Medieval castles acted as centralized strongholds of power, which facilitated marshalling and administration in a particular area. As defensive structures they provided refuge from invading forces and were often designed to be self-sufficient for long periods of time when under siege.

While they were ostensibly buildings in which a functional element might be seen to predominate, castles and other fortified buildings played an equally important symbolic role. They constituted grandiose statements of the lord's or other resident's power and authority, and were recognized as such by both his peers and subjects and potential invading forces.

The design of castles and fortified buildings naturally evolved as advances in offensive weaponry became widespread. Gunpowder and cannon fire dramatically altered how castles and fortified buildings were designed and constructed – ultimately rendering them somewhat redundant as military, as opposed to symbolic, structures. The threat of aerial bombardment in the twentieth century finally put paid to the symbolic fortified building when hidden – and therefore wholly functional – underground bunkers took on their role.

KEEP CASTLE
A castle with a *keep* at its centre, enclosed by one or more *curtain walls*. The keep castle derived from, and often superseded, the motte-and-bailey – a castle set upon a large earth mound (motte) adjoining a lower fortified enclosure (*bailey*) surrounded by a palisade (a fence of wooden stakes).

Keep or donjon
A large *tower* at the centre of a castle, sometimes set atop a motte (earth mound) which was usually enclosed by a ditch. The keep was the most strongly defended part of the castle, was where the lord would have resided, and also contained or adjoined the *great hall* and chapel.

Inner ward
A second upper fortified enclosure in which the *keep* was situated. The inner ward was usually inside or adjoining the *outer ward or bailey* and was enclosed by a further *curtain wall* or palisade.

Chapel

Kitchen

Great hall
The ceremonial and administrative centre of the castle. The great hall was also used for dining and receiving guests and visitors. Halls were often richly decorated, especially with heraldic ornaments.

Curtain wall
A fortified wall enclosing a *bailey* or *ward*. Curtain walls often feature elevated walkways and are usually linked by a series of *towers* to further aid defence. To deter undermining, curtain walls are often built with a projecting skirt at their base. Some curtain walls, especially in early motte-and-bailey castles, would have consisted of a simple palisade before being rebuilt in stone.

Outer ward or bailey
A fortified enclosure where the lord's household resided. It also contained stables, workshops and sometimes barracks.

Gatehouse
A fortified structure or *tower* protecting the gateway into the castle. A potential weak point in the castle's defences, the gatehouse was usually heavily fortified and often included a *drawbridge* and one or more *portcullises*.

Bastion
A structure or *tower* projecting from a *curtain wall* to aid defence.

Fortified Buildings › Concentric Castle

CONCENTRIC CASTLE
A castle composed from two or more concentric *curtain walls*. Concentric castles were usually built without a *keep* and in a variety of shapes depending on the terrain.

Tower
A narrow, tall structure projecting from, or attached to, a building or standing as an independent structure. In a castle, towers are fortified and usually positioned at the apexes formed at the intersections of different parts of *curtain walls*, to mitigate potential weaknesses. *See also Roofs, p. 154.*

Kitchen

Bastion
A structure or *tower* projecting from a *curtain wall* to aid defence.

Moat
A defensive ditch or large trench surrounding a castle for defensive purposes; usually with steep sides and often filled with water.

Great hall
The ceremonial and administrative centre of the castle. The great hall was also used for dining and receiving guests and visitors. Halls were often richly decorated, especially with heraldic ornaments.

Outer ward or bailey
A fortified enclosure where the lord's household resided. It also contained stables, workshops and sometimes barracks.

Inner ward
A second upper fortified enclosure, usually inside or adjoining the *outer ward or bailey* and enclosed by a further *curtain wall* or palisade.

Gatehouse
A fortified structure or *tower* protecting the gateway into the castle. A potential weak point in the castle's defences, the gatehouse was usually heavily fortified and often included a *drawbridge* and one or more *portcullises*.

Barbican
A further line of defence in front of a *gatehouse*, often designed to enclose attackers who could then be bombarded from above with missiles. Barbican also refers to the fortified outposts lying outside the main defences of a city's walls.

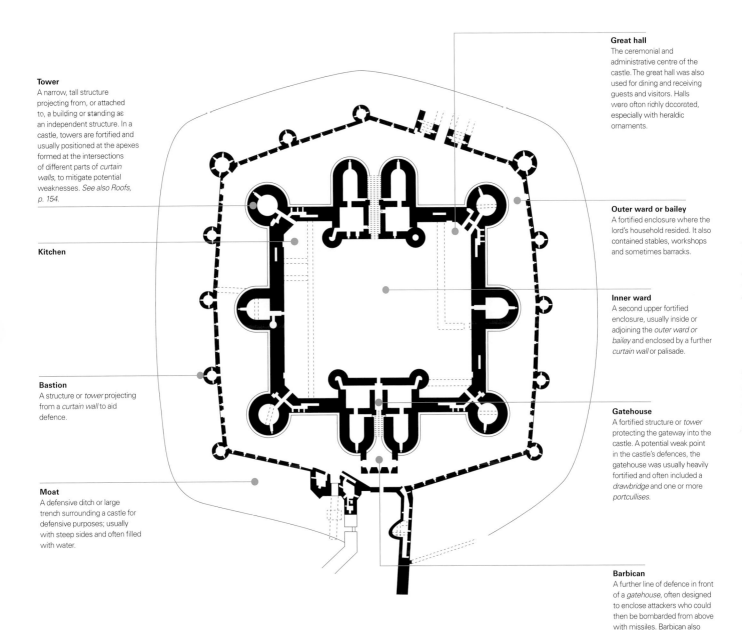

Fortified Buildings › Exterior

Machicolations
The holes in the floor between adjacent *corbels* supporting a crenellated *parapet*. Machicolations were designed for defensive purposes so that objects and liquids could be dropped on attackers below, but were later used for decorative purposes. *See also Roofs, p. 156.* (The Barbican at Lewes Castle, East Sussex, UK.)

Arrow slit
A very narrow window through which an archer could fire. Inside an arrow slit the wall was often cut away to provide the archer with a wider firing angle. One of the most common forms of arrow slit is the cross, which gives the archer further freedom in the direction and elevation of his arrow.

Crenellations
Regularly spaced teeth-like projections from the top of a wall. The projecting flaps are called 'merlons' and the gaps between, 'crenels'. Derived from defensive structures like castles or city walls, they were later used for decorative purposes. *See also Roofs, p. 156.*

Barbican
A further line of defence in front of a *gatehouse*, often designed to enclose attackers who could then be bombarded from above with missiles. Barbican also refers to the fortified outposts lying outside the main defences of a city's walls.

Portcullis
A wood or metal latticed gate in a *gatehouse* or *barbican* which could be quickly raised and lowered by a pulley system. It was common practice for a gatehouse to have two (or more) portcullises, one behind the other, which could be used to trap attackers where they would be vulnerable to missiles dropped from above. (Hever Castle, Kent, UK.)

Moat
A defensive ditch or large trench surrounding a castle for defensive purposes; usually with steep sides and often filled with water.

Crenellations

Arrow slit

Drawbridge
A movable bridge which can be raised or lowered over a *moat*. Drawbridges were usually made of wood and were often operated with a counterweight system. Some castles had two successive drawbridges which were intended to further inhibit and delay an attack.

Crenellations
(Old city walls, Avila, Spain.)

Bastion
A structure or *tower* projecting from a *curtain wall* to aid defence.

Curtain wall
A fortified wall enclosing a bailey or *ward*. Curtain walls often feature elevated walkways and are usually linked by a series of *towers* to further aid defence. To deter undermining, curtain walls are often built with a projecting skirt at their base. Some curtain walls, especially in early motte-and-bailey castles, would have consisted of a simple palisade before being rebuilt in stone.

Keep or donjon
A large *tower* at the centre of a castle, sometimes set atop a motte which was usually enclosed by a ditch. The keep was the most strongly defended part of the castle, where the lord would have resided, and also contained or adjoined the *great hall* and chapel. (Harlech Castle, Wales, UK.)

Curtain wall

Tower

Country Houses and Villas › Gothic

The country house type essentially derives from the medieval castle or fort. While the latter asserted its owner's power through the display of military might, the country house saw this reconfigured into a display of material and cultural supremacy. This could be rendered through heraldic ornamentation but also through new modes of architectural expression – especially Classicism and, later, Neoclassicism, as seen in the example of Kedleston Hall (p. 36). Despite this, the martial aspects of the medieval architectural vocabulary were not easily

forgotten, and such features as crenellation are found in country houses built right up to the nineteenth century, even on buildings, like Lichtenstein Castle (below), that had no pretence to any sort of military significance.

Roughly coterminous with the rise of the country house was the emergence of the villa typology – of which Palladio's Villa Capra (opposite) is the most enduring and well-known example. With the consolidation and expansion of the city in the early modern period, it became fashionable for the upper classes to seek refuge

from its perceived vices in the country and, moreover, reacquaint themselves with the very land from which they derived their power. With shared locales, over time the country house and villa typologies developed considerable overlap, so that, as seen in the example of Le Corbusier's famous Villa Savoye (p. 37), by the twentieth century they were inextricably intertwined.

Carl Alexander Heideloff, Lichtenstein Castle, Swabian Alb, Baden-Württemberg, Germany, 1840–42 (on medieval foundations).

Machicolations
The holes in the floor between adjacent *corbels* supporting a crenellated *parapet*. Designed for defensive purposes so that objects and liquids could be dropped on attackers below, but here used for purely decorative purposes. *See also Fortified Buildings, p. 32; Roofs, p. 156.*

Tower
A narrow, tall structure projecting from or attached to a building or standing as an independent structure. *See also Fortified Buildings, p. 31.*

Discharging arch
An arch built above a lintel to help carry the weight on either side of the opening. Also called a 'relieving arch'. *See also Arches, p. 83.*

Crow-stepped gable
A gable end projecting above the *pitched roof* line in a stepped manner. *See also Roofs, p. 153.*

Lancet windows
Tall, narrow pointed windows, named after their resemblance to the form of a lancet. *See also Windows and Doors, p. 141.*

Rubble masonry
Wall formed from irregularly shaped blocks of masonry, often laid with thick mortar joints. *See also Walls and Surfaces, p. 102.*

Crenellations
Regularly spaced teeth-like projections from the top of a wall. The projecting flaps are called 'merlons' and the gaps between, 'crenels'. Derived from defensive structures like castles or city walls, they were later used for decorative purposes. *See also Fortified Buildings, p. 32; Roofs, p. 156.*

Flèche
A small *spire* usually placed on the ridge of a *pitched roof* or at the intersection of the ridges of two perpendicular pitched roofs. *See also Roofs, p. 156.*

Orb finial
The sphere-shaped crowning ornament of a *pinnacle, spire* or roof. *See also Medieval Cathedral, p. 14; Renaissance Church, p. 23; Baroque Church, p. 25; Public Buildings, p. 47; Roofs, p. 154.*

Corner turret
A small *tower* projecting vertically from the corner or wall of a building. *See also Roofs, p. 156.*

Oriel window
A window that projects from one or more upper storeys but does not extend to the ground floor. *See also Windows and Doors, p. 143.*

Quoins
The cornerstones of a building. They are often composed of larger *rusticated* blocks and are sometimes in a different material to the building. *See also Walls and Surfaces, p. 103.*

Country Houses and Villas › Renaissance

Andrea Palladio, Villa Capra 'La Rotonda', Vicenza, Italy, begun 1566.

Chimney stack
A structure, usually of brick, used to convey smoke from internal fireplaces clear of the building. Where it protrudes above a roof it is often highly decorated. Chimney stacks are usually topped by a chimney pot. *See also Roofs, p. 152.*

Cupola
A small *dome*-like structure often placed on top of a larger roof and sometimes used as a viewing platform. *See also Roofs, p. 157.*

Attic window
A window that sits above the *entablature* level in a wall.

Hipped roof
A roof with sloping faces on all four sides. *See also Roofs, p. 148.*

Saucer dome
A dome that has a rise much smaller than its span, thus giving it a flatter, upturned-saucer shape. *See also Roofs, p. 159.*

Acroteria
Sculpture – usually *urns, palmettes* or *statues* – placed on flat *pedestals* on top of a *pediment*. If sculptures are placed at the outer angles of a pediment rather than at the apex, they are called 'acroteria angularia'. *See The Classical Temple, p. 9.*

Pedimented piano nobile window
A pediment-topped window on the building's principal storey. *See also Windows and Doors, p. 137.*

Basement window
A window that sits below the *piano nobile* at a level equivalent to that of a *plinth* or *pedestal*.

Hexastyle Ionic portico
A portico is a porch extending from the body of a building, usually, as here, with a temple front of a *colonnade* topped by a *pediment*. For hexastyles *see also The Classical Temple, p. 10;* for the Ionic order, *Arches p. 73.*

Perron
An exterior set of steps leading to a grand entranceway or *portal*.

Country Houses and Villas › Neo-Classical

*Robert Adam, Kedleston Hall (south front),
Derbyshire, England, 1760–70.*

Corinthian entablature
The superstructure above the *capital*
level composed of *architrave, frieze*
and *cornice.* For the Corinthian order
see also Columns and Piers, p. 74.

Lead roof
A roof surface consisting of
sheets of lead laid over wooden
battens. *See also Roofs, p. 151.*

Medallion
A circular or oval decorative
plaque usually adorned with a
painted or, as here, sculpted
figure or scene. *See also Walls
and Surfaces, p. 128.*

Blind central arch
An arch set into the wall
surface but with no actual
aperture. *See also Arches,
p. 82.*

Giant Corinthian column
A giant column is a typically
cylindrical upright shaft or
member composed of *base,
shaft* and *capital.* It extends
through two (or more) storeys.
For the Corinthian order *see
also Columns and Piers, p. 74.*

Attic panel relief
A panel relief is a rectangular
panel, decorated with a
rectangular recession or
projection in a surface; here it is
at attic level and decorated with
bas- or *low relief. See also Walls
and Surfaces, p. 130.*

Swag and paterae frieze
A frieze – the central section
of the *entablature* between
the *architrave* and *cornice* –
decorated in a repeating pattern
of suspended bowing cloth forms
(*swags*) and circular, dish-like
ornaments (*paterae*). *See also
Columns and Piers, p. 70; Walls
and Surfaces, pp. 129, 131.*

Mezzanine window
A window on a lower storey
between two main storeys,
usually the *piano nobile*
and *attic.*

Basement window
A window which sits below
the *piano nobile* at a level
equivalent to that of a *plinth*
or *pedestal.*

Sash window
A window consisting of one or more
sashes – glazed wooden frames
containing one or more glass panes
– which are set into grooves in the
jambs and slide vertically up and
down. A counterweight is usually
concealed in the window frame,
which is linked to the sash or sashes
by a cord and pulley system. *See also
Windows and Doors, p. 133.*

Voussoirs
Wedge-shaped blocks,
usually masonry, from which
an arch's curve is formed.
Here it is a flat arch above a
window. *See also Arches,
p. 78.*

Approach stair
A series of steps
leading up to a building's
entrance. *See also
Perron, p. 35.*

Niche with statue
A statue set in an arched
recess into a wall surface.
*See also Walls and
Surfaces, p. 129.*

Rustication
A style of working masonry
in which the joints between
adjacent blocks of stone are
accentuated. *See also Walls
and Surfaces, p. 103.*

**Pedimented piano nobile
window**
A *pediment*-topped window on
the building's principal storey.
*See also Windows and Doors,
p. 137.*

Country Houses and Villas › Twentieth-Century

Le Corbusier, Villa Savoye, Poissy, France, 1928–29.

Ribbon window
A series of windows of the same height and separated only by *mullions* which form a continuous horizontal band or ribbon across a building. *See also Windows and Doors, p. 142.*

Curvilinear concrete superstructure
A superstructure is a structure sitting on top of the main body of the building. This one is curvilinear – composed from one or several curved lines. *See also Contemporary Buildings, p. 65; Walls and Surfaces, p. 112.*

Flat roof
A roof whose pitch is almost horizontal (a slight incline is usually retained to ensure that water runs off). *See also Roofs, p. 149.*

Mullion
A vertical bar or member dividing an aperture. *See also Windows and Doors, pp. 132, 133, 135.*

Cement-rendered wall
A thick plaster or, here, cement coating applied to a wall to make it smooth and waterproof. *See also Walls and Surfaces, p. 113.*

Piloti
Pilotis are piers or columns that raise a building above ground level, freeing space for circulation or storage in the space underneath. *See also Columns and Piers, p. 69.*

Ground floor storage and service area

Street-Facing Buildings › Half-Timbered

Street-facing buildings include examples from every building type and every age, and consequently can be considered as a kind of building form that transcends type. All street-facing buildings are determined, to some extent, by the nature of their site. Street-facing sites have, of course, many practical advantages – for example, in terms of visibility and accessibility for trade. The convenience and commercial advantages of such sites has meant they have often been in high demand. As a result, street frontages are often comparatively narrow but,

because of their prominence, they are often important locations for architectural display.

A common set of characteristics exists among street-facing buildings, even those distant in time and place, because of the various particularities of street-facing sites. For example, such buildings tend to have one principal front which is usually the sole focus for architectural display. As the examples in this section illustrate, verticality is often emphasized, so subterranean basement storeys are frequently present, while Mansard roofs and dormer windows

extend usable space upwards. As the latter examples illustrate (pp. 44–45), over time such characteristics have been destabilized in various ways as architects seek to reinterpret and subvert this street-facing morphology. However, despite this, one can still reasonably make instructive parallels within this particular building form.

Staple Inn, London, 1580s
(with subsequent restoration).

Chimney stack
A structure, usually of brick, used to convey smoke from internal fireplaces clear of the building. Where it protrudes above a roof it is often highly decorated. Chimney stacks are usually topped by chimney pots. *See also Roofs, p. 152.*

Gable
The usually triangular part of the wall enclosing the sloping faces of a *pitched roof. See also Roofs, pp. 152, 153.*

Tiled pitched roof
A single-ridged roof with two sloping sides and *gables* at the two ends, here clad in tiles. *See also Walls and Surfaces, p. 110; Roofs, pp. 148, 152.*

Close-studded timber frame
Timber frame is the construction of a building from timber posts and cross beams (sometimes also with diagonal beams) in which the spaces between each beam are infilled with *lime plaster*, brick or stone. 'Close-studded' refers to the very narrow spacing between adjacent timber studs. *See also Walls and Surfaces, p. 108.*

Lime-rendered infill
The infilling of the spaces between timber members with a lime-based *cement render. See also Walls and Surfaces, p. 113.*

Casement window
A window which is attached to its frame by one or more hinges along one of its sides. *See also Windows and Doors, p. 132.*

Window lintel
The supporting, usually horizontal, member that surmounts a window. *See also Windows and Doors, p. 132.*

Oriel window
A window that projects from one or more upper storeys but does not extend to the ground floor. *See also Windows and Doors, p. 143.*

Mullion
A vertical bar or member dividing an aperture. *See also Windows and Doors, pp. 132, 133, 135.*

Timber studs
The smaller vertical members between larger posts. *See also Walls and Surfaces, p. 108.*

Window sill
The horizontal base on which a window rests. *See also Windows and Doors, p. 132.*

Overhanging jetty
A projection of an upper storey over a lower one in a timber-framed building. *See also Walls and Surfaces, p. 109.*

Transom
A horizontal bar or member dividing an aperture. *See also Windows and Doors, pp. 132, 133, 135.*

Cabinet window
The wooden, cabinet-like, traditionally multipaned window found in *shopfronts. See also Windows and Doors, p. 142.*

Street-Facing Buildings › Masonry

Andrea Palladio, Palazzo del Capitanio, Vicenza, Italy, 1571–72.

Balustraded attic balcony
A balcony is a platform attached to the outside of a building – cantilevered or supported on brackets – enclosed on its outer sides by a *railing* or, as here, by a balustrade, a series of *balusters* that supports a railing or coping. *See also Windows and Doors, p. 144.*

Dentil moulding
A repeating pattern of square or rectangular blocks that project from the underside of a Classical *cornice*. *See also Columns and Piers, pp. 73–75.*

Breaking forward Composite entablature
The entablature is the superstructure above the *pilaster capitals*, composed of *architrave*, *frieze* and *cornice*. When it projects further over the columns or pilasters it is said to be 'breaking forward'. For the Composite order, *see also Columns and Piers, p. 75.*

Piano nobile window
A window on the building's principal storey.

Window surround
The general term used to denote the often decorative framing of an aperture. *See also Windows and Doors, pp. 133, 136.*

Triglyph-like supporting bracket
A supporting bracket is a projection from a wall to support a structure above, here in the form of a *triglyph* – a grooved rectangular block in a Doric *frieze* characterized by its three vertical bars.

Semicircular arched opening
An arch whose curve has one centre with the rise equal to half the span giving it the form of a semicircle. *See also Arches, p. 79.*

Shouldered attic window surround
A window surround that has two symmetrical lateral projections from the top of the aperture. These are typically small rectangular flaps that form a shoulder, though they can take other, more decorated forms. *See also Windows and Doors, p. 136.*

Composite capital
The capital is the splayed and decorated uppermost part of the column on which the *entablature* sits. For the Composite order, *see also Columns and Piers, p. 75.*

Giant Composite column
A column is a typically cylindrical upright shaft or member composed of *base*, *shaft* and *capital*. A giant column extends through two (or more) storeys. *See also Columns and Piers, p. 69*; for the Composite order, *p. 75.*

Impost
The typically horizontal band (though it need not be delineated as such) from which the arch springs and on which the *springer voussoir* rests. *See also Arches, p. 78.*

Pedestal
The moulded block on which a column or *pilaster* is sometimes raised.

Street-Facing Buildings › Brick

Veere, The Netherlands, 1579.

Gable window
A window set into the gable. *See also Windows and Doors, p. 132; Roofs, p. 152.*

Discharging arch
An arch above a window or door which carries the weight on either side of the opening. Also called a 'relieving arch'. *See also Arches, p. 83.*

Quoins
The cornerstones of a building. They are often composed of larger *rusticated* blocks and are sometimes, as here, in a different material to the building. *See also Walls and Surfaces, p. 103.*

Cellar door
A door opening directly from the street to the building's cellar – a room or space in a building below ground level; typically used for storage.

Crow-stepped gable
A gable end projecting above the *pitched roof* line in a stepped manner. *See also Roofs, p. 153.*

Window lintel
The supporting, usually horizontal, member that surmounts a window. *See also Windows and Doors, p. 132.*

Transom light
A rectangular window sitting above a door but contained within the overall *surround*.

Shutter
A hinged panel, often *louvred*, sitting to the side of a window, which can be closed to keep light out or for security reasons. Shutters can be affixed to the inside or outside of windows. *See also p. 44; Public Buildings, p. 47; Windows and Doors, p. 144.*

26 Bedford Square, London, 1775–86.

Parapet
A low protective wall or *balustrade* running along the edge of a roof, *balcony* or bridge. Here, it obscures the *pitched roof* behind. *See also Roofs, p. 152.*

Flat-arched brick lintel
A flat arch is one with a horizontal *extrados* and *intrados* created from specially shaped, angled *voussoirs*. Flat arches are commonly used as *lintels* for windows and doors. *See also Windows and Doors, p. 132.*

Sash window
A window consisting of one or more sashes – glazed wooden frames containing one or more glass panes – which are set into grooves in the *jambs* and slide vertically up and down. A counterweight is usually concealed in the window frame, which is linked to the sash by a cord and pulley system. *See also Windows and Doors, p. 133.*

Fanlight
A semicircular or elongated window above a door but contained within the overall *surround*, with radiating glazing bars in the form of a fan or sunburst. *See also Windows and Doors, p. 135.*

Dormer window
A window that protrudes vertically from the plane of a *pitched roof. See also p. 42; Windows and Doors, p. 145.*

Mezzanine window
A window on a lower storey between two main storeys, usually the *piano nobile* and *attic*.

Piano nobile window
A window on the building's principal storey.

Balconette
A stone *balustrade*, or most often cast-iron *railing*, framing the lower section of usually an upper-storey window. *See also Windows and Doors, p. 144.*

Blocked rusticated door surround
The decorative framing of a door, here ornamented with rusticated blocks which are separated by evenly spaced gaps or apparent recessions. *See also Windows and Doors, p. 133;* for rustication *see also Walls and Surfaces, p. 103.*

Railing
A fence-like structure used to partially enclose a space or platform. The members supporting the rail are often treated decoratively. *See also Windows and Doors, p. 144.*

Panel door
A door constructed from a structural frame of *rails, stiles, mullions* and sometimes *muntins*, infilled with wooden panels. *See also Windows and Doors, p. 135.*

Street-Facing Buildings › Stone-Faced

Boulevard Haussmann, Paris, 1852–70.

Skylight
A window parallel with the face of a roof. *See also Windows and Doors, p. 145.*

Mansard roof
A roof with a double slope, the lower typically being steeper than the higher. Mansard roofs often contain *dormer* windows and are *hipped* at their ends. A typically French design, the term derives from its first proponent, the French architect François Mansart (1598–1666). If a Mansard roof terminates with a flat *gable* instead of hips, it is strictly called a 'gambrel' roof. *See also Roofs, p. 148.*

Dormer window
A window that protrudes vertically from the plane of a *pitched roof. See also p. 41; Windows and Doors, p. 144.*

Balconette
A stone *balustrade*, or most often cast-iron *railing*, framing the lower section of usually an upper-storey window. *See also Windows and Doors, p. 144.*

Side-hung casement window
A window which is attached to its frame by one or more hinges along one of its sides. *See also Windows and Doors, p. 132.*

Pilaster
Pilasters are flattened columns that project slightly from the face of a wall. *See also The Renaissance Church, pp. 22, 23, 28; Public Buildings, pp. 46, 47, 50; The Modern Block, p. 52; Columns and Piers, p. 68.*

Window surround
The frame surrounding a window, often moulded as here. *See also Windows and Doors, pp. 133, 136.*

Cornice
The highest level of the *entablature*, which projects over the lower levels. Here it supports *railing* and *balcony*. *See also opposite; Columns and Piers, pp. 70–75.*

Wrought-iron balcony railing
A balcony is a platform attached to the outside of a building – cantilevered or supported on brackets – and enclosed on its outer sides by a railing, here made from wrought iron – an iron alloy with a very low carbon content which makes it particularly malleable and weldable. It is often used for ornamental ironwork. For balcony *see also Street-Facing Buildings, p. 39; The Modern Block, pp. 53, 55; Windows and Doors, p. 144.* For railing, *see also Street-Facing Buildings, p. 41; Windows and Doors, p. 144; Stairs and Lifts, p. 166.*

Ground-floor arcade
A repeating series of arches set upon columns or piers. *See also Arches, p. 82.*

Banded rustication
A form of rustication in which only the top and bottom joints between blocks are accentuated. *See also Walls and Surfaces, p. 103.*

Keystone
The central wedge-shaped block at the top of the arch, which locks all the other *voussoirs* into place. *See also Arches, p. 78.*

Henry Janeway Hardenbergh,
The Dakota, New York City,
1880–84.

Oriel window
A window which projects from one or more upper storeys but does not extend to the ground floor. *See also Windows and Doors, p. 145.*

Small dome
A dome is a usually hemispherical structure whose shape derives from the rotation of a *vault* 360 degrees through its central axis. *See also Roofs, pp. 157, 158, 159.*

Finial
The crowning ornament of a *pinnacle*, *spire*, or roof. *See also Roofs, p. 154.*

Gable
The usually triangular part of the wall enclosing the sloping faces of a *pitched roof*. *See also Roofs, pp. 152, 153.*

Dormer window
A window that protrudes vertically from the plane of a *pitched roof*. *See also Windows and Doors, p. 145.*

Cornice
The highest level of the *entablature*, which projects over the lower levels. Here it supports *railing* and *balcony*. *See also opposite; Columns and Piers, pp. 70–75.*

Balconette
A stone *balustrade*, or most often cast-iron *railing*, framing the lower section of usually an upper-storey window. *See also Windows and Doors, p. 144.*

Quoins
The cornerstones of a building. Quoins are often composed of larger *rusticated* blocks and are sometimes, as here, in a different material to the building. *See also Walls and Surfaces, p. 103.*

Frieze
Strictly, the central section of the *entablature* between the *architrave* and *cornice*, often decorated in *relief*; the word is also used, as here, to refer to any continuous horizontal band of relief running along a wall. *See also Columns and Piers, pp. 70–75.*

Basement window
The general term used to refer to a window on the ground storey. In a Classical building, a basement window sits below the *piano nobile* at a level equivalent to that of a *plinth* or *pedestal*.

String course
A thin, horizontal moulded banding running across a wall. *See also Walls and Surfaces, p. 120.*

Rusticated basement storey
The basement is the lowest storey in a building, often partially or entirely underground. In a Classical building the basement sits below the *piano nobile* at a level equivalent to that of a *plinth* or *pedestal*. Rustication is the emphasizing of blocks of masonry by creating recessions at their joints and, in some examples, incising the wall surface in various ways. *See also Walls and Surfaces, p. 103.*

Street-Facing Buildings › Irregular

Antoni Gaudí, Casa Batlló,
Barcelona, Spain, 1877
(remodelled 1904–06).

Shutter
A hinged panel, often *louvred*, sitting to the side of a window, which can be closed to keep out light or for security reasons. Shutters can be affixed to the inside or outside of windows. *See also p. 40; Public Buildings, p. 47; Windows and Doors, p. 144.*

Balconette
A stone *balustrade*, or most often cast-iron *railing*, framing the lower section of usually an upper-storey window. *See also Windows and Doors, p. 144.*

Ovoidal window
A window that is roughly oval in shape.

Rectilinear window
A window formed entirely by straight lines in the form of a rectangle or square.

Polychromatic ceramic wall surface
The decoration of a wall with ceramic tiles of differing colours. *See also Walls and Surfaces, p. 111.*

Decorative mullion
A vertical bar or member dividing an aperture, here treated with decoration. *See also Windows and Doors, pp. 132, 133, 135.*

Balustrade
A series of *balusters* that supports a *railing* or *coping*. *See also Windows and Doors, p. 144.*

Amorphous light arrangement
An irregular arrangement that has no easily definable form.

*Frank Gehry, Ray and Maria Stata Center,
Massachusetts Institute of Technology,
Cambridge, MA, 2000–04.*

Aluminium cladding
Cladding is the covering or application of one material over another to protect the underlying layer against the weather or for aesthetic purposes. Aluminium is often used as a cladding material as it is relatively lightweight, and resistant to corrosion thanks to the durable oxide layer on its surface. *See also Walls and Surfaces, p. 117.*

Deconstructivist forms
An appearance characterized by vehemently non-rectilinear forms and the juxtaposition of divergent and often angular components. *See also Contemporary Buildings, p. 65.*

Mullion
A vertical bar or member dividing an aperture. *See also Windows and Doors, pp. 132, 133, 135.*

Projecting window
A window protruding from the surface of a wall.

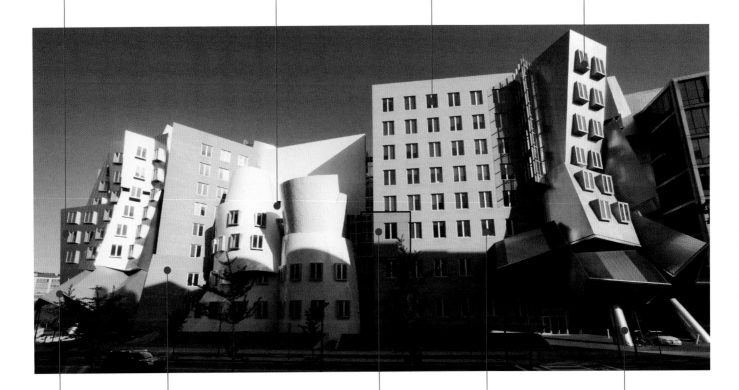

Corrugated canopy
A canopy is a projection from a building, providing cover from precipitation or sunlight. Here it is corrugated – composed of a series of alternating grooves and peaks. *See also Walls and Surfaces, p. 118.*

Batter
An inclined face of wall, sloping towards the top. *See also Contemporary Buildings, p. 64.*

Brick panel
A prefabricated *curtain-wall* panel faced with brick. *See also Walls and Surfaces, p. 105.*

Recessed window
A window whose face is sunken behind the wall surface.

Concrete pier
A pier is an upright member providing vertical structural support; here it is formed from concrete. *See also Columns and Piers, p. 68; Concrete, p. 88.*

Public Buildings › Neo-Gothic / 1

For as long as societies have existed there has been a need for public buildings – ones that represent a community rather than an individual. Not important just for the particular functions they facilitated, they have always been great statements of identification and prestige for a town, city or nation.

Public buildings have, of course, evolved considerably. Initially their function was purely administrative, but especially during the nineteenth century many new types emerged, from civic halls and public libraries to museums and train stations. Despite this multitude of types, public buildings can be seen to share certain fundamental characteristics to do with their civic and social functions, which often set them apart.

As the examples in this section illustrate, public buildings tend to be situated in highly visible sites. They are often large in relation to their (original) architectural context. They are usually highly architectural; that is, they are often conscious architectural statements through their use of particular architectural languages and ornament. Therefore, despite the plethora of architectural languages from which public buildings have been constructed over the ages, they are often apogees of architectural expressiveness – extremely grand or ornate, or with a great clarity of expression as befits their important symbolic purpose.

Hendrick de Keyser, Stadhuis, Delft, The Netherlands, 1618–20.

Weather vane
A movable structure for showing the direction of the wind, typically at the highest point of a building.

Finial
The crowning ornament on a *pinnacle, spire* or roof. *See also Roofs, p. 154.*

Bell tower
A tower is a narrow, tall structure rising above the rest of the building. Here it houses a bell. *See also The Medieval Cathedral, p. 14; Fortified Buildings, p. 31; Country Houses and Villas, p. 34; Public Buildings, pp. 46, 51; Roofs, p. 154.*

Coat of arms
A heraldic symbolic design representing an individual, family or corporate body.

Niche
An arched recess into a wall surface, designed to hold a statue (as in the central niche here) or simply to provide surface variegation. *See also Walls and Surfaces, p. 129.*

Urn finial
The vase-shaped crowning ornament on a *pinnacle, spire* or roof. *See also Roofs, p. 154.*

Ionic entablature
The superstructure above the *capital* level composed of *architrave, frieze* and *cornice.* For the Ionic order, *see also Columns and Piers, p. 73.*

Fluted Ionic pilaster
Pilasters are flattened columns that project slightly from the face of a wall. Fluting is the indentation of a column or pilaster with vertical recessed grooves. For the Ionic order, *see also Columns and Piers, p. 73.*

Triglyph
A grooved rectangular block in a Doric *frieze,* characterized by its three vertical bars. *See also Columns and Piers, pp. 71, 72.*

Shouldered window surround
A window surround that has two symmetrical lateral projections from the top of the aperture. These are typically small rectangular flaps that form a shoulder, though they can take other, more decorated forms. *See also Windows and Doors, p. 136.*

Rusticated Roman Doric pilasters
Pilasters are flattened columns that project slightly from the face of a wall. Rustication is the emphasizing of blocks of masonry by creating recessions at their joints and, in some examples, incising the wall surface in various ways. *See also Walls and Surfaces, p. 103.* For the Roman Doric order, *see also Columns and Piers, p. 71.*

Clock lucarne
A lucarne is a small *dormer* window set into a *spire*, though here with a clock face instead of a window. *See also Windows and Doors, p. 145.*

Tetrastyle temple front
A temple front composed of four *pilasters* (or columns). *See also The Classical Temple, p. 10.*

Corinthian pilaster
Pilasters are flattened columns that project slightly from the face of a wall. For the Corinthian order, *see also Columns and Piers, p. 74.*

Obelisk
A narrow, tall, roughly rectangular structure tapering upwards with a pyramidal top. *See also Columns and Piers, p. 69.*

Balustraded parapet
A parapet is a low protective wall running along the edge of a roof, *balcony* or bridge. A balustrade is a series of *balusters* that supports a *railing* or *coping*. *See also Windows and Doors, p. 144; Roofs, p. 152.*

Segmental pediment
Similar to a triangular pediment except that the triangle is replaced by a shallow curve. *See also Windows and Doors, p. 137.*

Keystone mask
A keystone decorated with a sculpted stylized human or animal face. *See also Walls and Surfaces, p. 128.*

Shutter
A hinged panel, often *louvred* (though not here), sitting to the side of a window, which can be closed to keep out light or for security reasons. Shutters can be affixed to the inside or outside of windows. *See also pp. 40, 44; Windows and Doors, p. 144.*

Volute
A scroll in the form of a spiral, most often found in Ionic, Corinthian and Composite *capitals*, but also, as here, used in a much larger form as an individual element in a façade. *See also Columns and Piers, pp. 73, 75.*

Distyle temple front
A temple front composed of two columns (or *pilasters*). *See also The Classical Temple, p. 10.*

Transom
A horizontal bar or member dividing an aperture. *See also Windows and Doors, pp. 132, 133, 135.*

Mullion
A vertical bar or member dividing an aperture. *See also Windows and Doors, pp. 132, 133, 135.*

Public Buildings › Neo-Gothic / 2

Frederick William Stevens,
Chhatrapati Shivaji Terminus
(formerly Victoria Terminus)
Mumbai, 1878–87.

Parapet spire
A typically octagonal spire whose triangular faces are set back from the edge of the *tower*. With such spires a parapet runs around the top of the tower with *turrets* or *pinnacles* set in the four corners. *See also Roofs, p. 155.*

Parapet
A low protective wall or *balustrade* running along the edge of a roof, *balcony* or bridge. *See also Roofs, p. 152.*

Gargoyle
A carved or moulded grotesque figure usually protruding from the top of a wall, designed to carry water away from the wall surface below. *See also The Medieval Cathedral, p. 14.*

Corner turret
A small tower projecting vertically from the corner or wall of a building. *See also Roofs, p. 156.*

Frieze
Strictly, the central section of the *entablature* between the *architrave* and *cornice*, often decorated in *relief*; the word is also used, as here, to refer to any continuous horizontal band of relief running along a wall. *See also Columns and Piers, pp. 70–75.*

Geometric tracery
A simple tracery type consisting of series of circles often infilled with *foils*. *See also Windows and Doors, p. 139.*

Tympanum
The often decorated space created between a horizontal *lintel* and enclosing arch above. Tympanum also denotes the triangular (or segmental) space created by a *pediment*. *See also Windows and Doors, p. 137.*

Crocketed dome rib

A rib is a typically curved masonry member which, when set in an evenly spaced arrangement with others, provides the structural support for a *vault* or dome with the space between infilled. Here, the ribs are visible from the exterior and are decorated with crockets – scroll-like, projecting leaf forms. *See also Roofs, p. 157.*

Melon dome

A dome in which the structural support is provided by a series of curved *ribs* with the space between infilled. *See also Roofs, p. 159.*

Finial

The crowning ornament of a *pinnacle*, *spire* or roof. *See also Roofs, p. 154.*

Parapet

Gable clock face

A gable is the usually triangular part of the wall enclosing the sloping faces of a *pitched roof*, here set with a clock face.

Dormer window

A window that protrudes vertically from the plane of a *pitched roof*. *See also Windows and Doors, p. 145.*

Loggia

A covered space partially enclosed on one or more sides by an *arcade* or *colonnade*. It may form part of a larger building or stand as an independent structure. *See also Walls and Surfaces, p. 118.*

Public Buildings › Neo-Classical

Paul Wallot and Foster + Partners, Reichstag, Berlin, Germany, 1884–94 (renovated 1961–64, 1992).

Breaking forward Composite entablature
The entablature is the superstructure above the *pilaster capitals* composed of *architrave*, *frieze* and *cornice*. When it projects over columns or pilasters it is said to be 'breaking forward'. For the Composite order, *see also Columns and Piers, p. 75.*

Finial
The crowning ornament of a *pinnacle*, *spire* or *roof*. *See also Roofs, p. 154.*

Modern steel and glass dome
A dome is a usually hemispherical structure whose shape derives from the rotation of a *vault* 360 degrees through its central axis. Here it is made of metal and glass. *See also Roofs, p. 157.*

Tympanum
In Classical architecture, the triangular (or segmental) space created by a *pediment*, typically recessed and decorated, often with figurative sculpture, as here. *See also Windows and Doors, p. 137.*

Corner pavilion
A structure that marks the end of a range by featuring a discrete architectural arrangement or an increase in scale.

Rusticated basement storey
The basement storey sits below the ground storey, and is often partially or entirely underground. Rustication is the emphasizing of blocks of masonry by creating recessions at their joints and, in some examples, incising the wall surface in various ways. *See also Walls and Surfaces, p. 103.*

Round-headed piano nobile window
A round-headed window on the building's principal storey. *See also Windows and Doors, p. 141.*

Hexastyle Composite temple front
A temple front composed of six columns (or *pilasters*). *See also The Classical Temple, p. 10.* For the Composite order *see also Columns and Piers, p. 75.*

Giant Composite engaged column
Engaged columns are not free-standing but built into a wall or surface. A giant column extends through two storeys. For the Composite order, *see also Columns and Piers, pp. 68, 69, 75.*

Distyle Composite temple front
A temple front composed of two columns (or *pilasters*). *See also The Classical Temple, p. 10.* For the Composite order, *see also Columns and Piers, p. 75.*

Giant Composite column
A column is a typically cylindrical upright shaft or member composed of *base*, *shaft* and *capital*. A giant column extends through two storeys. For the Composite order, *see also Columns and Piers, pp. 69, 75.*

Public Buildings › Twenty-First-Century

Snøhetta, New Norwegian National Opera and Ballet, Oslo, Norway, 2003–07.

Stone cladding
Cladding is the covering or application of one material over another to protect the underlying layer against the weather or for aesthetic purposes. Here the material used is stone.

Glass curtain wall
A non-load-bearing enclosure or envelope of a building, attached to the structure but standing separate from it. Here made of glass. *See also Steel, p. 92.*

Angled pier
An angled member providing vertical structural support.

Viewing platform
An elevated space for sightseeing, here located on the building's roof.

Fly tower
The larger space over a stage in which a theatre's fly system – the series of counterweights and pulleys that allows scenery to be moved on and off stage – operates.

Parapet
A low protective wall or *balustrade* running along the edge of a roof, *balcony* or bridge. *See also Roofs, p. 152.*

Municipal space
Publicly accessible open areas such as parks or ceremonial squares. Here, the municipal space normally associated with a public building merges with the building itself with its sloping, publicly accessible roof.

Ribbon window
A series of windows of the same height and separated only by *mullions* which form a continuous horizontal band or ribbon across a building. *See also Windows and Doors, p. 142.*

Aluminium panel
A prefabricated *curtain-wall* panel faced with aluminium. *See also Walls and Surfaces, p. 117.*

The Modern Block › Pre-War

Transcending the confines of a single type, the modern block encompasses buildings whose essential cuboidal form derives from the structural qualities and resultant uses of modern materials, especially steel and concrete. This building form is subsequently a key and recurring part of modern architecture's aesthetic vocabulary.

The development in the late nineteenth century of rectilinear steel and concrete frames enabled interior spaces to be designed unencumbered by supporting walls. This allowed greater freedom and adaptability in interior plans, and led to the widespread adoption of such structures in a great variety of building types. Therefore, the buildings included here traverse a range of types, from commercial and residential in Jenney's Leiter II Building (below) and Mies's Am Weissenhof 14–20 (opposite) respectively, to public and, in Niemeyer's Palácio da Alvorada (p. 54), even ceremonial buildings.

So great was the impact of this building form in the twentieth century, that in some quarters the 'Modernist box' came to be seen as a dull and predictable cliché. Consequently, architects have sought to reinterpret the form and subvert some of the aesthetic and structural certainties it is seen to embody. This is illustrated vividly in Toyo Ito's Sendai Mediatheque (p. 55) with its apparently typical box-like form which is in fact supported internally by hollow diagrid-lattice tubes.

William Le Baron Jenney, Leiter II Building, Chicago, 1891.

Flat roof
A roof whose pitch is almost horizontal (a slight incline is usually retained to ensure that water runs off). *See also Roofs, p. 149.*

Massive corner pier
A pier is an upright member providing vertical structural support. Here, the corner pier carries more of the load than the subsidiary façade piers, hence its increased size.

Rectilinear grid structure
A structural frame composed entirely from a series of vertical and horizontal elements. *See also Concrete, p. 88, and Contemporary Buildings, p. 64.*

Entablature
The superstructure above the *capitals*, composed of *architrave, frieze* and *cornice. See also Columns and Piers, pp. 70–75.*

Colossal Doric pilaster
Pilasters are flattened columns that project slightly from the face of a wall. A colossal pilaster (or column) extends through more than two storeys. For the Greek/Roman Doric order *see also Columns and Piers, pp. 69, 71, 72.*

Shopfronts
The usually heavily fenestrated street-facing ground-floor façade of a shop or commercial building. *See also Windows and Doors, p. 142.*

Transfer beam
A horizontal member intended to transfer loads to the vertical supports. Here a concrete beam is clad in stone for aesthetic purposes.

Pier articulated with Classical ornament
A pier is an upright member providing vertical structural support. Here, the piers are ornamented with Classical decoration. *See also Columns and Piers, p. 68.*

*Ludwig Mies van der Rohe, Am Weissenhof
14–20, Weissenhof Settlement, Stuttgart, 1927.*

Whitewashed cement render
Cement render is a form of *lime plaster* to which cement has been added. Mostly impervious to water, cement renders are most often used on exterior surfaces. Here, as is common, the render has been whitewashed. *See also Walls and Surfaces, p. 113.*

Flat roof
A roof whose pitch is almost horizontal (a slight incline is usually retained to ensure that water runs off). *See also Roofs, p. 149.*

Reinforced-concrete canopy
A canopy is a projection from a building that provides cover from precipitation or sunlight. Here it is formed from reinforced concrete. *See also Walls and Surfaces, p. 118.*

Roof garden or terrace
A paved garden or terrace situated on the roof of a building. As well as providing a place for recreation – especially useful when space at ground level is at a premium – roof gardens help to regulate the temperature of the spaces below.

Ribbon windows
A series of windows of the same height and separated only by *mullions*, which form a continuous horizontal band or ribbon across a building. *See also Windows and Doors, p. 141.*

Balcony
A platform attached to the outside of a building – cantilevered or supported on brackets – and enclosed on its outer sides by a *railing* or *balustrade*. *See also Windows and Doors, p. 144.*

The Modern Block › Post-War

Oscar Niemeyer, Palácio da Alvorada,
Brasília, 1957.

Glass curtain wall
A curtain wall is a non-load-bearing enclosure or envelope of a building, attached to the structure but standing separate from it. Here, it is constructed from glass with steel *transoms* and *mullions*. *See also Steel, p. 92.*

Flat roof
A roof whose pitch is almost horizontal (a slight incline is usually retained to ensure that water runs off). *See also Roofs, p. 149.*

Canopy
A projection from a building, providing cover from precipitation or sunlight. *See also Walls and Surfaces, p. 118.*

Applied trim
Supplementary elements applied to the surface of a building or *curtain wall*, often designed to highlight the underlying structural frame. Here, the trim is applied in long *louvre*-like vertical strips and deflects sunlight from the glass curtain wall.

Low-rise segmental arch arcade
A repeating series of arches set upon columns or piers. A *segmental arch's* curve is one segment of a semicircle whose centre is below *impost* level; thus its *span* is much larger than its *rise*. *See also Arches, p. 79.*

Inverted parabolic arch arcade
A repeating series of upside-down arches whose curves are formed from the inverted shape of an idealized hanging chain supported at each end. *See also Arches, p. 81.*

Toyo Ito, Sendai Mediatheque, Sendai, Japan, 2001.

Recessed balcony
A balcony is a platform attached to the outside of a building – cantilevered or supported on brackets – and enclosed on its outer sides by a *railing* or *balustrade*. However, here the balcony is recessed, sitting within the building shell. No external supports are needed and a continuation of the *curtain wall* makes a railing unnecessary. *See also Windows and Doors, p. 144.*

Rectilinear brise-soleil
A structure attached to the exterior of a glass-*curtain-walled* building (though not exclusively so) that provides shade and reduces solar heat gain. Here, it is rectilinear, composed entirely from a series of vertical and horizontal elements. *See also Walls and Surfaces, p. 118.*

Curtain-wall side protrusion
An extension of the curtain wall beyond the side of the building.

Semi-opaque spandrel panels
A spandrel panel is the part of a *curtain wall* between the head of a window and the bottom of the window immediately above. Spandrel panels often serve to obscure various service pipes and cables running between floors. Here, they are distinguished from the glass panels by the repeating semi-opaque rectangular patches. *See also Walls and Surfaces, p. 114.*

Balcony
A platform attached to the outside of a building – cantilevered or supported on brackets – enclosed on its outer sides by a *railing* or *balustrade. See also Windows and Doors, p. 144.*

Point-loaded glass curtain wall
A curtain wall is a non-load-bearing enclosure or envelope of a building, attached to the structure but standing separate from it. In a point-loaded system, the reinforced-glass panes are held in place through point attachments in each corner to the arms of a spider, or other point attachment, which is attached by a bracket to a structural support. *See also Walls and Surfaces, p. 115.*

Ground-floor entranceway canopy
A canopy is a projection from a building, providing cover from precipitation or sunlight, here set above the ground-floor entranceway. *See also Walls and Surfaces, p. 118.*

Hollow diagrid supporting tube
A supporting tube is an elongated hollow structure formed from a steel frame composed of diagonal steel members. Here they form a repeating diamond pattern (diagrid). This tube provides structural support.

High-Rise Buildings › Art Deco

As with buildings encompassed by the 'modern block', high-rise buildings are facilitated by (and thus inextricably bound up with) the modern materials used in their construction, principally steel and concrete. While some of the earliest examples clothed this most modern of building forms incongruously in Classical or Gothic dress, the expression of structure, and its very modernity, soon became the primary aesthetic strategy.

While high-rise buildings pose a fairly homogeneous building form – elongated structures composed from a repeating stacked plan – great variety exists in how that form is constituted and articulated. The International Style embodied in Mies's Seagram Building (opposite), with its sternly cuboidal form, repeating grid and refusal of ornament, sought to transcend contingencies of place or context in architectural production. This was an approach quite unlike that embodied by Van Allen's Chrysler Building (right), built 30 years earlier, whose emblematic Art Deco design was partly inspired by the speed and glamour of the cars Chrysler manufactured.

In the High-Tech buildings that emerged in the 1970s and 1980s, such as Foster's HSBC Headquarters (p. 58), the structure became the aesthetic as never before. More usable internal space (and thus greater financial returns on rents charged per square foot) could be realized by removing structural and service components to the exterior, which in turn became the building's primary aesthetic statement.

This synergy between a building's form and its commercial function has come to the fore most strikingly in the so-called 'iconic' architecture of the 1990s and 2000s. The unconventional and arresting form of buildings such as Jean Nouvel's Torre Agbar (p. 59) is designed to create a wholly unique building, intended to be symbolically tied to its location or a particular commercial entity.

William Van Allen, Chrysler Building, 1928–30.

Ribbed stainless-steel cladding
When alloyed with other metals, steel can become almost entirely resistant to corrosion, especially, as here, in its stainless variety. Rather than being laid in flat sheets, in this instance the cladding is articulated with series of long thin projections described as 'ribs'. *See also Walls and Surfaces, p. 117.*

Squinch
An arch constructed across the corner created by the intersection of two perpendicular walls. Squinches are often used to provide additional structural support, especially for a *dome* or *tower*. *See also Arches, p. 82.*

Masonry cladding
The use of masonry purely to face a building rather than to provide structural support. *See also Walls and Surfaces, p. 102.*

Needle spire
A slender, spike-like spire. *See also Roofs, p. 155.*

Chevrons
A repeating pattern of V-shaped forms. *See also Walls and Surfaces, p. 126.*

Concentric arches
A series of arches with the same centre, stacked above each other.

Eagle gargoyle
A gargoyle is a carved or moulded grotesque figure usually protruding from the top of a wall, designed to carry water away from the wall surface below, here in the form of an eagle. *See also The Medieval Cathedral, p. 14; Public Buildings, p. 48.*

Stacked arrowheads
Pointed, wedge-shaped forms similar to the head of an arrow. Here, three arrowheads are stacked above each other.

High-Rise Buildings › International Style

Ludwig Mies van der Rohe and Philip Johnson, Seagram Building, New York City, 1958.

Glass curtain wall
A non-load-bearing enclosure or envelope of a building, attached to the structure but standing separate from it. Glass has the benefit of allowing light to penetrate deep into a building. *See also Walls and Surfaces, p. 115.*

Spandrel panel
A spandrel panel is the usually opaque or semi-opaque part of a *curtain wall* between the head of one glass pane and the bottom of the one immediately above. Spandrel panels often serve to obscure service pipes and cables running between floors. *See also Walls and Surfaces, p. 114.*

I-beam trim
A metal beam, I- or H-shaped in cross section, found in almost all steel-framed structures. Here, I-beams are used as supplementary elements applied to the surface of the building to highlight the underlying structural frame.

Canopy
A horizontal or slightly pitched projection from a building, providing cover from precipitation or sunlight. *See also Walls and Surfaces, p. 118.*

Pier
An upright member providing vertical structural support. *See also Columns and Piers, p. 68.*

Concrete inner core
As in many high-rise buildings, a concrete inner core provides lateral rigidity to the building's steel frame. For *concrete* see also Walls and Surfaces, p. 112.

High-Rise Buildings › High-Tech

Foster + Partners, HSBC Headquarters,
Hong Kong, 1979–86.

Superstructure
A structure sitting on top of the main body of the building.

Aluminium cladding
The second most widely extracted metal after iron, aluminium is most often used as a cladding material as it is relatively lightweight, and resistant to corrosion thanks to the durable oxide layer on its surface. *See also Walls and Surfaces, p. 117.*

'Coathanger' suspension truss
A truss is a structural framework of one or more triangular units combined with straight members that can be used to span large distances and support a load. Here, the truss transfers loads to the *masts*. *See also Roofs, p. 160.*

Hanger beam
Vertical post suspended from the 'coathanger' *truss* to which other parts of the building are attached.

Building maintenance unit
A permanently installed crane set atop a high-rise building, allowing a platform to be suspended to facilitate maintenance and cleaning of its façades.

Mast
A tall, upright post or structure from which other elements can be suspended. Here they suspend the *trusses*.

Emergency stairs
A staircase running the full length of the building, included to facilitate evacuation during an emergency such as a fire. For other staircases *see also Stairs and Lifts, pp. 166, 167.*

Two-storey recession
A section in the building's façade that is set back from the rest of the wall surface.

Glass curtain wall
A non-load-bearing enclosure or envelope of a building, attached to the structure but standing separate from it. A glass curtain wall has the benefit of allowing light to penetrate deep into a building. *See also Walls and Surfaces, p. 115.*

High-Rise Buildings › Twenty-First-Century

Jean Nouvel, Torre Agbar,
Barcelona, 2001–04.

Curvilinear form
A building whose shape is
composed from one or more
curved surfaces rather than a series
of planes. *See also Contemporary*
Buildings, p. 65.

Irregular fenestration
An unevenly spaced
arrangement of windows,
often of differing sizes. *See*
also Concrete, p. 88, and
Contemporary Buildings, p. 64.

Glass louvres
Louvres are rows of angled slats
placed over a window, door or wall
surface, designed to allow light
and air to circulate but provide a
barrier against direct sunlight. Here,
the louvres are formed from semi-
opaque glass. *See also Windows*
and Doors, p. 144.

Regularly spaced banding
Banding is a thin horizontal
stripe or band running around
a building or façade. Here,
it denotes the distinction
between floors.

Aluminium cladding
The second most widely extracted
metal after iron, aluminium is most
often used as a cladding material
as it is relatively lightweight and
resistant to corrosion thanks to the
durable oxide layer on its surface.
As in this example, aluminium can
also be anodized, allowing a variety
of coloured finishes. *See also Walls*
and Surfaces, p. 117.

Contemporary Buildings / 1

Contemporary architecture encompasses an ever-growing multitude of different building types as a result of both increasing specialization and hybridization, with buildings today often combining many different uses. One of the consequences of this is an almost incomprehensible formal variety: buildings of all shapes and sizes, utilizing a vast range of different materials, and employing a diversity of architectural styles.

Yet within this apparent confusion it is possible to detect a series of recurring and visually identifiable trends that point to common underlying ideas, theories and approaches. This section introduces eight of the most significant and widespread trends. In keeping with the other sections of this chapter, each of these trends is identified according to its visual characteristics, which are then related to the

ideas, pressures and contexts of which they are manifestations.

The second part of this section goes beyond these key trends to look at some constituent formal characteristics that have emerged from them. The vocabulary used to describe the formal appearance of contemporary architecture evolves as quickly as architecture itself, so this section should be treated as inherently incomplete.

Minimalist ›
Minimalism in architecture is the paring-back of a design to all but the essentials of a space or structure. It is identifiable by the rejection of decoration and ornament in favour of clean, smooth surfaces; simple, often natural lighting; and the clearly expressed arrangement of spaces and volumes. Minimalism often extends to colour, combining white surfaces with the natural colours of materials, although bolder colours are sometimes used.

Tony Fretton Architects, Fuglsang Art Museum, Toreby, Denmark, 2008.

Parametric ›
Parametric design is characterized by curving, sinewy and amorphous forms. It emerged during the 1990s as a way of using computer algorithms to model the impact of a series of parameters on an architectural design in real time. It is seen by its promoters as enabling buildings to dynamically integrate into their social and topographical contexts, while for its critics it is arbitrary form making.

Zaha Hadid Architects, Heydar Aliyev Cultural Center, Baku, Azerbaijan, 2013.

Local ›

Architects are increasingly looking to the crafts, traditions and materials local to where they are building. Driving this is the aspiration to better integrate buildings into local cultures and communities. In addition, many architects now look to learn from vernacular architectures which have, for example, evolved techniques for dealing with climatic conditions that do not rely on mechanical ventilation or cooling.

Francis Kéré, Gando Primary School, Burkina Faso, 2001.

Reuse and retrofit ›

Buildings have always been adapted, remade and reused, but as a result of the climate emergency, this has acquired new urgency and vigour. Retrofitting – the augmentation and reimagining of existing structures – allows the embodied energy and carbon held within existing buildings to be retained while opening them up to new uses. From a symbolic perspective, the reworking of existing buildings also has powerful implications for culture and memory.

David Chipperfield Architects, Neues Museum, Berlin, Germany, 1997–2009.

Contemporary Buildings / 2

Sustainable ›

Sustainable architecture aims to limit a building's impact on the environment. Sustainable design considers both the building's construction and use. Typical strategies include an efficient structure that minimizes the use of carbon-intensive materials such as concrete, and features that reduce a building's energy usage once it is complete, for example high-specification glazing, passive ventilation, green walls and shading.

WOHA, Kampung Admiralty, Singapore, 2018.

Iconic ›

This term describes the trend towards buildings that are typically large in scale, bold or idiosyncratic in form, and which are readily translatable into an image and a symbol of the city, and even country, in which they are located. There are numerous examples of iconic buildings throughout history, but the trend became particularly pronounced during the 1990s and 2000s and was associated with a number of so-called 'starchitects'.

OMA, CCTV Headquarters, Beijing, China, 2012.

Diagrammatic ›

In the early stage of a building's design, diagrams are frequently used to schematize the various requirements of the brief and help conceive the building's programme (the activities that it is intended to support). In some instances that diagram is translated directly into its built form. For this reason, such diagrammatic buildings vary considerably, but are generally characterized by being formed from a series of constituent parts, bold use of colour and reliance on a signature spatial or formal device.

BIG, VIA 57 West, New York, USA, 2016.

Pop ›

Pop architecture is conceived to appeal directly to the public. Buildings of this type are frequently stylistically bold and playful, using bright colours and striking forms in ways that are intended to be visually appealing, approachable and enchanting. The approach is particularly prevalent in retail, community buildings and temporary pavilions created for cultural events and festivals.

MVRDV, Markthal, Rotterdam, Netherlands, 2014.

Contemporary Buildings › Building Forms

Today, buildings are unconstrained by traditional plans and elevations, and can be constructed in seemingly any shape, often formed with the help of computer-aided design (CAD) software. While several of the terms illustrated here – such as canted, battered and rectilinear – can be used to describe features in pre-modern buildings, in modern and contemporary architecture they have a quite different expression. Other terms are wholly specific to architecture of the last 50 years, and they helpfully allow building forms to be described that cannot be defined using traditional architectural terminology.

Rectilinear structures ›
A building or façade composed from a series of vertical and horizontal elements. *See also The Modern Block, p. 52.* (Steven Holl Architects, Simmons Hall, MIT, Cambridge, Massachusetts, USA, 2002.)

Irregular fenestration ›
An unevenly spaced arrangement of windows, often of differing sizes. *See also p. 88; High-Rise Buildings, p. 59.* (Zaha Hadid, Phaeno Science Centre, Wolfsburg, Germany, 2005.)

Crystalline ››
Three-dimensional structures in which identical or very similarly shaped units are repeated. (Foster + Partners, The Great Court, British Museum, London, UK, 2000.)

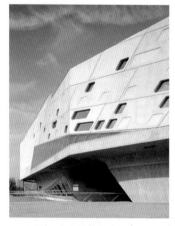

Projection ›
A projection supported solely at one end, with no supporting piers underneath. (GBQC, Douglas Cardinal, Ltd., Jones & Jones Architects and SmithGroup, National Museum of the American Indian, Washington, DC, USA, 2004.)

Batter ››
An inclined wall face, sloping towards the top. *See also Street-Facing Buildings, p. 45.* (OMA, Public Library, Seattle, Washington, USA, 2004.)

Cant ›
A wall face angled less than 90 degrees from the façade surface. (WZMH, Sun Life Center, Toronto, Canada, 1984.)

Stacked ››
A building composed of multiple box-like components, which might be stacked vertically or connected horizontally. (SANAA, New Museum, New York City, USA, 2007.)

Curvilinear ›
A building whose shape is composed from one or more curved surfaces rather than a series of planes. *See also High-Rise Buildings, p. 59.* (Eero Saarinen, TWA Terminal, JFK Airport, New York, USA, 1962.)

Undulating ››
A building whose shape is composed from intersecting convex and concave curves, creating a wave-like form. (Oscar Niemeyer, Copan Building, São Paulo, Brazil, 1966.)

Amorphous ›
An irregularly shaped building that has no easily definable form. (Frank Gehry, Guggenheim Museum, Bilbao, Spain, 1997.)

Columns and Piers

Columns and Piers

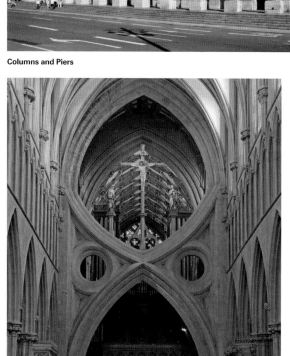

Arches

Timber

Concrete

Steel

CHAPTER 2 **Structures**

In the most fundamental sense, all buildings are structures designed to enclose space. The very act of constructing even in the simplest building creates an interior space, physically separated and distinct from the outside, yet also separated socially in terms of how spaces operate and are ascribed meaning. A building's structure is, therefore, key not only in the obvious way that without it there would be no building, but in terms of how buildings are perceived and understood. As such, all modes of building structure have achieved architectural significance beyond that simply related to their function.

The articulation of a building's structure, often encoded and manifested in a variety of ways, recurs throughout the history of architecture. In many ways, the articulation of structure can be seen as fundamental to architecture, occurring in all styles and periods. Indeed, it is often the most basic component in the constitution of many diverse and seemingly unrelated architectural languages. Thus, this chapter is intended to transcend stylistic classifications to present the key structural elements encountered in a whole range of buildings of different styles and periods. These are distilled into five broad groupings: **Columns and Piers** and **Arches** deal with fundamental structural devices. **Timber**, **Concrete** and **Steel** then focus on the various types of structures that are enabled by – and characteristic to – these materials.

Columns and Piers are integral to almost all forms of architecture, from primitive prehistoric structures up to the architecture of the present day. While providing a consistent structural function, they are ascribed meaning within architectural languages in a variety of ways. For example, in Classical architecture the column has evolved from having a purely structural function to, as part of the broader Classical orders, being key to the proportional logic of the entire building. Often a column or pier is ascribed meaning through sculptural ornamentation and, as illustrated on the following pages, the capital of a column or pier is a frequent site for this. In other examples, such as an unadorned Modernist piloti, an element can be ascribed meaning because of its placement and the way it transforms how a building is formed.

Arches are similarly structural elements which are central to architecture of very different styles and effects. The arch was the structural innovation that facilitated many of the great architectural and civil engineering developments of the Roman world. Moreover, in the triumphal arch – many of which still survive – it acquired important symbolic and ceremonial status. Arches are, of course, also key to Gothic architecture. Here, the new structural possibilities of the pointed arch allowed masons to build higher and more ornately. When traceried, the Gothic arch acted as an important frame for ornamental and symbolic decoration.

Materials have their own structural characteristics, and these enable certain types of structures that are particular to them. Before the twentieth century, almost all columns and piers were masonry and all arches were masonry or brick – these structural systems emerging in response to the structural properties of those materials. Similarly, the structural characteristics of timber have enabled certain types of structures that are particular to it. **Timber** has been used in architecture for millennia, and over that time particular techniques and structural forms have emerged and evolved. Today, timber is used in architecture in a way that is little changed from centuries ago, while, at the same time, new material innovations and cutting-edge engineering has seen a number of novel techniques and structural forms emerge.

In contrast, **Concrete** and **Steel** are the defining structural materials of the twentieth century. Synonymous with the modern age and its architectural manifestation – Modernism – concrete and steel are manufactured or synthetic materials, of a fundamentally different nature to stone (which is dug out of a quarry) or timber (from cutting down trees). Their structural characteristics have allowed architects to build bigger, faster, taller – if not always better – and have seen the emergence of a range of structural systems that utilize those characteristics in different ways.

Columns and Piers › Types

Columns and piers are upright structural members which act in compression to transmit loads from the structure above to the ground or to further structures below. They are most often used in post-and-lintel – or 'trabeated' – systems in which the horizontal lintels or beams are supported by posts – either piers or columns. Trabeated systems range from those found in primitive Neolithic architecture to providing the core of modern-day steel-framed structures.

Originating independently in several locations, columns and piers are found in all periods and styles of architecture. They are key elements in Ancient Egyptian, Persian and most famously Ancient Greek and Roman architecture. In these examples, and especially when deployed as part of the Classical orders, columns and piers are used not just for structural purposes but according to particular representational or symbolic values they are seen to embody.

Free-standing column ›
A detached, typically cylindrical upright *shaft* or member. (Classical façade of the Grand Theatre, Bordeaux, France.)

Engaged column ››
A column which is not free-standing but is built into a wall or surface. (San Lorenzo de El Escorial, Madrid, Spain.)

Pier ›
Any upright member providing vertical structural support. (Duomo di Siena, Italy.)

Pilaster ››
A flattened column that projects slightly from the face of a wall. (57–58 Lincoln's Inn Fields, London, UK.)

Caryatid ›
A heavily draped sculpted female figure that takes the place of a column or pier in supporting an *entablature*. (Erechtheion, Acropolis, Athens, Greece.)

Solomonic column ››
A helical column with a twisting *shaft*. Said to derive from the temple of Solomon in Jerusalem, Solomonic columns can be topped by any *capital*. Especially ornate, they are rarely used in architecture but more often found in furniture. (St Peter's, Rome, Italy.)

Fluted column ›
A column indented with vertical recessed grooves called *flutes*. The flat strips between flutes are called *fillets*. When the flutes wind around a column rather than running vertically the fluting is called 'serpentine'. (Ritz Carlton Hotel, Philadelphia, Pennsylvania, USA.)

Coupled columns ››
When two columns are placed side by side they are said to be coupled. When the *capitals* of coupled columns overlap they are called 'geminated' capitals. (St Paul's Cathedral, London, UK.)

Giant column ›
A column or pier that extends through two storeys. (Château de Vaux-le-Vicomte, Maincy, France.)

Colossal column ››
A column or pier that extends through more than two storeys. Because of their size, colossal columns are rarely used. (National Building Museum, Washington, DC, USA.)

Monumental column ›
A tall, *free-standing column* erected to commemorate a great military victory or hero. Monumental columns are sometimes topped by a sculpted figure and decorated with *relief* carving. (Trajan's Column, Rome, Italy.)

Compound column or pier ››
A column or pier composed of several *shafts*; also described as 'clustered'. *See also The Medieval Cathedral, pp.15, 18.* (New Cathedral, Salamanca, Spain.)

Obelisk ›
A narrow, tall, roughly rectangular structure tapering upwards with a pyramidal top. Derived from Egyptian architecture, obelisks are often used in Classical architecture. *See also Public Buildings, p. 47.* (Luxor Obelisk, Place de la Concorde, Paris, France.)

Piloti ››
Piers or columns that raise a building above ground level, freeing space for circulation or storage. *See also Country Houses and Villas, p. 37.* (Unité d'Habitation, Marseilles, France.)

Columns and Piers › The Classical Orders / 1

The Classical orders are the principal components of a Classical building, composed of base, shaft, capital and entablature. There are usually considered to be five orders – the Tuscan, Doric, Ionic, Corinthian and Composite – which vary in size and proportions. Their form and use is prescribed in numerous architectural treatises, especially those of the Renaissance which drew heavily on the writings of the Roman architect Vitruvius. As well as varying in size and proportions, the orders sit in a hierarchy of prestige. At the bottom the Tuscan, a Roman

order, is the plainest and largest, rarely used except where its massiveness and solidity are required. The Doric is usually found on a building's ground floor and there are two distinct varieties: the Roman Doric may have a fluted or unfluted shaft but has a base; the Greek Doric is characterized by its fluted shaft and lack of base. Used in the storey above the Doric, the Ionic is Greek in origin but was used extensively by the Romans; it is distinguished by its voluted capital and often fluted shaft. At the top of the hierarchy is the Corinthian order, reserved for

a building's principal storey or most important part. The Corinthian is characterized by acanthus leaves decorating its capital. The fifth order is the Composite, a Roman creation that combines the volutes of the Ionic with the acanthus leaves of the Corinthian. The Composite is present only in some treatises where it sits between the Ionic and Corinthian, or in some instances above the Corinthian as a summation of the other two orders.

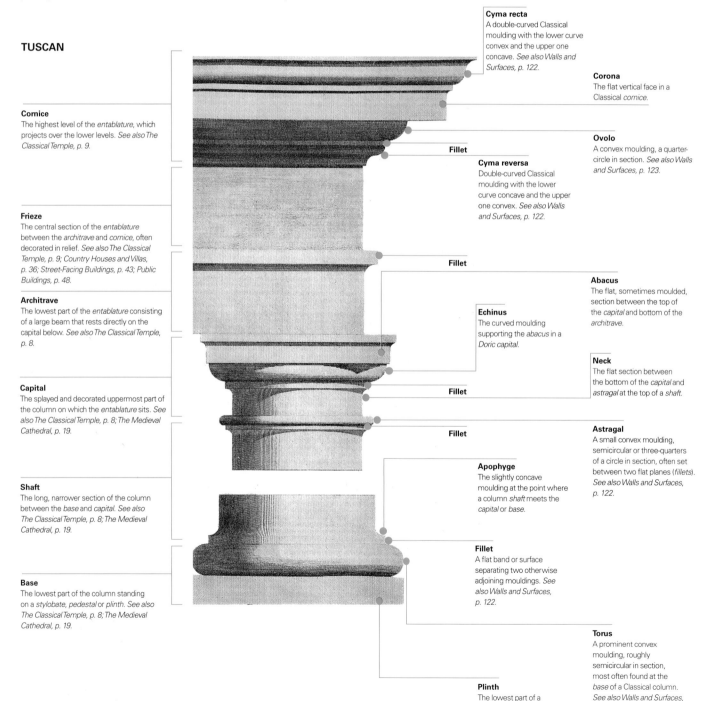

TUSCAN

Cornice
The highest level of the *entablature*, which projects over the lower levels. *See also The Classical Temple, p. 9.*

Frieze
The central section of the *entablature* between the *architrave* and *cornice*, often decorated in relief. *See also The Classical Temple, p. 9; Country Houses and Villas, p. 36; Street-Facing Buildings, p. 43; Public Buildings, p. 48.*

Architrave
The lowest part of the *entablature* consisting of a large beam that rests directly on the capital below. *See also The Classical Temple, p. 8.*

Capital
The splayed and decorated uppermost part of the column on which the *entablature* sits. *See also The Classical Temple, p. 8; The Medieval Cathedral, p. 19.*

Shaft
The long, narrower section of the column between the *base* and *capital*. *See also The Classical Temple, p. 8; The Medieval Cathedral, p. 19.*

Base
The lowest part of the column standing on a *stylobate*, *pedestal* or *plinth*. *See also The Classical Temple, p. 8; The Medieval Cathedral, p. 19.*

Cyma recta
A double-curved Classical moulding with the lower curve convex and the upper one concave. *See also Walls and Surfaces, p. 122.*

Corona
The flat vertical face in a Classical *cornice*.

Fillet

Ovolo
A convex moulding, a quarter-circle in section. *See also Walls and Surfaces, p. 123.*

Cyma reversa
Double-curved Classical moulding with the lower curve concave and the upper one convex. *See also Walls and Surfaces, p. 122.*

Fillet

Abacus
The flat, sometimes moulded, section between the top of the *capital* and bottom of the *architrave*.

Echinus
The curved moulding supporting the *abacus* in a Doric *capital*.

Neck
The flat section between the bottom of the *capital* and *astragal* at the top of a *shaft*.

Fillet

Astragal
A small convex moulding, semicircular or three-quarters of a circle in section, often set between two flat planes (*fillets*). *See also Walls and Surfaces, p. 122.*

Fillet

Apophyge
The slightly concave moulding at the point where a column *shaft* meets the *capital* or *base*.

Fillet
A flat band or surface separating two otherwise adjoining mouldings. *See also Walls and Surfaces, p. 122.*

Torus
A prominent convex moulding, roughly semicircular in section, most often found at the *base* of a Classical column. *See also Walls and Surfaces, p. 123.*

Plinth
The lowest part of a column *base*.

ROMAN DORIC

See also The Renaissance Church, pp. 22, 23; Public Buildings, p. 46.

Bucranium
A decorative motif in the form of a bull's skull, often flanked by *garlands*. *See also Walls and Surfaces, p. 126.*

Metope
The space between the *trigylphs* in a Doric *frieze*. *See also The Classical Temple, p. 9.*

Triglyph
A grooved rectangular block in a Doric *frieze* characterized by its three vertical bars. *See also The Classical Temple, p. 9; Public Buildings, p. 46.*

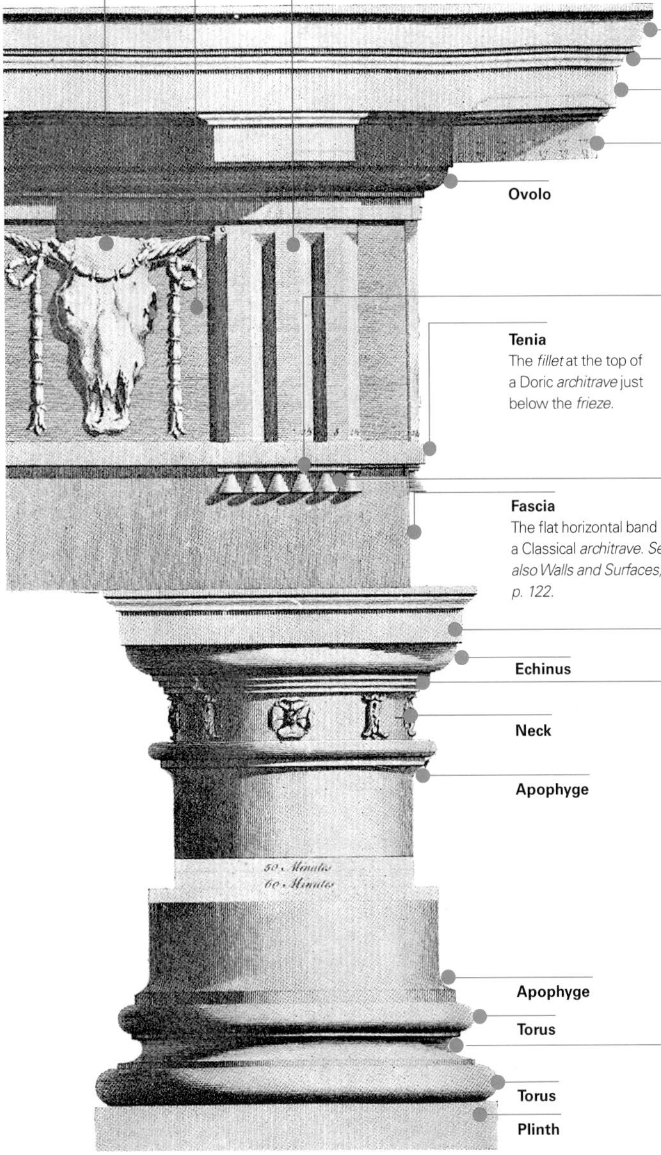

Cavetto
A concave moulding, usually a quarter-circle in section. *See also Walls and Surfaces, p. 122.*

Cyma reversa

Corona

Mutule
A projecting block, whose underside is sometimes inclined, sitting below the *corona* in a Doric *cornice*.

Ovolo

Cornice

Regula
The small rectangular band just below the *tenia* in a Doric *architrave* from which the *guttae* protrude.

Tenia
The *fillet* at the top of a Doric *architrave* just below the *frieze*.

Entablature
The superstructure above the capital level composed of *architrave*, *frieze* and *cornice*.

Frieze

Guttae
The small conical projections from the underside of the *regula* in a Doric *entablature*.

Fascia
The flat horizontal band in a Classical *architrave*. *See also Walls and Surfaces, p. 122.*

Architrave

Abacus

Echinus

Fillet

Neck

Capital

Apophyge

Shaft

Apophyge

Torus

Scotia
The concave moulding at the *base* of a Classical column between two *tori*. *See also Walls and Surfaces, p. 123.*

Torus

Plinth

Base

Columns and Piers › The Classical Orders / 2

GREEK DORIC
See also The Baroque Church, p. 24;
The Modern Block, p. 52.

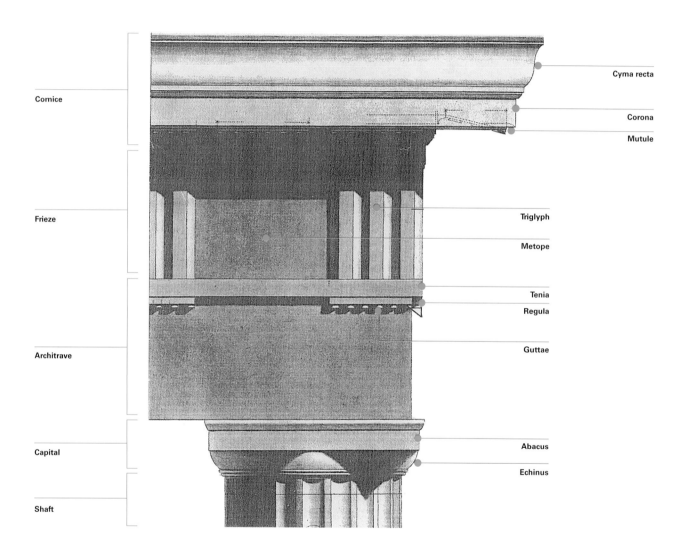

Cornice

Frieze

Architrave

Capital

Shaft

Cyma recta

Corona

Mutule

Triglyph

Metope

Tenia

Regula

Guttae

Abacus

Echinus

IONIC

See also The Renaissance Church, p. 22; The Baroque Church, p. 24; Public Buildings, p. 46.

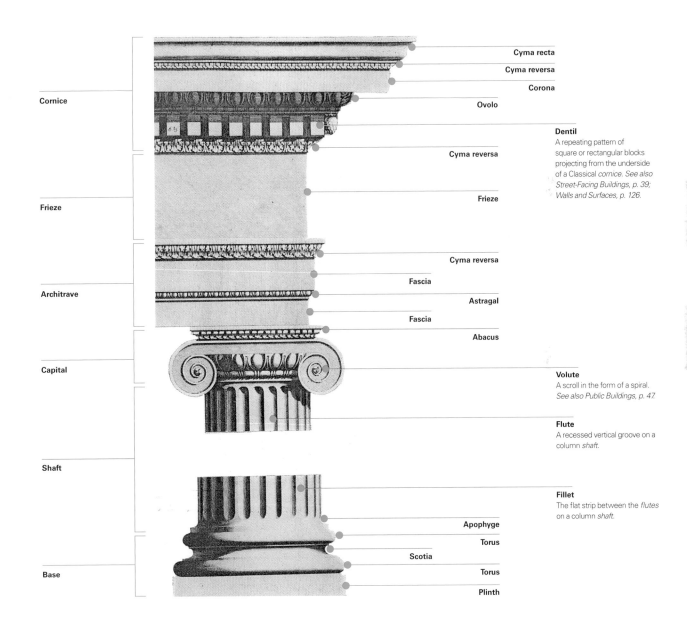

Cornice

Frieze

Architrave

Capital

Shaft

Base

Cyma recta

Cyma reversa

Corona

Ovolo

Dentil
A repeating pattern of square or rectangular blocks projecting from the underside of a Classical *cornice*. *See also Street-Facing Buildings, p. 39; Walls and Surfaces, p. 126.*

Cyma reversa

Frieze

Cyma reversa

Fascia

Astragal

Fascia

Abacus

Volute
A scroll in the form of a spiral. *See also Public Buildings, p. 47.*

Flute
A recessed vertical groove on a column *shaft*.

Fillet
The flat strip between the *flutes* on a column *shaft*.

Apophyge

Torus

Scotia

Torus

Plinth

Columns and Piers › The Classical Orders / 3

CORINTHIAN

See also The Renaissance Church, p. 28; The Baroque Church, p. 24; Country Houses and Villas, p. 36; Public Buildings, p. 47.

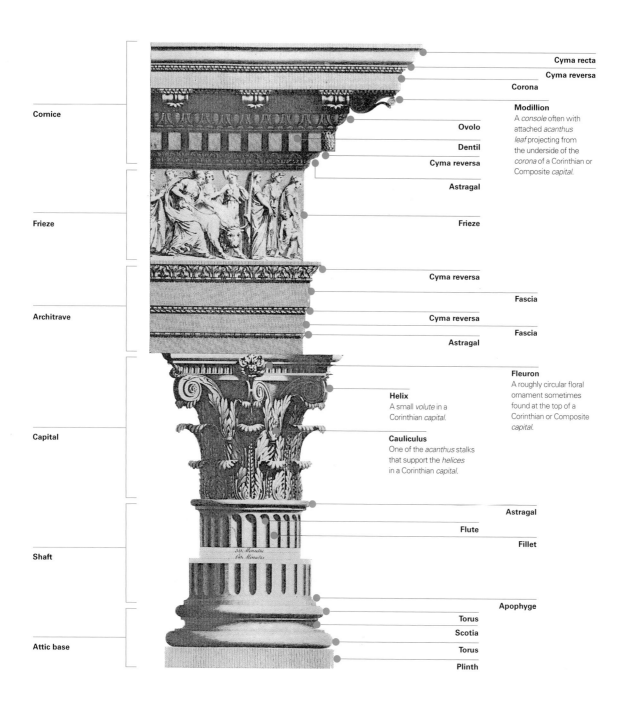

Cornice

Frieze

Architrave

Capital

Shaft

Attic base

Cyma recta

Cyma reversa

Corona

Modillion
A *console* often with attached *acanthus leaf* projecting from the underside of the *corona* of a Corinthian or Composite *capital.*

Ovolo

Dentil

Cyma reversa

Astragal

Frieze

Cyma reversa

Fascia

Cyma reversa

Fascia

Astragal

Fleuron
A roughly circular floral ornament sometimes found at the top of a Corinthian or Composite *capital.*

Helix
A small *volute* in a Corinthian *capital.*

Cauliculus
One of the *acanthus* stalks that support the *helices* in a Corinthian *capital.*

Astragal

Flute

Fillet

Apophyge

Torus

Scotia

Torus

Plinth

COMPOSITE

See also The Baroque Church, p. 29; Street-Facing Buildings, p. 39; Public Buildings, p. 50.

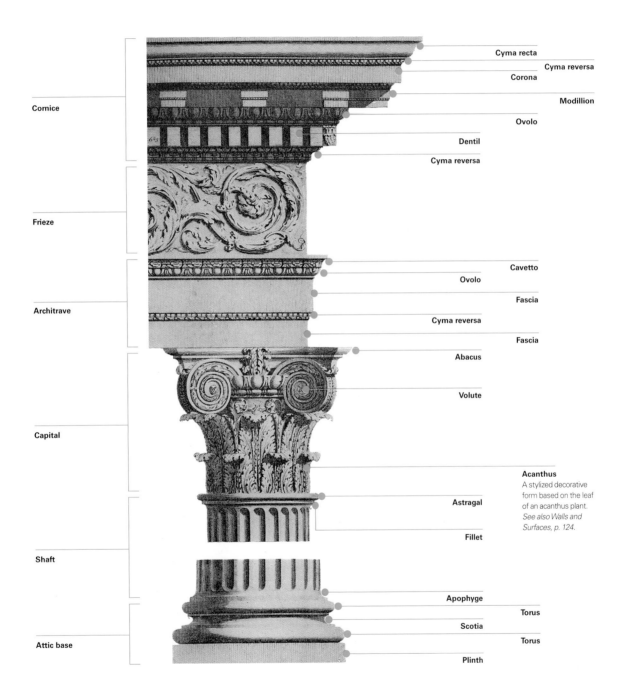

Cornice

Frieze

Architrave

Capital

Shaft

Attic base

Cyma recta

Cyma reversa

Corona

Modillion

Ovolo

Dentil

Cyma reversa

Cavetto

Ovolo

Fascia

Cyma reversa

Fascia

Abacus

Volute

Acanthus
A stylized decorative form based on the leaf of an acanthus plant. *See also Walls and Surfaces, p. 124.*

Astragal

Fillet

Apophyge

Torus

Scotia

Torus

Plinth

Columns and Piers › Non-Classical Capitals

The capital of a column or pier is the splayed and often decorated uppermost part on which the lintel or beam sits; or, in a Classical example, it supports the entablature. Capitals are found in most columns because they help to transmit the load from the lintel or beam above to the shaft below. Because of their prominent position at the top of the column, capitals are often decoratively carved, sometimes highly ornately.

While in Classical architecture the capital carving mainly corresponds to one of the five orders, in Gothic architecture, by contrast, there is no such rigid prescription and there is a great variety of different types of capital, used in many different contexts. This variety is, of course, not confined to the Gothic but, as the examples in this section illustrate, exists in all styles of architecture. Indeed, even in Classical architecture itself, there is more variation in how each capital is carved than many architectural treatises generally accept.

Block capital ›
The simplest capital form with a gradual change in profile from the round bottom to the square top. This otherwise plain capital type is often decorated in various forms of *relief*.

Cushion capital ››
A capital shaped like a cube with its lower corners rounded off. The resultant semicircular faces are called 'shields'. Its angles may sometimes be incised with narrow grooves called 'tucks'.

Foliated capital ›
The generic term for any capital incorporating foliage.

Crocket capital ››
A capital adorned with crockets – scroll-like, projecting leaf forms.

Flat-leaf capital ›
A simple *foliated* capital with broad leaves at each corner.

Stiff-leaf capital ››
A *foliated* capital usually with three-lobed leaves whose tops are folded outwards.

Scallop capital ›
A tapering cube-shaped capital, corrugated with several raised cones between recessed grooves, forming a shell-like pattern. When the cones do not reach the full height of the capital, they are described as 'slipped'.

Basket capital ››
A capital with interlaced carving resembling wickerwork, usually found in Byzantine architecture.

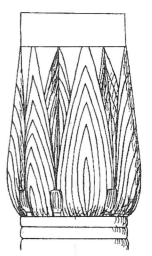

Historiated or figured capital ›
A capital decorated with human or animal figures, often combined with foliage. In some examples the scene is intended to portray a story.

Lotus capital ››
An Egyptian capital in the form of a lotus bud.

Palm capital ›
An Egyptian capital with splayed leaf forms resembling the branches of a palm tree.

Campaniform capital ››
An Egyptian bell-shaped capital resembling an open papyrus flower.

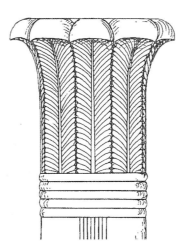

Arches › Elements

An arch is a structure composed from one or more curves, which spans a distance and typically supports a load. Arches were first used extensively by the Romans. They were a key element of their civil engineering projects as they were able to span longer distances than a simple trabeated system. Arches were used in bridges, aqueducts, viaducts, ceremonial triumphal arches, and, in the related development of the vault and dome, roofing large interior spaces.

While the Romans made use of round arches, the advent of the pointed arch in the eleventh and twelfth centuries – formed in its most basic form from two intersecting curves – allowed medieval masons to build taller structures with thinner supports. Indeed, arches need not be made with one continuous curve but can be formed from several intersecting ones. Moreover, despite the etymology of the word and its usual definition as a curved structure, not all arches are curved; a flat arch with horizontal extrados and intrados can be formed from specially shaped angled voussoirs.

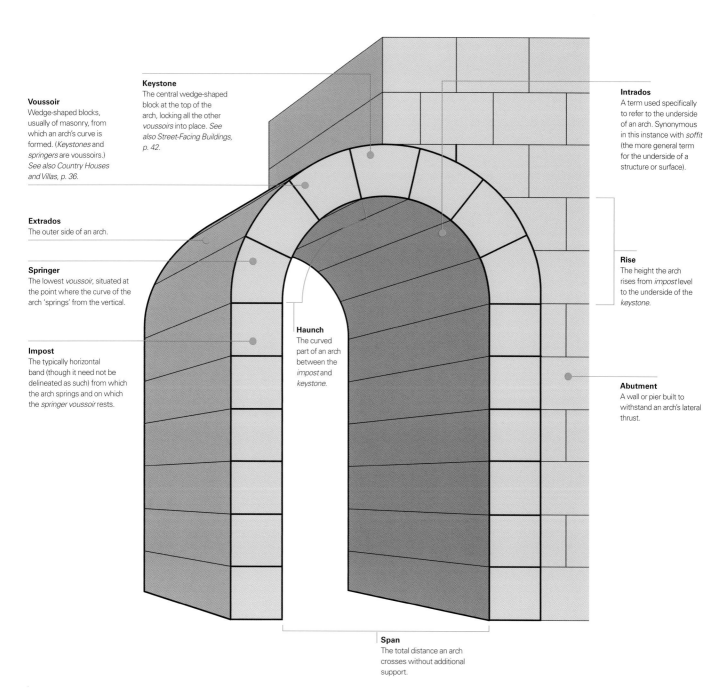

Voussoir
Wedge-shaped blocks, usually of masonry, from which an arch's curve is formed. (*Keystones* and *springers* are voussoirs.) *See also Country Houses and Villas, p. 36.*

Keystone
The central wedge-shaped block at the top of the arch, locking all the other *voussoirs* into place. *See also Street-Facing Buildings, p. 42.*

Intrados
A term used specifically to refer to the underside of an arch. Synonymous in this instance with *soffit* (the more general term for the underside of a structure or surface).

Extrados
The outer side of an arch.

Springer
The lowest *voussoir*, situated at the point where the curve of the arch 'springs' from the vertical.

Rise
The height the arch rises from *impost* level to the underside of the *keystone*.

Haunch
The curved part of an arch between the *impost* and *keystone*.

Impost
The typically horizontal band (though it need not be delineated as such) from which the arch springs and on which the *springer voussoir* rests.

Abutment
A wall or pier built to withstand an arch's lateral thrust.

Span
The total distance an arch crosses without additional support.

Arches › Round Arches

A round arch is any arch formed from a smooth continuous curve with no apices (pl. of apex). The simplest type is a semicircular arch composed from a curve with one centre whose rise is equal to half its span. Other round arches can be made from segments of larger curves or from multiple intersecting curves. *See also The Medieval Cathedral, p. 18; Windows and Doors, p. 141.*

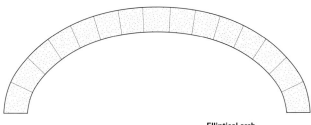

Elliptical arch
An arch whose curve is formed from half an ellipse – a regular oval shape formed from the intersection of a cone by a plane.

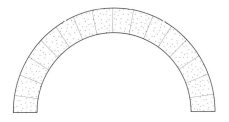

Semicircular arch
An arch whose curve has one centre with the *rise* equal to half the *span*, giving it the form of a semicircle.

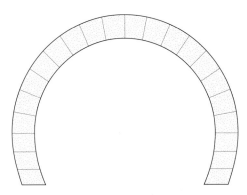

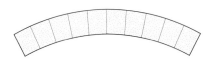

Segmental arch
An arch whose curve is one segment of a semicircle whose centre is below *impost* level; its *span* is thus much larger than its *rise. See also The Modern Block, p. 54.*

Horseshoe arch
An arch whose curve is in the form of a horseshoe; it is wider at *haunch* level than at *impost* level. Horseshoe arches are emblematic of Islamic architecture.

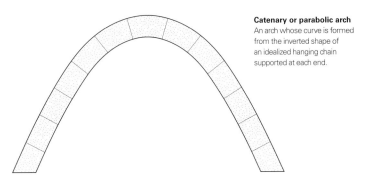

Catenary or parabolic arch
An arch whose curve is formed from the inverted shape of an idealized hanging chain supported at each end.

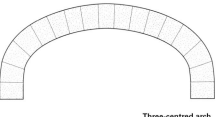

Three-centred arch
An arch formed from three intersecting curves. The central one has a larger radius than the two on either side, with its centre located below *impost* level.

Arches › Pointed Arches

A pointed arch is formed from two or more intersecting curves (straight members in the case of the triangular arch), two of which meet in a central apex. Pointed arches are an integral feature of Gothic architecture, as well as Islamic architecture which may have been the inspiration for the use of the pointed arch in Europe. *See also Windows and Doors, p. 141.*

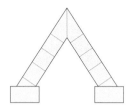

Triangular arch
The simplest pointed arch, formed from two diagonal members standing on *imposts* and resting on each other at the apex.

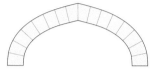

Four-centred or depressed arch
An arch made up from four intersecting curves. The centres of the outer two curves sit at *impost* level within the *span* while the centres of the inner two curves similarly sit within the span but below impost level.

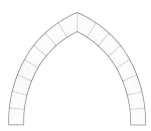

Equilateral arch
An arch formed from two intersecting curves, the centres of which are at the opposing *imposts.* The chords of each curve are equal to the arch *span. See also The Medieval Cathedral, p. 19.*

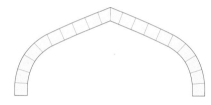

Tudor arch
Often regarded as being synonymous with a *four-centred arch*, a Tudor arch strictly denotes an arch formed from two outer curves whose centres sit within the *span* at *impost* level. The curves are carried on in diagonal straight lines to a central apex.

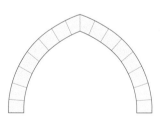

Drop arch
Squatter in shape than the *equilateral arch.* In a drop arch the centres of each curve are located within the *span.*

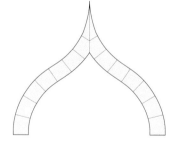

Ogee arch
A pointed arch, each side of which is composed of a lower concave curve intersecting a higher convex one. The centres of the outer two concave curves sit at *impost* level within the *span* or, as here, at its centre. The centres of the inner two convex curves stand above the arch *rise. See also Roofs, p. 159.*

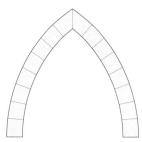

Lancet arch
More slender than the *equilateral arch.* In a lancet arch the centres of each curve are located outside the *span.*

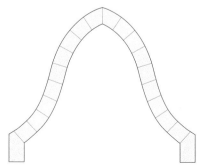

Reverse ogee arch
Similar to an ogee arch, except that the lower two curves are convex while the higher two are concave.

Arches › Other Arch Forms

Arches are not confined to the regular round or pointed types, but are found in a variety of other forms. Especially common examples include foiled arches, flat arches and gauged arches.

Three-foiled arch
A three-centred arch with the centre of the central curve standing above *impost* level, creating three distinct arcs or foils.

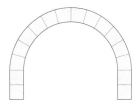

Stilted arch
An arch whose *springer* is some distance above its *impost* level.

Multifoiled or cusped arch
An arch composed of several small round or pointed curves, creating recessions called foils and triangular protrusions called cusps.

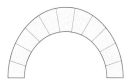

Florentine arch
A semicircular arch whose *extrados* is formed from a curve whose centre sits higher than that of its *intrados*.

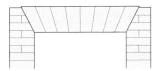

Flat arch
An arch with horizontal *extrados* and *intrados* created from specially shaped angled *voussoirs*.

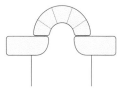

Bell arch
Similar to a *shouldered arch*, a bell arch consists of a curved arch resting on two *corbels*.

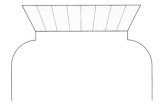

Shouldered arch
A flat arch supported by two outer arcs, sometimes seen as separate *corbels*.

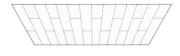

Gauged arch
An arch of any shape but usually either round or flat, in which the *voussoirs* have been shaped to radiate from a single centre. *See also Walls and Surfaces, p. 105.*

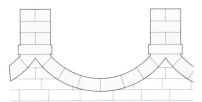

Inverted arch
An upside-down arch often used in foundations. *See also The Modern Block, p. 54.*

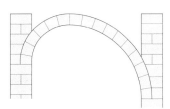

Unequal or rampant arch
An asymmetrical arch whose *imposts* are at different heights.

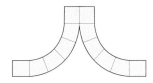

Inflexed arch
A pointed arch composed from two convex curves rather than the more typical concave curves.

Arches › Types

There are a number of arches or series of arches whose types are classified according to their function rather than being dependent upon a particular form. For example, an arcade – a repeating series of arches set upon columns or piers – may be composed from round or pointed arches. This section includes some of the most important and prevalent arch types.

Arcade ›
A repeating series of arches set upon columns or piers. An arcade is termed 'blind' when it is applied to a surface or wall. *See also Street-Facing Buildings, p. 42.* (Spedale degli Innocenti, Florence, Italy.)

Respond
An *engaged column* or *corbel* usually deployed at the end of an *arcade* against a wall or pier.

Spandrel
The roughly triangular space created between the outer side of an arch's curve, a horizontal bounding above (such as a *string course*) and the curve of an adjacent arch or some kind of vertical moulding, column or wall. *See also The Medieval Cathedral, pp. 14, 19.*

Squinch ›
An arch constructed across the corner created by the intersection of two perpendicular walls. Squinches are often used to provide additional structural support, especially for a *dome* or *tower* above. *See also High-Rise Buildings, p. 56.* (Mausoleum of Abu Sa'id at Meana Baba, Turkmenistan.)

Blind arch ››
An arch set into a wall or surface but with no actual opening. *See also Country Houses and Villas, p. 36.* (Waterhouse Square, Holborn, London, UK.)

Compound arch ›
An arch formed by two or more arches of diminishing size set concentrically within one another. (Law Courts, London, UK.)

Discharging arch ››
An arch built above a *lintel* to help carry the weight on either side of the opening. Also called a 'relieving' arch. *See also Street-Facing Buildings, p. 40.* (Eighteenth-century house, London, UK.)

Strainer arch ›
An arch placed between opposing piers or walls to provide additional lateral support. (Wells Cathedral, Somerset, UK.)

Triumphal arch ››
An ancient motif of a central archway flanked by two smaller openings. Deployed as a free-standing structure in the Classical world, it was revived in the Renaissance and used as a motif on a variety of structures. (Arch of Constantine, Rome, Italy.)

Proscenium arch ›
An arch surmounting the stage in many theatres, framing the opening between stage and auditorium. (Royal Opera House, Stockholm, Sweden.)

Timber / 1

Timber structures go back to the very origins of what we understand as architecture. Theorists in the eighteenth century went so far as to postulate that Adam himself had built the first building out of wood in the Garden of Eden. But by the beginning of the twentieth century, timber was increasingly perceived as backward and traditional, in contrast to the modern materials of steel and concrete. Nevertheless, timber has remained an important building material across the world, though typically employed on small scales and in vernacular settings.

Today, timber is enjoying a resurgence as architects rediscover a material that lends itself to intricate and precise off-site manufacture,

is incredibly quick to assemble on-site, is safe and durable, and has a drastically smaller environmental footprint than conventional steel and concrete. While concrete is one of the largest single contributors to global CO_2 emissions, timber is a renewable material allowing the possibility of net zero or even carbon positive construction. In addition, technical innovations in materials and engineering, particularly around the use of cross-laminated timber, has offered architects new structural and expressive possibilities.

PARA Project, Brugge Diptych Pavilion, Bruges, Belgium, 2021.

Roof panel
A flat component lying on top of rafters which acts as or provides support to the roof cladding.

Timber stud
The smaller vertical members between larger posts in a timber-framed building. *See Street-Facing Buildings, p. 38.*

Lintel
The supporting horizontal member that surmounts a window or door. *See Windows and Doors, p. 132.*

Principal rafter
In a *truss* roof, the rafters that form the truss structure. *See Roofs, p. 160.*

Ridge beam
In a *truss* roof, a beam that runs along the top of the truss against which the *rafters* rest. *See Roofs, p. 160.*

Top plate
The horizontal beam on which the rafters sit (equivalent to a wall plate).

Collar beam
In a *truss* roof, a transverse horizontal beam which spans the underside of two opposing rafters, sitting above the *wall plate* but below the apex. *See Roofs, p. 161.*

Purlin
In a truss roof, a longitudinal beam on top of the *principal rafters* that gives support to the *common rafters* (where applicable) and the roof cladding above. *See Roofs, p. 162.*

Nogging
A horizontal piece of timber inserted between two vertical ones to provide structural rigidity.

Wall plate
In a *truss* roof, the beam along the top of the wall on which the *common rafters* sit. *See Roofs, p. 160.*

Traditional timber frame ›
Until fairly recently, the
structural use of timber in
building construction was
limited to relatively small-scale
structures, such as private
houses. Broadly speaking,
most of these examples
tended to employ structures
and techniques that were little
different to those established
and employed centuries before.

*The Great Barn,
Harmondsworth, UK, early
fifteenth century.*

Cross-laminated timber ›
First developed in the 1990s,
cross-laminated timber is a
so-called engineered wood,
produced by sawing a piece
of timber into layers, turning
every other layer 90 degrees,
and then gluing them together.
This gives the timber greater
and more consistent structural
rigidity, while maintaining its
comparative lightness. This
allows it to be used in situations
where steel or concrete would
usually be required.

*Waugh Thistleton Architects,
Murray Grove housing,
London, UK, 2009.*

Timber / 2

Waffle grid ›

Waffle grids are most often used to create roofs or canopies. They are formed of intersecting panels of cross-laminated timber, which are glued and then usually braced by steel threads. Timber waffle grids can take the form of flat panels, but also allow for more sculptural curving forms that would be very difficult to achieve using other materials.

Jürgen Mayer and ARUP, Metropol Parasol, Seville, Spain, 2011.

Gridshell ›
A gridshell is a gridded structure
in the shape of a double curve,
from which it derives its
strength. Gridshells are typically
constructed from steel but
are increasingly being realized
in timber thanks to advanced
engineering and the necessary
incredibly precise fabrication
that can be achieved through
the combination of traditional
hand techniques and cutting-
edge computer automation.

Cullinan Studio, Downland
Gridshell, Weald and Downland
Living Museum, West Sussex,
UK, 2002.

Concrete / 1

As a construction material, concrete has been around certainly since the Roman world. There, it released builders from the constraints of brick and stone, and allowed the construction of some of the great structures of the ancient world – aqueducts, bridges, baths and temples. The Pantheon's second-century AD domed concrete roof was Rome's greatest achievement in this field, and remains the largest unreinforced concrete dome in the world.

Concrete was not widely used again until the end of the nineteenth century, after which it went on to become the key material of early twentieth-century Modernism. In its reinforced form – set with steel bars or grids which increase its tensile strength – concrete facilitated some of the great architectural advances of the twentieth century. Although often hidden within the core of a building, during the 1960s and 1970s many architects chose to leave concrete exposed in its raw and unfinished state. The French *béton brut* – which translates literally as 'raw concrete' – gave the movement its name: Brutalism.

Concrete is now the most widely produced man-made material and currently contributes around one-twentieth of man-made CO_2 emissions each year. As a result, the designers of many ecologically aware building projects often seek to reduce dependency on concrete in favour of more sustainable materials.

Kallmann, McKinnell and Knowles, Boston City Hall, Boston, 1963–68.

Rectilinear concrete grid
A concrete frame composed entirely from a series of vertical and horizontal elements. *See also The Modern Block, p. 52.*

Flat roof
A roof whose pitch is almost horizontal (a slight incline is usually retained to ensure that water runs off). *See also Roofs, p. 149.*

Corbels
A series of brackets projecting from the wall to support the structure above. Here they are supporting the projecting upper storeys. *See also Roofs, p. 152.*

Concrete pier
A pier is an upright member providing vertical structural support. Here it is formed from concrete. *See also Columns and Piers, p. 68.*

Brick base-structure
The lower part on which a building sits or from which it appears to emerge.

Irregular fenestration
An unevenly spaced arrangement of windows, often of differing sizes. *See also High-Rise Buildings, p. 59.*

Municipal space
Publicly accessible open areas such as parks or ceremonial squares. Here, the municipal space is paved with the same brick as the building's substructure to visually link the two.

Exposed concrete
Concrete that is unclad and left unpainted and exposed on the exterior or interior of a building, for either aesthetic or cost-saving reasons. This use of concrete is also known by its French description – *béton brut* – which literally means 'raw concrete'.

Cast in-place structure ›
Also known as poured in-place
or cast in-situ, cast in-place is a
construction technique in which
a building's foundations, floor
slabs and structural members
are cast on-site. Formwork,
most often of timber, is used
to create the mould in which
the concrete is poured and is
removed once it has hardened.
Cast in-place concrete is
usually covered on the exterior
and interior of buildings, but
is sometimes deliberately
exposed, for example in
polished concrete floors or
fair-faced surfaces.

Le Corbusier, Unité d'Habitation,
Marseille, France, 1952.

Pre-cast construction ›
Pre-cast concrete differs
from cast in-place concrete
by being cast off-site before
being transported to site for
construction. The advantages
of pre-cast structures over cast
in-place are the lower costs
associated with standardization,
the speed of construction
on-site, and the higher quality
control over colour and finish;
its downsides are higher
transportation costs and the
difficulty of making any changes
once the components have
been cast.

Grafton Architects, Town
House, Kingston University,
London, UK, 2019.

Concrete / 2

Panel construction ›
Concrete panel construction is
a form of pre-cast construction
where standardized panels
are cast off-site before being
brought on-site and lifted
into place. The technique
was popular for housing
developments in the 1960s and
early 1970s, with a number of
companies offering different
panel construction systems
which could be adapted to
different sites and scales.

*Hans Peter 'Felix' Trenton and
London Borough of Southwark
Architects' Department,
Aylesbury Housing Estate,
London, UK, 1967–77.*

Sculptural ›

The structural properties of reinforced concrete allow it to be used structurally in a highly sculptural way, with wide spans, dramatic cantilevers, sweeping curves and sharp angles. This was one of the defining characteristics of the Brutalist movement of the 1960s and early 1970s, notable for its bold use of concrete which it typically left in its raw, 'unfinished' state.

Gottfried Böhm, Church of the Pilgrimage, Neviges, Germany, 1968.

Steel / 1

The potential of metal as a building material became most visibly apparent in Joseph Paxton's ground-breaking Crystal Palace for the Great Exhibition of 1851, held in London's Hyde Park. Built almost entirely from cast iron and glass, it prefigured later developments in steel-framed structures.

As a building material cast iron is limited, being relatively brittle. However, steel – which contains lower amounts of carbon – has far greater tensile strength. With the advent of industrial steel-making in the latter half of the

nineteenth century, steel soon became a key building material. During the twentieth century, it was frequently used to provide a structural 'skeleton' for buildings of all types – a practice that remains central to architecture today. As in the examples illustrated here, modern steel frames are usually composed from a network of steel posts, sometimes tubular and filled with concrete, which support horizontal beams. This structure is sometimes strengthened by further diagonal members. Corrugated steel sheets, on to which concrete is poured to provide floors

as well as structural rigidity, usually sit on top of this structural framework. Sometimes, the corrugated sheets are omitted in favour of precast concrete panels.

While steel is used because of its strength and comparative resistance to erosion, it is susceptible to fire, which could lead to structural failure. For this reason, steel frameworks are usually encased in concrete or sprayed with insulating fibre to protect them from heat.

Richard Rogers and Renzo Piano, Centre Georges Pompidou, Paris, 1971–77.

Lift
A vertical transportation device, essentially an enclosed platform moved up and down by mechanical means, either by a system of pulleys (a 'traction lift') or hydraulic pistons (a 'hydraulic lift'). *See also Stairs and Lifts, p. 168.*

Steel tie beam
A horizontal beam between two adjacent piers. *See Roofs, p. 161.*

External escalator
A moving staircase formed from a motor-driven chain of steps. Usually found inside a building's envelope, here it is attached to the steel exoskeleton. *See also Stairs and Lifts, p. 169.*

Emergency stairs
A staircase that runs the full length of the building, included to facilitate evacuation during an emergency such as a fire.

Rectilinear steel frame
A steel frame composed principally from series of vertical and horizontal members. Here, the steel frame forms an exoskeleton with a series of steel *piers* supporting the building interior. A further layer of external steel framework supports various service ducts, *escalators*, stairs and lifts.

Diagonal braces
Angled members that create a system of triangles to provide additional bracing to a *rectilinear structure*. The addition of diagonal members to a steel-framed structure is known as 'triangulation'.

Steel pier
A pier is an upright member providing vertical structural support. Here it is formed from steel. *See also Columns and Piers, p. 68.*

Glass curtain wall
A curtain wall is a non-load-bearing enclosure or envelope of a building, attached to the structure but standing separate from it. Glass has the benefit of allowing light to penetrate deep into a building. *See also Public Buildings, p. 51; The Modern Block, p. 54; Walls and Surfaces, p. 115.*

Rectilinear steel frame ›
The simplest steel structure is a grid of vertical posts and horizontal beams that have been bolted together, and which provide the structural support for a building's floors, walls and roof. The characteristic I-beam shape is used to provide greater structural strength and rigidity. Steel frames are used for their speed of construction, ease of manufacture off-site and adaptability to a variety of scales and shapes.

Charles and Ray Eames, Eames House, Los Angeles, California, USA, 1949.

Space frame ›
A space frame is a three-dimensional truss formed from a series of interlocking triangles that in turn form interlocking tetrahedrons. The resulting structure is lightweight and rigid, allowing it to be used to span wide distances with relatively few supports, whether they are straight or curved. For this reason, space frames are frequently used in factories, warehouses and indoor arenas.

Kenzo Tange, Arata Isozaki and Atsushi Ueda, Festival Plaza, Expo '70, Osaka, Japan, 1970.

Steel / 2

Diagrid ›

A diagrid, as its name suggests, is a diagonal grid of structural members. Each unit combines both vertical and lateral support in a way that is lighter and more efficient than conventional rectilinear structures. Diagrids can also be used to produce curving structures, giving architects more freedom in the shapes they are able to create. Diagrids are often used as exoskeletons, with the exposed structure becoming a key aspect of the building's expressive power.

Foster + Partners, 30 St Mary Axe ('The Gherkin'), London, UK, 2004.

Tube structure ›

Tube structures are found in
high-rise buildings. First used in
the 1960s, tube structures treat
the building as a hollow tube,
which has strong resistance to
lateral loads imposed by wind.
The tube itself is created by
a tight perimeter of columns,
sometimes supported by
exterior cross-bracing, with
additional vertical supports
around the building's core.
Derivations of this technique
employ 'bundles' of adjacent
tubes, which allow buildings to
reach over 100 floors high.

*SOM, John Hancock Center,
Chicago, Illinois, USA, 1969.*

Steel / 3

Geodesic dome ›
Popularized by the American architect and thinker, Richard Buckminster Fuller in the 1950s and 1960s, a geodesic dome is a spherical dome formed from a thin, shell-like structure of interlocking triangles. Geodesic domes are light and structurally very rigid, but, despite Fuller's various attempts, their shape has limited their use beyond theme parks, temporary pavilions and botanical gardens.

Buckminster Fuller, United States Pavilion, Expo '67, Montreal, Canada, 1967.

Tensile structure ›
Tensile structures are those in which the structural components are held in place via tension rather than compression (although they are often supported by structures in compression). They typically take the form of tent-like structures, with a membrane pulled tight over masts by cables and wires. The advantages of tensile structures are their lightness and economic use of materials, as well as their formal flexibility and ability to be quickly assembled and disassembled.

Günther Behnisch and Frei Otto, Olympic Stadium, Munich, Germany, 1972.

Exoskeleton ›

As the word suggests, an exoskeleton is an external skeleton or building structure. The rationale for moving the structure to a building's exterior is to leave the interior space completely unencumbered by structural supports. The Pompidou Centre in Paris was a high-profile example of this approach, where it allowed radically open-plan gallery spaces, but it is now most often employed in commercial buildings requiring open-plan offices or trading floors, such as Eric Parry Architects' office building in King's Cross.

Eric Parry Architects, 4 Pancras Square, London, UK, 2018.

Monocoque ›

A monocoque structure is where a building's envelope or skin is doing all of the structural work. The word derives from the French, meaning 'single hull' in the context of boats. Monocoque structures are relatively unusual in architecture, being more common in car or aircraft design. Where they are used, however, they offer the potential for extremely efficient and striking designs.

Make Architects, Portsoken Pavilion, London, UK, 2008.

Walls and Surfaces

Windows and Doors

Roofs

Stairs and Lifts

Irrespective of style, scale or form, a building is formed from several key elements. All buildings have walls, apertures (windows and doors), roofs and, if they consist of more than one storey, stairs (or lifts and/ or escalators). Moreover, both conceptually and in practice, these elements usually stand as separate and discrete components of a building. As this chapter outlines in four sections, walls, windows and doors, roofs and stairs can take many different forms and be articulated in a huge variety of ways. They are all integral to a building's architectural display.

Walls and Surfaces are fundamental to the way buildings enclose space – both in creating a physical barrier between a building's interior and exterior, and in its internal compartmentalization. While the main functional requirement of a wall is to provide a barrier against the elements, they are the principal sites for architectural display. The choice of materials and how they are articulated – for example, in terms of finish or decorative moulding – both externally and internally is central to the way a building can be made to evoke meaning.

Windows and Doors are necessary in all buildings to let light into interior spaces and allow the movement of air, heat and people between outside and internal spaces. Because almost all walls feature them, the number, spacing and style of windows and doors is one of the most often used ways of articulating a façade. Windows and doors are here treated together because of their related functions, which have often led them to be treated similarly in architecture.

All buildings have **Roofs**, whether standing as semi-autonomous structures, such as domes or spires, merging imperceptibly and seamlessly with walls in irregularly shaped modern buildings, or simply enclosing from above the space created by walls. While in some buildings the roof is hidden behind a parapet, in others, because of its prominent position it is an important part of the architectural display. A roof's aesthetic impact is not necessarily confined to a building's exterior; the interior roof structure can be visible and in some instances – types of medieval rib vaults or timber ceilings are examples – is highly decorated.

Once buildings of more than one storey began to be constructed, a means of moving easily between storeys became a necessity. Two principal structures that facilitate this are: **Stairs** (which can take the mechanized form of escalators) **and Lifts** (elevators). All buildings over more than one storey have stairs and, although the main elements are constant they can be deployed in a whole variety of ways depending on the particular architectural context. Lifts tend to be found where disability access is required or in buildings of multiple storeys where stairs are less practical.

Walls and Surfaces › Masonry › Common Types of Stone

Stone is one of the most widely used building materials, due to its durability, great compressive strength and, in many locations, ready availability. Stone can also be hewn to create a variety of finishes and is a frequent medium for ornamental features such as moulding or relief.

There are, of course, many different types of stone each with its own properties, which affect how it is used. Because of its great weight, transporting it has, until comparatively recently, been very difficult and expensive. Thus, it is often possible to ascertain the type and relative availability of stone in a particular region from its prevalence in the local architecture. Moreover, in areas where stone is not readily available it is often found only in buildings of the highest prestige, as a display of the wealth and power required to procure it.

Marble ›
A metamorphic rock created by the metamorphism of sedimentary rocks such as *limestone*. Its characteristic veins as well as various colours come from impurities in the original rock. Marble is found in many places in the world; one of the most famous examples is Italy's Carrara marble, from which some of the greatest artistic and architectural achievements of antiquity and the Renaissance were created. (Pantheon, Rome, Italy.)

Granite ›
An igneous rock characterized by its large-grained crystals and hardness. For this reason, it is an extremely durable stone with good resistance to weathering but is consequently less suitable for decorative carving. Porphyry, the reddish-purple stone found in Egypt, is one of the most famous examples of granitic stone, used especially in ancient architecture. (Machu Picchu, Peru.)

Limestone ›

A sedimentary rock which, because it has not undergone metamorphosis, often contains thick veins as well as many fossils. While not as hard-wearing as *marble* or *granite*, limestone is relatively durable compared to other sedimentary rocks. Famous examples include travertine and Portland stone. (St Peter's Square, Rome, Italy.)

Man-made stone ›

An artificial stone-like substance composed from clay, ground stone and a binding agent or synthetic materials. 'Coade' stone is perhaps the most famous man-made stone. Composed from clay cast in moulds, during the late eighteenth and early nineteenth centuries it represented a way of reproducing otherwise expensive Classical elements and decoration in a relatively cheap way. The name comes from the founder of the firm that produced the stone, Mrs Eleanor Coade. (Westminster Bridge, London, UK.)

Masonry › Surfaces

Ashlar ›
A wall formed from flat-faced oblong blocks of stone laid with very precise joints so as to create an almost entirely smooth wall surface.

Boasted ashlar ››
An ashlar surface incised with horizontal or diagonal grooves.

Rubble masonry ›
A wall formed from irregularly shaped blocks of masonry often laid with thick mortar joints. When the gaps between the blocks are filled with rectangular stones of varying heights called 'snecks', it is described as 'snecked rubble' masonry.

Coursed rubble masonry ››
Like rubble masonry except that similarly sized blocks are grouped together to form horizontal courses of varying heights.

Knapped flint ›
The use of flint stones on a wall face with their cut, black faces turned outwards.

Flushwork ››
The use of *knapped flint* and dressed stone to create decorative schemes, often in a chequerboard pattern.

Dry-stone wall ›
A stone wall constructed from interlocking stones without using mortar.

Gabions ››
Metal cages filled with a dense material such as stone, but also sand and soil. They are usually used for purely structural purposes, especially in civil engineering projects, but can be found as architectural features in many modern buildings.

Masonry veneer ›
Also called 'masonry cladding', a masonry veneer is the use of masonry purely to face a building rather than to provide structural support. In multistorey buildings, it is frequently used, often with glass as here, in a *curtain wall. See also High-Rise Buildings, p. 56.*

Masonry › Rustication

Rustication is a style of masonry in which the joints between adjacent blocks of stone are accentuated. In some forms of rustication, the faces of the stone blocks are further delineated in a variety of ways. *See also Country Houses and Villas, p. 36; Street-Facing Buildings, pp. 42, 43; Public Buildings, pp. 46, 50.*

Banded ›
Only the top and bottom joints between blocks are accentuated.

Diamond-faced ››
The faces of the blocks are hewn into regular, repeating patterns of small shallow pyramids.

Chamfered ›
The sides of the blocks are angled, creating V-shaped grooves at the joints.

Frosted ›
The faces of the blocks are hewn into stalactite or icicle forms.

Quarry-faced ››
The faces of the blocks are treated roughly and look as if they are unfinished.

Vermiculated ›
The faces of the blocks are incised to give the appearance of being, literally, 'worm-eaten'.

Blocked ›
Rusticated blocks are separated by evenly spaced gaps or apparent recessions. This form of rustication, especially on a window or door surround, was popularized in Britain and beyond by the architect, James Gibbs; hence it is sometimes called the 'Gibbs surround'. *See also Windows and Doors, p. 141.*

Quoins ››
The cornerstones of a building. They are often composed of larger rusticated blocks, and are sometimes in a different material to the one used for the rest of the walls. *See also Country Houses and Villas, p. 34; Street-Facing Buildings, pp. 40, 43.*

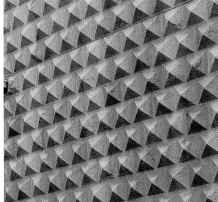

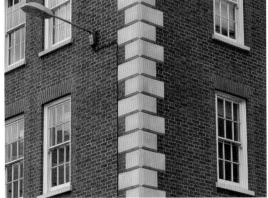

Brick › Positions

Bricks are cuboidal blocks generally of fired clay, although in some locations they are sun-dried rather than fired. Many early civilizations used them, and they are still a key component in current building practices. The shapes and sizes of bricks are standardized so that they can be laid in regular rows to form walls; the different arrangements of these bricks are called 'bonds'. There is a variety of bonds and their prevalence varies according to the traditions of particular locations as well as the structural properties of each type of bond.

When laid out in rows, bricks are separated by a thin layer of mortar – a paste which when set bonds adjacent bricks together in a wall. Mortar is made from sand mixed with a binder such as cement or lime, to which water is added. When a mortar joint has been manipulated by a tool before the mortar has set it is said to be 'tooled'.

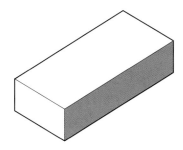

Stretcher
A brick laid horizontally with its broad, long face on the bottom and its narrow, long face exposed on the outer face of the wall.

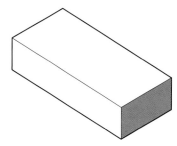

Header
A brick laid horizontally with its broad, long face on the bottom but with the short end exposed on the outer face of the wall.

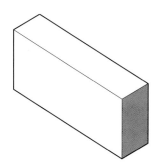

Rowlock header
A brick laid horizontally on its narrow, long side with the short end exposed on the outer face of the wall.

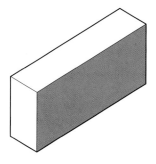

Rowlock stretcher or shiner
A brick laid horizontally with the long, narrow side on the bottom and the broad, long side exposed on the outer face of the wall.

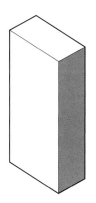

Soldier
A brick laid vertically with its long, narrow side exposed on the outer face of the wall.

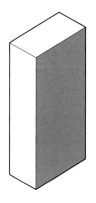

Sailor
A brick laid vertically but with the broad, long side exposed on the outer face of the wall.

Brick › Bonds

Stretcher bond
The simplest bond type consisting of repeating courses of *stretcher* bricks overlapping the bricks below by half their length. As such, stretcher bond is usually reserved for walls one brick thick, and is often used to face a cavity wall, or timber or steel structures.

Header bond
A simple bond type in which the bricks are laid with their *header* faces showing.

Common bond
A bond type combining rows of *headers* and *stretchers* – five courses of stretchers alternating with one course of headers.

Flemish bond
Alternating *stretchers* and *headers* in the same course. Each stretcher overlaps a quarter of the one below it while the headers are aligned with the ones two courses below.

English bond
Alternating courses of *stretchers* and *headers*.

Stacked bond
Stretchers stacked on top of each other with the vertical joints aligned. For this reason, it is a relatively weak bonding type so is often used to face a cavity wall or, especially, a steel structure.

Herringbone bond
A zigzag pattern usually composed from *stretcher* bricks set diagonally.

Diaper
Technically not a bond type as it can be achieved in any number of ways, diaper is a rectangular, square or diamond pattern created by the particular placement of different-coloured bricks. *See also p. 127.*

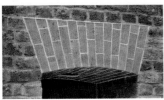

Gauged brickwork
Brickwork with very fine joints, often with bricks cut to shape and used in *lintels*. *See also Arches, p. 81.*

Brick › Mortar Joints

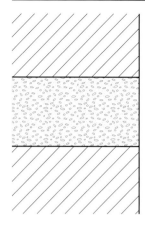

Flush
The mortar is flat with the adjacent brick faces.

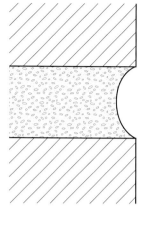

Concave
The mortar is finished in a recessed arc.

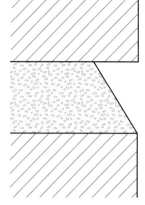

Weathered
The mortar is angled so that it slopes inwards from the face of the lower brick.

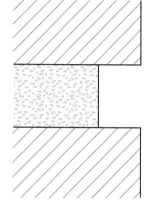

Raked
The mortar sits parallel with the brick faces but is recessed into the joint.

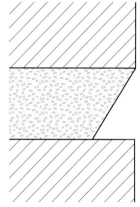

Struck
The mortar is angled so that it slopes inwards from the face of the upper brick.

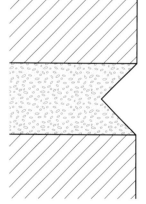

V-shaped
The mortar is finished in a V-shaped recession.

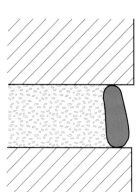

Galletting
Insertion of small pieces of stone into the mortar joints while they are still wet, for decorative purposes.

Brick › Types

Although most commonly composed of fired clay, bricks can be composed of several different materials. Irrespective of material, however, bricks are almost always formed in moulds, which ensure their standardized shape. Thus, bricks can be moulded in a variety of shapes depending on their intended usage. Bricks with a chamfered side, for example, are often found in copings, while non-rectangular, angled bricks are often used in the joints between two non-perpendicular walls.

Solid brick
A small cuboid of fired clay.

Glazed brick
A brick to which a layer of glaze has been applied before firing to give it a different colour and finish.

Perforated brick
A standard brick but with two or three vertical perforations to reduce weight and aid ventilation.

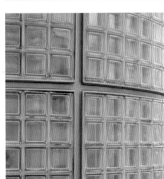

Glass brick
Originating in the early twentieth century, glass bricks are usually square. Because they are relatively thick, they provide partial obscuration but still admit natural light into and between internal spaces.

Hollow brick
A brick with oblong or cylindrical horizontal hollows to reduce the weight of the brick and provide insulation.

Frogged brick
A commonly found brick with indentations on the top and bottom when laid in the stretcher position. The term 'frog' usually refers to the indentation, though it can also refer to the block which makes the indentation in the moulding process. Frogged bricks are lighter than solid bricks and the frogging also provides a great surface area for the mortar to adhere to when laid in courses.

Timber

Like stone and brick, timber is a very widely used building material, found in the buildings of almost all civilizations and cultures. Because of its strength, relative lightness and ability to be easily cut into required shapes, timber is frequently used for the structural frameworks, especially roofs, of a whole variety of building types.

In a timber-framed building, the structural framework is most often formed from upright timber posts and horizontal cross beams (sometimes also with diagonal beams). The spaces in between the framework are usually infilled with brickwork, masonry, plaster, cement,

or wattle and daub. When the spacing between studs – the smaller vertical members between larger posts – is very narrow, the timber frame is described as 'close-studded'. Sometimes the timber frame is obscured by external timber cladding or, in some instances, tiled or brick walls.

Timber is also frequently used as a cladding material. In these situations, it is attached to an underlying structural framework, sometimes also of timber though not necessarily so. The timber cladding is often painted or stained with a wood preservative.

Below, clockwise from top left:
Lohkäs, Strasbourg, France; Jutul'n & Blessomen café, Vågåmo, Norway; nineteenth-century interior, traditional house, Kyoto, Japan; Nordic Watercolour Museum, Skärhamn, Sweden.

Overhanging jetty ›
The projection of an upper storey over a lower one in a timber-framed building. *See also Street-Facing Buildings, p. 38.* (Little Hall Market Place, Lavenham, Suffolk, UK.)

Brick nog ››
The use of brick or small blocks of masonry to fill the gaps in a building's timber frame. For other infill types, *see Concrete and Renders, p. 112.* (Medieval timber-frame building, UK.)

Log cabin ››
A timber building type common in North America, constructed from cut logs laid horizontally. The logs have notched ends so that they form a strong interlocking arrangement at the corners. Gaps between the logs can be filled with plaster, cement or mud. (Log cabin, Kuusamo, Finland.)

Weatherboarding ›
Cladding a building with long, overlapping slats or boards laid horizontally, to protect the interior from the elements or for aesthetic effect. Sometimes the joints between adjacent slats are strengthened by the use of a tongue-and-groove joint. Weatherboarding can be painted, stained or left unfinished. Recently timber weatherboarding has, in some instances, been superseded by plastic though the aesthetic remains similar. (Nineteenth-century house, Litchfield, Connecticut, USA.)

Timber cladding ›
Timber is frequently used as a cladding material in modern architecture. While in *weatherboarding* it is almost always laid with the slats horizontal and overlapping, in other forms of timber cladding slats are laid at any of a whole variety of angles without necessarily overlapping. Timber cladding is most often left stained or untreated rather than painted, to retain the rhythmic effect of colour and grain variation between series of slats. (SPF Architects, Brosmith Residence, Los Angeles, California, USA, 2004.)

Tiles and Ceramics

Tiles are thin blocks of fired clay which are used to cover a surface either by being hung from a frame or by being fixed directly on to an underlying surface (and to each other) using a fine mortar or grouting – known as being 'set'. Tiles are often hung from a building's exterior – especially its roof, though also sometimes from walls – because of their imperviousness to water. Set tiles are frequently used to waterproof walls and floors, most often in bathrooms and kitchens.

Because they can be formed in moulds and then applied with various glazes, tiles are often used to provide decorative and polychromatic effects on a surface. A frequent ornamental use is in mosaics, where small pieces of coloured tile (also sometimes glass or stone) can be used to produce geometric patterns or figurative scenes to decorate both walls and floors.

Today, almost all tiles are mechanically produced and various types of artificial ceramic, in tile or panel form, are often used in contemporary architecture.

Hung tiles ›
Not just confined to roofs where they are most often found, ceramic tiles can be used to cover external walls and are usually hung from an underlying timber or brick frame in overlapping rows – an arrangement called 'imbrication'. Different-coloured tiles can be used to create a variety of geometrical patterns. *See also Roofs, p. 150.*

Hung slate ››
Slate is strictly masonry, but because it can be broken into thin sheets, it is often used in a similar way to *hung tiles*. *See also Roofs, p. 150.*

Set tiles ›
Rather than being hung from a frame, tiles can be fixed directly on to a surface and to each other using a fine mortar or grouting.

External set tiles ››
Tiles used on the exterior of buildings, principally to provide waterproofing. Because of the relative ease of producing coloured tiles of varying shapes and with decorative details, they are often used to provide various types of surface ornamentation.

Mosaic ›

An abstract pattern or figurative scene created by arranging small pieces of coloured tile, glass or stone – called 'tesserae' – on a surface. The tesserae are fixed into position with mortar or grouting. Mosaics are used as both wall and floor decoration.

Floor tiles ››

Usually ceramic or slate, floor tiles can be used throughout buildings, but because of their durability and water resistance they are most often found in public areas or, especially in domestic settings, in bathrooms and kitchens.

Interior wall tiles ››

Usually ceramic or slate, interior wall tiles are most often used in bathrooms and kitchens to provide waterproofing.

Ceiling tiles ››

Made from polystyrene or mineral wool, ceiling tiles are usually lightweight and hung from a metal frame suspended from a ceiling. They are often used to provide sound and heat insulation, and also to hide service pipes and ducts that may lie above the ceiling.

Ceramic curtain-wall panels ›

Ceramic sheets can be mass-produced and used as opaque panels in a *curtain wall* – a non-load-bearing enclosure or envelope of a building. *See also Street-Facing Buildings, p. 44.*

Concrete and Renders

Concrete is a man-made material composed from cement, an aggregate usually of crushed stone and sand, and water. To this are sometimes added various natural or artificial admixtures designed to alter the concrete's properties according to the particular purposes for which it is intended. As outlined in Chapter 2, concrete is a key component of the structure and aesthetic of much modern architecture.

Render is a thick, viscous substance applied to a wall when wet. When dry, it provides a hard coating, but unlike concrete has no structural function. Renders, usually various types of plaster, are used to cover underlying, often brick, structures and provide a smooth finish to an exterior or interior wall. Render finishes are sometimes augmented by various types of moulding. Cement renders are often set with small stones when wet to provide a further protective layer.

Cast-in-place concrete ›
Concrete that is cast cumulatively in vertical layers on-site, usually using wooden slats. The impressions left by wooden slats can be kept visible for aesthetic purposes.

Precast concrete ››
A standardized concrete panel or pier cast off-site for quick assembly on-site.

Bush-hammered concrete
Concrete with an exposed aggregate finish usually produced with a power hammer after the concrete has set.

 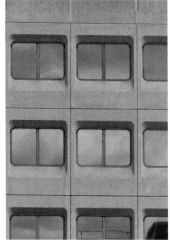 

Exposed aggregate ›
Concrete whose outer surface is removed before it has fully hardened, revealing the aggregate.

Plaster ››
A substance consisting of an aggregate and binder which, when combined with water, forms a malleable paste that is applied to a surface before it sets. Plaster can be used in its various forms to render both exterior and interior surfaces, and can be moulded to provide surface decoration.

Lime plaster ›
Historically one of the most common plasters, lime plaster is formed from sand, lime and water; animal fibres are sometimes used for additional binding. Lime plaster is used for fresco painting, as here.

Gypsum plaster ››
Also known as plaster of Paris, gypsum plaster is made by heating gypsum powder, then adding water to form a paste which can be used to cover a surface before the mixture hardens. Gypsum plasters are usually used only for interior surfaces because of their susceptibility to water damage (as seen here).

Stucco ›
Traditionally, a hard form of *lime plaster* used to render the exterior surfaces of buildings, often to hide an underlying brick structure and provide surface decoration. In this example, it is combined with stone dressings with the stucco reserved for the flat wall surfaces. Modern stuccos are typically forms of *cement plaster*.

Wattle-and-daub ›
A primitive construction method in which a lattice of thin wooden strips – the 'wattle' – is literally daubed with a render of mud, soil or clay which is then smoothed off. Wattle-and-daub is most often found infilling *timber frames* but in some examples is used to construct entire walls.

Pargetting ››
The decoration of the exterior plaster surfaces of *timber-framed buildings* with embossed or recessed ornamental patterns.

Cement plaster or render ›
A form of *lime plaster* to which cement has been added. Mostly impervious to water, cement plasters are frequently used to render exterior surfaces. Modern cement renders sometimes have acrylic additives to further enhance water resistance and provide colour variation.

Pebble-dash ››
An exterior rendering of *cement plaster or render* which is then set with pebbles and sometimes small shells. A variation of the procedure sees the pebbles (and shells) added to the render before application to the wall – called 'roughcast'.

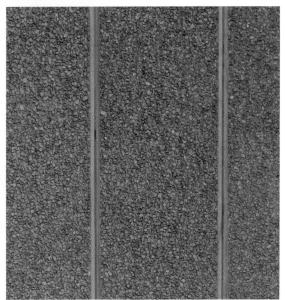

Glass

It is only comparatively recently that it has been possible to use glass as a building surface material as distinct from using it in windows. Advances in concrete and steel-frame construction allowed walls to be freed from load-bearing duties so that materials such as glass could be used to form curtain walls – a non-load-bearing enclosure or envelope of a building, attached to the structure but standing separate from it.

Curtain walls can consist of a variety of materials – brick, masonry, wood, stucco, metal – but most typically in contemporary architecture, they are made from glass. So prevalent as to have become something of a cliché, the glass curtain wall has been a key part of the vocabulary of modern architecture since the mid twentieth century.

In office blocks, where they are frequently seen, glass curtain walls have the benefit of allowing daylight to penetrate deep into the building. However, a major disadvantage of cladding a building in glass is that it is difficult to regulate solar heat gain, which is why the curtain walls are often deployed with semi-opaque panels, louvres or brise-soleils. Despite these devices, buildings with glass curtain walls typically have to rely upon air conditioning to regulate their internal climates.

GLASS CURTAIN WALL

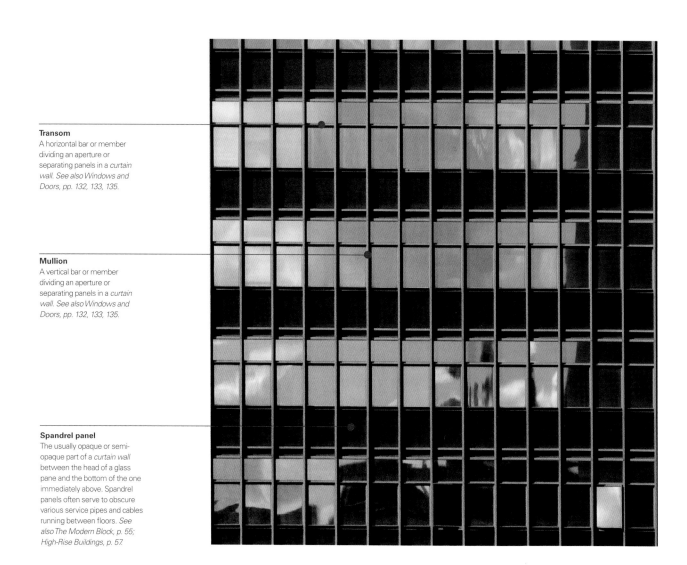

Transom
A horizontal bar or member dividing an aperture or separating panels in a *curtain wall*. *See also* Windows and Doors, pp. 132, 133, 135.

Mullion
A vertical bar or member dividing an aperture or separating panels in a *curtain wall*. *See also* Windows and Doors, pp. 132, 133, 135.

Spandrel panel
The usually opaque or semi-opaque part of a *curtain wall* between the head of a glass pane and the bottom of the one immediately above. Spandrel panels often serve to obscure various service pipes and cables running between floors. *See also* The Modern Block, p. 55; High-Rise Buildings, p. 57.

Point-loaded/supported glass curtain wall ›
Reinforced-glass panes held in place through point attachments in each corner to the arms of a spider, which is then attached by a bracket to a structural support. *See also The Modern Block, p. 55.*

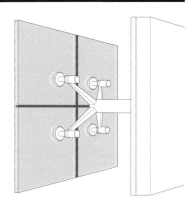

Unitized glass curtain wall ›
Prefabricated panels containing one or more glass panes attached via a bracket to a structural support. Such panels may also include *spandrel panels* and *louvres. See also Steel, p. 92.*

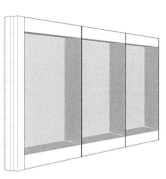

Hidden-frame curtain wall ›
The glass panes are set into a regular steel frame in a way that largely obscures the frame.

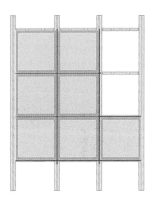

Exposed-frame curtain wall ›
Unlike the *hidden-frame curtain wall*, here the frame stands proud of the glass surface and may include some additional trim. Although the frame is highlighted, its only structural function is to attach the glass panes to the supporting frame behind.

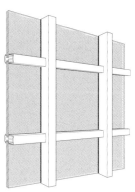

Metal and Synthetic Materials

Metal has a long history of being used in buildings. However, because of the difficulty and expense involved in extracting most metals in large quantities, it was most often used sparingly as a cladding material; lead and copper were usually confined to cladding roofs, and even then were used very little except in the most prestigious buildings.

As chapter 2 outlined, it was in the nineteenth century that metal, principally steel, came to the fore as an important construction material. Today steel, like concrete, is used in almost every construction project.

While its most important impact has been as a structural material, steel is also frequently used for wall and roof cladding as it is relatively cheap

and quick to assemble. Lead and copper continue to be used for this purpose, and electrolytically extracted metals like aluminium and titanium are, like various synthetic materials, increasingly being used for their aesthetic effects and resistance to corrosion and weathering.

Lead ›
Malleable and resistant to corrosion, lead is often used to provide a water-resistant membrane on roofs, though it is sometimes used on other parts of buildings. It is usually laid in sheets over wooden battens. *See also Roofs, p. 151.* (Renzo Piano, Parco della Musica, Rome, Italy, 2002.)

Copper ›
Like lead, copper is often used to provide a water-resistant membrane on roofs, though it is sometimes used on other parts of buildings. When first applied it is a shiny pinky-orange. This quickly corrodes to copper's characteristic green patina, which is resistant to further corrosion. *See also Roofs, p. 151.* (Will Alsop, Peckham Library, London, UK, 2000.)

Titanium ›
As a structural material, titanium has the advantages of being extremely strong but relatively lightweight; it is also subject to little thermal expansion. Titanium is highly resistant to corrosion and has found use as a cladding material that offers a variety of finishes; when it is anodized a reflective, shimmering effect is produced. (Frank Gehry, Guggenheim Museum, Bilbao, Spain, 1997.)

Steel ›
An alloy of iron and carbon and sometimes other metals, steel has a long history as a building material, and its mass production in the mid nineteenth century made it one of the most important. It is extremely strong and durable and can be welded together, and is, thus, one of the most versatile and important elements in modern construction and design. When alloyed with other metals it can become almost entirely resistant to corrosion, especially in its stainless variety. Corrugated sheets of steel – pressed with a series of alternating peaks and troughs for rigidity – are often used as cladding material when low cost and speed of construction are necessary. *See also High-Rise Buildings, p. 56; Roofs, p. 151.* (Philips Avent Factory, Sudbury, Suffolk, UK.)

Aluminium ›
The second most widely extracted metal after iron, aluminium is most often used as a *cladding material* as it is relatively lightweight and is resistant to corrosion thanks to the durable oxide layer on its surface. Aluminium can also be anodized allowing a variety of coloured finishes. *See also Street-Facing Buildings, p. 45; Public Buildings, p. 51; High-Rise Buildings, pp. 58, 59.* (Daniel Libeskind, Royal Ontario Museum, Toronto, Canada, 2007.)

Synthetic membrane ›
Synthetic membranes are used for building envelopes or surface layers. They are usually deployed in tension and are matched with compression elements such as *masts. See also Roofs, p. 151.* (Rogers Stirk Harbour + Partners, Millennium Dome, London, UK, 1999.)

Wall Articulations

Walls and surfaces are rarely simply planar, broken up solely by windows and doors. They are, of course, the primary places for various modes of architectural display, but are also a primary means of negotiating the threshold between a building's interior and exterior. This section includes examples of a number of large-scale features that augment walls and surfaces, recessing or projecting from a wall – which often transcend any particular architectural language.

Loggia ›
A covered space, partially enclosed on one or more sides by an *arcade* or *colonnade*. It may form part of a larger building or stand as an independent structure. *See also Public Buildings, p. 49.* (Loggia della Signoria, Florence, Italy.)

Veranda ››
A partially enclosed gallery-type space usually attached to the ground level of a house. If located on upper floors it is usually described as a *balcony*. (The DuBignon Cottage, Jekyll Island, Georgia, USA.)

Brise-soleil ›
A structure attached to the exterior of a *glass-curtain-walled* building (though not exclusively so) that serves to provide shade and reduces solar heat gain. *See also The Modern Block, p. 55.* (Grimshaw, Roberts Engineering Building, UCL, London, UK, 2008.)

Canopy ››
A horizontal or slightly pitched projection from a building, providing cover from precipitation or sunlight. *See also The Modern Block, pp. 54, 55; High-Rise Buildings, p. 57.* (Herzog & de Meuron, Pérez Art Museum Miami, Florida, USA, 2013.)

Buttress ›
A masonry or brick structure providing lateral support to a wall. (The Guildhall, London, UK.)

A An 'angle' buttress is used at corners, usually of *towers*, and consists of two buttresses set at 90 degrees on the adjoining faces of the two perpendicular walls.

B A 'diagonal' buttress consists of a single buttress set at the corner where two perpendicular walls meet.

C When sides of the buttresses do not meet at the corner they are called 'setback'.

D A buttress is said to be 'clasping' when the two angle buttresses are conjoined into a single buttress enveloping the corner.

See also The Medieval Cathedral, pp. 14, 15, 17, 19.

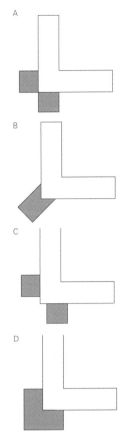

A

B

C

D

Flying buttress ›
These are typical in cathedrals and consist of 'flying' half-arches that help to carry down the thrust of the *nave*'s high vault or roof.

Amortizement
The sloping portion of a *buttress*, designed to shed water.

Aedicule ››
An architectural frame set into a wall, deployed to indicate a shrine in a sacred building, draw attention to a particular work of art or to provide additional surface variegation. Similar to *Niche, p. 129; See also The Baroque Church, p. 25.* (Church of Orsanmichele, Florence, Italy.)

Surface Articulations

The surfaces of a building can be articulated in a variety of ways. One of the most common is the use of mouldings. These consist of continuous, usually projecting, specially shaped bands. Moulding – so-called because of the wooden moulds that are sometimes used to ensure a consistent profile along its course – can be rendered in stone, ceramic, brick, wood, stucco and especially plaster.

A number of widely found elements such as wood panelling, hood moulds, skirting and dado rails are included in this section, and usually feature mouldings of which there are numerous types. Unenriched mouldings are characterized by their relatively simple curving profiles. Other, more complicated mouldings are enriched with complex repeating patterns rather than forming a continuous band. Decorative elements are sometimes included within the moulding itself as part of the pattern. Many of these elements also stand on their own as they are commonly found within various architectural vocabularies.

Cove ›
The concave moulding between a wall and ceiling; also sometimes known as a 'bed moulding'. When a coving is very large, it is viewed as part of the ceiling rather than a moulding – a 'coved ceiling'.

Hood mould ››
A projecting moulding often found in medieval architecture, (though not confined to it) that drapes over an aperture. A rectilinear hood mould is called a 'label'. *See also Windows and Doors, p. 138.*

String course ›
A thin, horizontal moulded banding running across a wall. *See also The Medieval Cathedral, p. 19; Street-Facing Buildings, p. 43.*

Skirting ››
The typically wooden slat, often moulded, affixed to the bottom of an internal wall where it meets the floor. Also known as a 'baseboard'.

Wood panelling ›
The covering of an interior wall with thin sheets of wood set within a frame of thicker strips, usually running vertically and horizontally. When the wood panelling only goes up as high as the *dado* level it is called 'wainscot'.

Stile
The vertical strip or member in *wood panelling* or *panel door*. A subsidiary, usually thinner, vertical strip or member is called a *muntin*.

Rail
The horizontal strip or member in *wood panelling* or *panel door*.

Panel door
A door constructed from a structural frame of *rails*, *stiles*, *mullions* and sometimes *muntins*, which is infilled with wooden panels. *See also Windows and Doors, p. 135.*

Dado ›
The marked-off region of an interior wall equivalent to the *base* or pedestal level of a *Classical order*. The continuous moulding that often marks the top of the dado level is called a 'dado rail'.

Sunk panel ››
A recessed panel in a façade, here blank but usually filled with sculptural *relief* or ornament.

Unenriched Mouldings

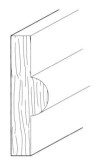

Astragal
A small convex moulding, semicircular or three-quarters of a circle in section, often set between two flat planes (*fillets*). *See also Columns and Piers, pp. 70, 73, 74, 75.*

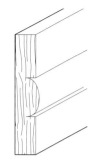

Bead
A narrow convex moulding, usually semicircular in section.

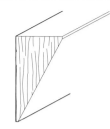

Bevelled or chamfered
A simple moulding, created when a right-angled edge is cut away at an angle. Described as 'hollow' when the chamfer is concave rather than flat; 'sunk' when it is recessed; and 'stopped' when the moulding is not carried the whole length of an angle.

Bolection
A bold moulding, either concave or convex, providing a link between two parallel surfaces in different planes.

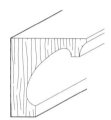

Casement
A concave moulding with a deep curved indentation, often found in late medieval door and window casements. *See also Windows and Doors, p. 132.*

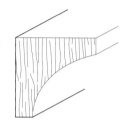

Cavetto
A concave moulding usually a quarter-circle in section. *See also Columns and Piers, pp. 71, 75.*

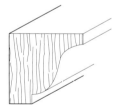

Cyma recta
A double-curved Classical moulding with the lower curve convex and the upper concave. *See also Columns and Piers, pp. 70–75.*

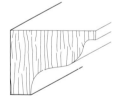

Cyma reversa
A double-curved Classical moulding with the lower curve concave and the upper convex. *See also Columns and Piers, pp. 70, 71, 73, 74, 75.*

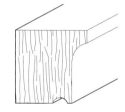

Drip
A projection on the underside of a moulding or *cornice*, intended to ensure that rainwater drips clear of the face of the wall.

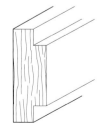

Fascia
The flat horizontal divisions in a Classical *architrave*, or in any decorative scheme. *See also Columns and Piers, pp. 71, 73, 74, 75.*

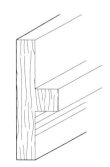

Fillet
A flat band or surface separating two otherwise adjoining mouldings, it sometimes stands proud of the surrounding surface. *See also Columns and Piers, pp. 70–75.*

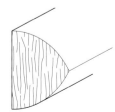

Keel
A moulding whose two curves form a pointed edge much like the keel of a ship.

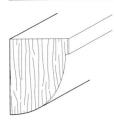

Ovolo
A convex moulding, a quarter-circle in section. *See also Columns and Piers, pp. 70, 71, 73, 74, 75.*

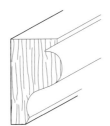

Quirked
A moulding with a continuous, horizontal V-shaped indentation.

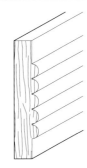

Reed
A series of two or more parallel convex or projecting mouldings.

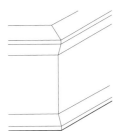

Return
A 90-degree turn in a moulding. *See also Windows and Doors, p. 136.*

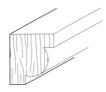

Roll
A simple convex moulding, usually semicircular in section but sometimes more than semicircular. It is usually found in medieval architecture. A variant is the 'roll-and-fillet' moulding which consists of a roll moulding combined with one or two *fillets*.

Scotia
The concave moulding at the *base* of a Classical column, between two *tori*. *See also Columns and Piers, pp. 71, 73, 74, 75.*

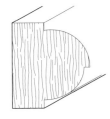

Scroll
A projecting moulding, somewhat like a *roll* moulding but composed from two curves with the upper one projecting further than the lower one.

Torus
A prominent convex moulding, roughly semicircular in section. It is most often found at the *base* of a Classical column. *See also Columns and Piers, pp. 70, 71, 73, 74, 75.*

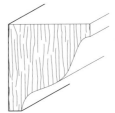

Wave
A moulding formed from three curves: a convex curve set between two concave ones.

Enriched Mouldings and Decorative Elements / 1

Acanthus ›
A stylized decorative form based on the leaf of an acanthus plant. It is an integral element of *Corinthian* and *Composite capitals*, but is also used as a discrete element or as part of a moulded ensemble. *See also Columns and Piers, p. 75.*

Agraffe ››
A carved *keystone*.

Addorsed ›
Two figures, usually animals, placed back-to-back. When the figures are facing each other they are said to be 'affronted'.

Alcove ›
A typically bowed recession into the surface of a wall. Alcoves differ from *niches* by extending down to the floor.

Apron ››
An embossed (occasionally recessed) panel immediately below a window or *niche*, often enriched with further decorative elements. *See also Windows and Doors, p. 136.*

Anthemion ›
A stylized decorative form based on honeysuckle, the lobes of which point inwards (unlike a *palmette*).

Arabesque ››
The term given to intricate decorative mouldings that consist of foliation, scrolls and mythical creatures but omit human figures. As the term suggests, it derives from Islamic decoration.

Ball flower ›
A roughly spherical ornament composed of a ball inserted into the bowl of a three-petalled flower visible through its trefoiled opening.

Bay-leaf ››
A decorative element in the form of a bay leaf. It is a common motif in Classical architecture, often present in pulvinated (convex) *friezes*, *festoons* and *garlands*.

Bead-and-reel ›
A motif consisting of an alternating arrangement of elliptical (or sometimes elongated lozenge-shaped) forms and semicircular discs.

Beak-head ››
A figurative enrichment composed of a repeating pattern of birds' heads, usually with prominent beaks.

Bezant ›
A coin- or disc-shaped ornament.

Billet ››
A moulding consisting of regularly spaced rectangular or rounded blocks.

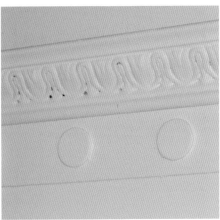

Enriched Mouldings and Decorative Elements / 2

Bucranium ›
A decorative motif in the form of a bull's skull, often flanked by *garlands*. It is sometimes found (usually alternating with *paterae*) in the *metopes* in a *Doric frieze*. *See also Columns and Piers, p. 71.*

Cable ››
A convex moulding whose winding form resembles that of a rope or cable.

Cartouche ›
A typically oval tablet form surrounded by scrolling and sometimes with a carved inscription. *See also The Baroque Church, p. 25.*

Chevron ››
A moulding or decorative motif consisting of a repeating pattern of V-shaped forms, often found in medieval architecture. *See also High-Rise Buildings, p. 56.*

Console ›
A double-scrolled bracket.

Cornucopia ››
A decorative element symbolizing plenty, usually consisting of a goat's horn overflowing with flowers, corn and fruit.

Crossette ›
A corner of a rectangular moulding with small vertical and horizontal flaps or off-sets; often found in window and door *surrounds*.

Dentil ››
A repeating pattern of square or rectangular blocks projecting from the underside of a Classical cornice. *See also Columns and Piers, pp. 73, 74, 75.*

Diaper ›
Any decorative pattern in the form of a repeating grid. *See also p. 115.*

Dog-tooth ››
A four-lobed pyramidal form; often found in medieval architecture (here shown underneath arch joins).

Drop ›
A surface ornament that appears to be suspended from a single point.

Egg-and-dart ››
An alternating pattern of egg-shaped and pointed arrow-like elements.

Festoon ›
A chain of flowers that appears to be suspended in a bow or curve from any number of (usually evenly) spaced points on a surface.

Fret ››
A repeating geometrical moulding composed entirely from straight lines.

Foliated ›
The general term referring to any ornament incorporating foliage.

Garland ››
A moulded ring or wreath of flowers and foliage.

Grotesquery ›
Arabesque-like intricate decorative mouldings including human figures. This type of decoration was inspired by rediscovery of Ancient Roman decorative forms. *See also Arabesque, p. 125.*

Guilloche ››
A repeating moulding of two or more interleaved curved bands or narrow strips.

Grisaille ››
A form of painting whose tonal shades of grey are intended to imitate sculptural *relief*.

Enriched Mouldings and Decorative Elements / 3

Herm or term ›
A *pedestal* that tapers towards the bottom and is topped by a bust of a mythological figure or animal. The name 'term' derives from Terminus, the Roman god of boundaries. A variant is the 'herm' – when the head is a representation of Hermes/Mercury, the Greek/Roman messenger god. *See also The Baroque Church, p. 25.*

Husk ››
A bell-shaped motif; husks are sometimes linked in *festoons, garlands* or *drops.*

Intarsia ›
The inlaying of strips or different shapes of wood into a surface, forming decorative patterns or figurative scenes. Intarsia also refers to the process of inlaying marble stones in a highly polished decorative arrangement on walls and especially floors, as in this example.

Mask ›
A decorative motif of an often stylized human or animal face. *See also The Baroque Church, p. 25; Public Buildings, p. 47.*

Medallion ››
A circular or oval decorative plaque usually adorned with a sculpted or painted figure or scene. *See also The Baroque Church, p. 25; Country Houses and Villas, p. 36.*

Modillion ›
A *console* with attached *acanthus* leaf projecting from the underside of the *corona* of a Corinthian or Composite *cornice*, though sometimes also used elsewhere. *See also Ancon, p. 136; Console, p. 136.*

Nail-head ›
A moulding consisting of a repeating pattern of projecting pyramidal forms, said to resemble the heads of nails. When the pyramid forms are indented into the wall surface the moulding is described as 'hollow-square'. Both are often found in Norman and Romanesque architecture.

Niche ›
An arched recess into a wall surface, designed to hold a statue or simply to provide surface variegation. *See also Aedicule, p. 119; The Medieval Cathedral, p. 15; The Baroque Church, pp. 25, 27, 29; Country Houses and Villas, p. 36; Public Buildings, p. 46.*

Palmette ››
A decorative motif in the form of a fan-shaped palm leaf, whose lobes face outwards (unlike an *anthemion*).

Patera ›››
A circular, dish-like ornament. Paterae are sometimes found (usually alternating with *bucrania*) in the *metopes* in a Doric *frieze*.

Pelta ›
A decorative motif in the form of an elliptical, circular or crescent-shaped shield.

Putto ››
A figure of a small male child usually unclothed and winged; sometimes called an 'amorino'. *See also The Baroque Church, p. 29.*

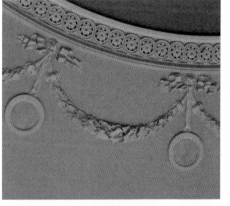

Overdoor ›
A decorative panel often set with a painting or a bust, placed over a door; sometimes incorporated with the doorcase.

Ovum ››
An egg-shaped ornamental element found, for example, in an *egg-and-dart* enrichment.

Enriched Mouldings and Decorative Elements / 4

Raffle leaf ›
A scrolling, serrated leaf-like ornament, often found in Rococo decoration.

Rinceau ››
A decorative motif in the form of multistemmed and intertwining vines and leaves.

Relief ›
A sculpted surface in which the modelled forms project from – or in some examples are recessed into – the surface plane. Bas-relief or 'basso-relievo' is a low relief with the sculpted scene extending less than half its depth from the relief plane. In high relief or 'alto-relievo' the scene typically extends more than half its depth from the relief plane. 'Mezzo-relievo' is an intermediate relief between high and low relief. In 'cavo-relievo' the scene recedes, rather than projects, from the relief plane; it is also known as 'intaglio' or 'diaglyph'. 'Rilievo stiacciato' is an extremely flat relief most often found in Italian Renaissance sculpture.

Rosette ›
A circular ornament resembling the form of a rose.

Roundel ››
A circular panel or moulding. Roundels can be used as independent motifs, as here, but are often part of a larger decorative scheme. *See also Roofs, p. 158.*

Running ornament ›
The name given to a continuous and often intertwining band of ornament.

Scallop ›

A corrugated ornament with raised cones between recessed grooves forming a shell-like pattern. *See also Scallop capital, Columns and Piers, p. 77.*

Swag ››

Like a *festoon* except that in place of a chain of flowers, a swag has the form of a cloth that appears to be suspended in a bow or curve from any number of (usually evenly) spaced points on a surface.

Trompe-l'œil ›

French for trick of the eye, trompe-l'œil is the technique of painting a surface to give the illusion that what is portrayed exists in three-dimensional space.

Vitruvian scroll ››

A repeating pattern of wave-like forms; sometimes called 'wave-scroll' moulding.

Water-leaf ›

A moulding enriched with a repeating pattern of leaves whose tops are folded like small scrolls, sometimes alternating with darts.

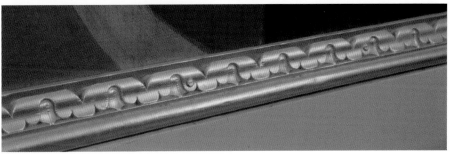

Windows and Doors › Types / 1

Windows and doors are integral elements of almost every building. If a building's primary characteristic is considered to be that of enclosing space, the function of windows and doors is to facilitate the movement of light, air, heat and people between the outer and inner spaces defined by a building.

While early windows were left open or covered by shutters, the advent of glass and glazed windows allowed a building's interior to be much better protected from outside elements while still allowing daylight into its interior. Doors most often consisted of movable hinged barriers of durable wood or metal until the advent of sliding doors, and of large-scale reinforced-glass panels that blurred the distinction between windows and doors.

Because they both pierce external or internal walls, which are often supporting, doors and windows share structural characteristics which frequently extend into, or are manifested as, aesthetic ones. Given their prominence in all buildings, their arrangement and architectural articulation often provides the basis of a building's façade.

Fixed window
Any window that does not contain sections that open or close. Windows may be fixed for any number of reasons. Early windows were often fixed because of the difficulty and expense of fashioning opening mechanisms, especially, for example, for intricate tracery windows. More recently, windows may be fixed to ensure the efficiency of building-wide environmental and air-conditioning systems, or, in the case of high-rise buildings, as a safety measure.

Saddle bar
The horizontal supporting bar, typically lead, of the subsidiary *lights* in a fixed window.

Light
The opening in a window enclosed by one or more panes of glass.

Lintel
The supporting horizontal member that surmounts a window or door. *See also Street-Facing Buildings, pp. 38, 40, 41.*

Jamb
The vertical side of a window *surround*.

Transom
A horizontal bar or member dividing a window. *See also Street-Facing Buildings, p. 38; Public Buildings, p. 47.*

Stanchion bar
The vertical supporting bar, typically lead, of the subsidiary *lights* in a fixed window.

Mullion
A vertical bar or member dividing a window. Can also be used to describe a central member running vertically down a *panel door. See also p. 135; Country Houses and Villas, p. 37; Street-Facing Buildings, p. 38, 44, 45; Public Buildings, p. 47.*

Sill
The horizontal base of a window *surround. See also Street-Facing Buildings, p. 38.*

Casement window

A window attached to its frame by one or more hinges along one of its sides. *See also Street-Facing Buildings, pp. 38, 42; Walls and Surfaces, p. 122.*

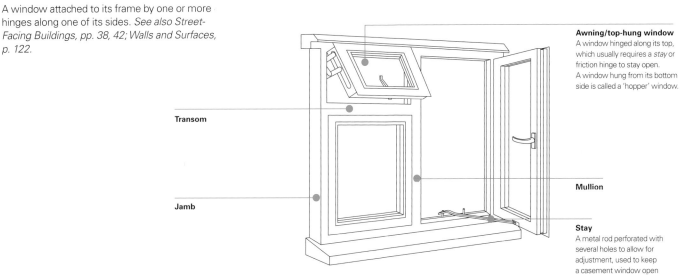

Transom

Jamb

Awning/top-hung window
A window hinged along its top, which usually requires a *stay* or friction hinge to stay open. A window hung from its bottom side is called a 'hopper' window.

Mullion

Stay
A metal rod perforated with several holes to allow for adjustment, used to keep a casement window open or closed.

Sash window

A window consisting of one or more 'sashes' – glazed wooden frames containing one or more glass panes. These are set into grooves in the jambs and slide vertically up and down. A counterweight is usually concealed in the window frame and is linked to the sash by a cord and pulley system. *See also Country Houses and Villas, p. 36; Street-Facing Buildings, p. 41.*

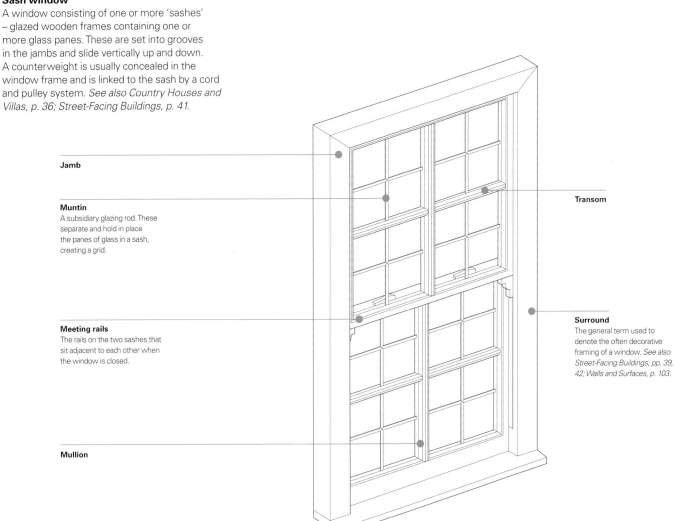

Jamb

Muntin
A subsidiary glazing rod. These separate and hold in place the panes of glass in a sash, creating a grid.

Meeting rails
The rails on the two sashes that sit adjacent to each other when the window is closed.

Mullion

Transom

Surround
The general term used to denote the often decorative framing of a window. *See also Street-Facing Buildings, pp. 39, 42; Walls and Surfaces, p. 103.*

Windows and Doors › Types / 2

Hinged door

The most commonly found kind of door, having one side attached to the door frame via movable hinges, which act as pivots allowing the door to be swung open and closed. Hinged doors are found in a variety of materials and sizes, though are most often rectangular. Some hinged doors are fitted with 'self-closers' (contraptions that allow the door to close when left ajar) or are even automated.

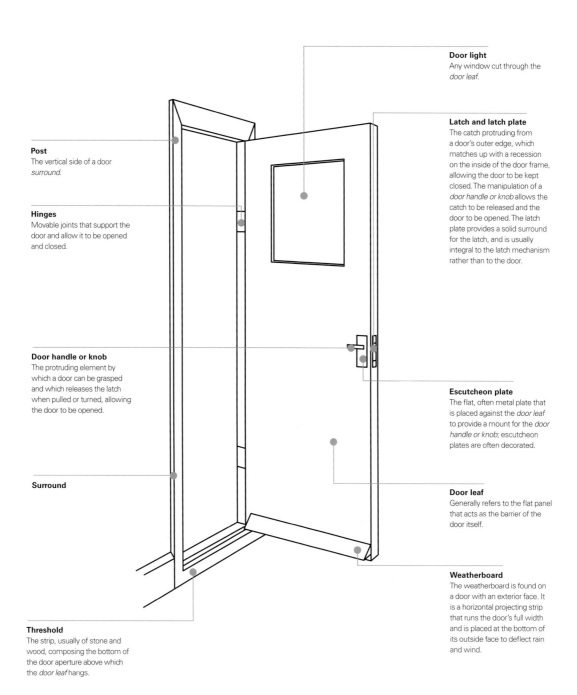

Door light
Any window cut through the *door leaf*.

Latch and latch plate
The catch protruding from a door's outer edge, which matches up with a recession on the inside of the door frame, allowing the door to be kept closed. The manipulation of a *door handle or knob* allows the catch to be released and the door to be opened. The latch plate provides a solid surround for the latch, and is usually integral to the latch mechanism rather than to the door.

Post
The vertical side of a door *surround*.

Hinges
Movable joints that support the door and allow it to be opened and closed.

Door handle or knob
The protruding element by which a door can be grasped and which releases the latch when pulled or turned, allowing the door to be opened.

Escutcheon plate
The flat, often metal plate that is placed against the *door leaf* to provide a mount for the *door handle or knob*; escutcheon plates are often decorated.

Surround

Door leaf
Generally refers to the flat panel that acts as the barrier of the door itself.

Weatherboard
The weatherboard is found on a door with an exterior face. It is a horizontal projecting strip that runs the door's full width and is placed at the bottom of its outside face to deflect rain and wind.

Threshold
The strip, usually of stone and wood, composing the bottom of the door aperture above which the *door leaf* hangs.

Panel door

A panel door is constructed from a structural frame of rails, stiles, mullions and sometimes muntins, infilled with wooden panels. *See also Street-Facing Buildings, p. 41; Walls and Surfaces, p. 121.*

Fanlight
A semicircular (or elongated semicircular) window above a door but contained within the overall *surround*, with radiating glazing bars in the form of a fan or sunburst. If there is a window above a door but it is not in the form of a fan it is usually called a *transom light*. *See also Street-Facing Buildings, p. 41.*

Transom bar
The bar that runs horizontally above a door separating it from a *fanlight* or other *transom light*.

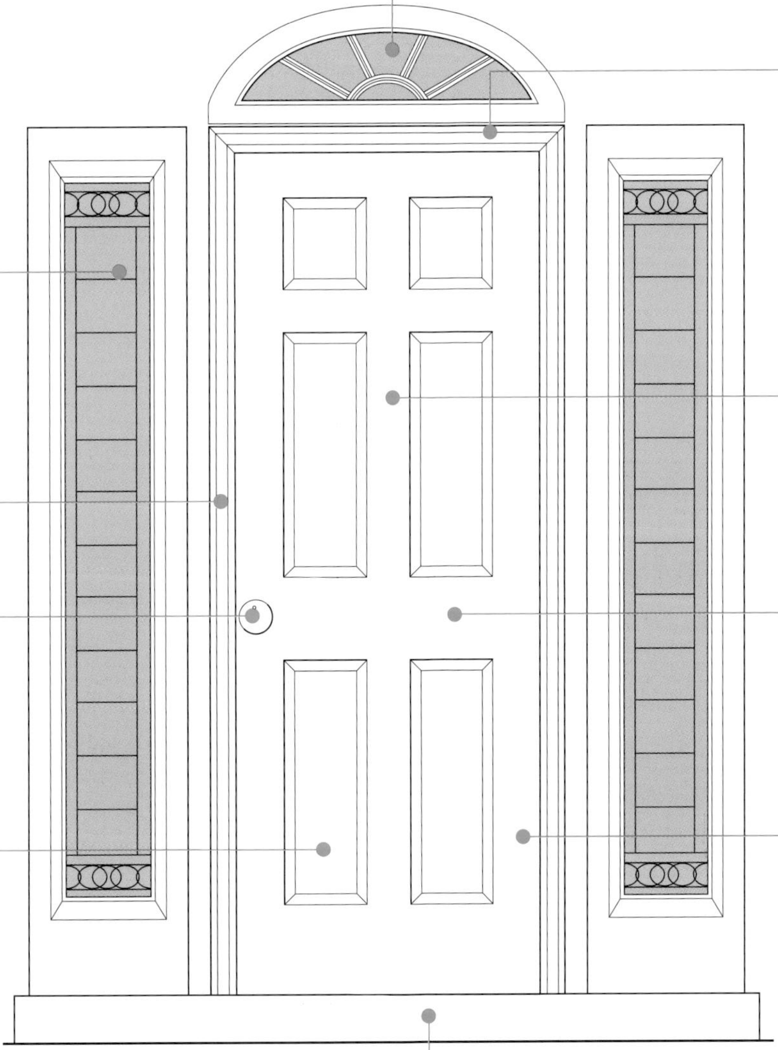

Sidelight
Window to the side of a doorway.

Post

Door handle or knob

Mullion
The central member running vertically down the door. Any subsidiary vertical members further dividing the door into smaller panels are called *muntins*.

Rail
The bar that runs horizontally across a door. Subsidiary rails may be included, such as an intermediate rail that breaks the door up into further smaller panels.

Panel
The boards between the *rails, stiles, mullions* and *muntins.*

Stile
A member that runs vertically down the door, composing its left and right sides.

Threshold

Delineating Apertures › Classical Apertures

The size and spacing of windows and doors are key elements in the proportional logic of a Classical façade. Classical apertures are most often rectangular in form although round-headed windows and doors (if the fanlight is included) are also found. In a Classical façade the windows vary in height; the tallest windows light the piano nobile – the building's principal storey – while the basement, attic and any mezzanine floors are lit by shorter windows.

The architectural treatment of Classical windows and doors is quite similar; it is usually delineated by a moulded surround, with a cornice above. The cornice is often supported by consoles – scrolled brackets – attached to the jambs or posts on either side of the opening. In many cases a Classical window or door is topped by a pediment, so as to form the motif of a small-scale distyle temple front. The triangular pediment is the most common, but several other types are frequently found. For example, the segmental pediment is often seen, alternating with triangular pediments, topping rows of windows in Palladian architecture. *See also The Classical Temple, p. 8; The Renaissance Church, pp. 22, 23; Country Houses and Villas, pp. 35, 36.*

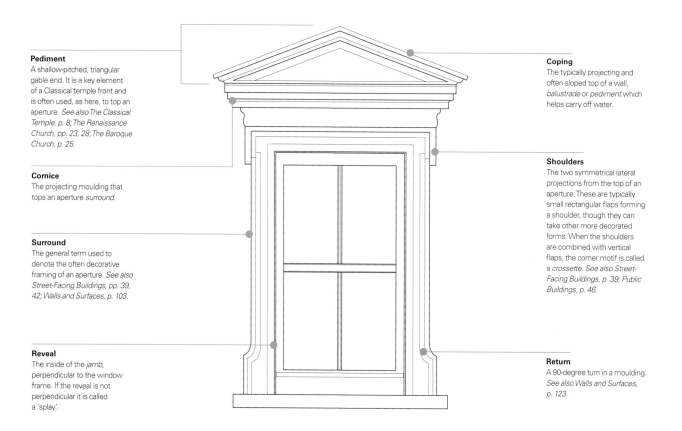

Pediment
A shallow-pitched, triangular gable end. It is a key element of a Classical temple front and is often used, as here, to top an aperture. *See also The Classical Temple, p. 8; The Renaissance Church, pp. 23, 28; The Baroque Church, p. 25.*

Cornice
The projecting moulding that tops an aperture *surround*.

Surround
The general term used to denote the often decorative framing of an aperture. *See also Street-Facing Buildings, pp. 39, 42; Walls and Surfaces, p. 103.*

Reveal
The inside of the *jamb*, perpendicular to the window frame. If the reveal is not perpendicular it is called a 'splay'.

Coping
The typically projecting and often sloped top of a wall, *balustrade* or *pediment* which helps carry off water.

Shoulders
The two symmetrical lateral projections from the top of an aperture. These are typically small rectangular flaps forming a shoulder, though they can take other more decorated forms. When the shoulders are combined with vertical flaps, the corner motif is called a *crossette*. *See also Street-Facing Buildings, p. 39; Public Buildings, p. 46.*

Return
A 90-degree turn in a moulding. *See also Walls and Surfaces, p. 123.*

Ancon ›
A bracket supporting the *entablature* of a window *surround* or door *surround*. *See also Modillion, p. 128.*

Console ››
A double-scrolled bracket, here supporting the *entablature* of a window *surround* or door case. *See also Modillion, p. 128.*

Apron ›››
An embossed (occasionally recessed) panel immediately below a window or *niche*, sometimes articulated with further decoration. *See also Walls and Surfaces, p. 122.*

Delineating Apertures › Pediment Types

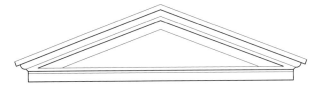

Tympanum
The triangular (or *segmental*)
space created by a *pediment*,
typically recessed, and
often decorated with
figurative sculpture. *See also
The Classical Temple, p. 8;
The Medieval Cathedral, p. 19;
Public Buildings, pp. 48, 50.*

Segmental pediment
Similar to a *triangular* pediment
except that the triangle shape
is replaced by a shallow curve.
*See also The Renaissance
Church, p. 28; Public Buildings,
p. 47.*

Broken-based pediment
Any type of pediment whose
horizontal base is broken in
the centre.

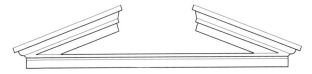

Open pediment
A pediment – *triangular* or
segmental – left open at the top
so that the ends do not meet in
the centre.

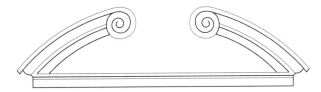

Scrolled pediment
Similar to an *open, segmental
pediment* except that the ends
are turned in on themselves
as scrolls.

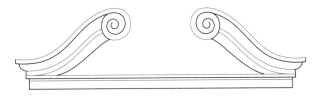

Swan-neck pediment
Similar to a *scrolled pediment* but
composed from two opposing
flattened S-shape curves.

Gothic Apertures › Tracery Elements

Gothic windows and doors are characterized by their pointed-arch elevation which, as Chapter 2 outlines, can be formed from a whole variety of arch shapes. Like windows and doors in Classical architecture, Gothic windows are key to how the internal and external elevations of medieval and medievalized buildings, especially cathedrals, are articulated. In a medieval church or cathedral the window arrangement corresponds to the number of bays and thus provides a way of clearly forging a visual link between the interior and exterior elevations.

The actual apertures of Gothic windows are usually 'traceried' – set with thin bars of stonework, creating an ornamental pattern or figurative scene. Stained glass is set between the masonry bars to complete the decorative stonework. The many styles of tracery vary according to period and location.

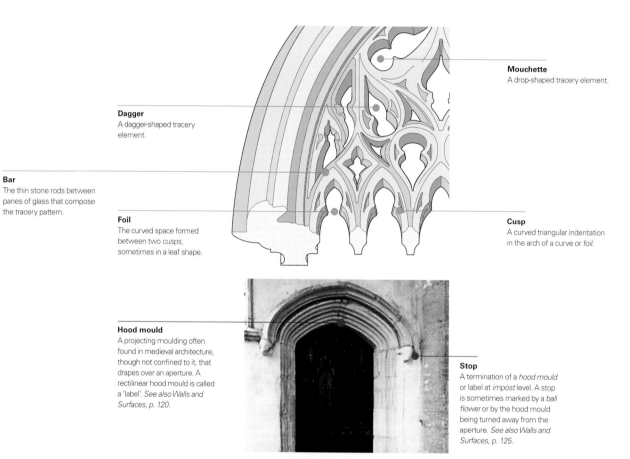

Mouchette
A drop-shaped tracery element.

Dagger
A dagger-shaped tracery element.

Bar
The thin stone rods between panes of glass that compose the tracery pattern.

Foil
The curved space formed between two *cusps*, sometimes in a leaf shape.

Cusp
A curved triangular indentation in the arch of a curve or *foil*.

Hood mould
A projecting moulding often found in medieval architecture, though not confined to it, that drapes over an aperture. A rectilinear hood mould is called a 'label'. *See also Walls and Surfaces, p. 120.*

Stop
A termination of a *hood mould* or label at *impost* level. A stop is sometimes marked by a *ball flower* or by the hood mould being turned away from the aperture. *See also Walls and Surfaces, p. 125.*

Trumeau ›
The central *mullion* in an arched window or doorway, supporting a *tympanum* above two smaller arches. *See also The Medieval Cathedral, p. 19.*

Gothic Apertures › Tracery Types

Plate ›
A basic type of tracery in which the pattern is seemingly incised into, or cut through, a solid layer of stone.

Geometric ››
A simple tracery type consisting of series of circles often infilled with *foils. See also Public Buildings, p. 48.*

Y-tracery ›››
A simple tracery form in which a central *mullion* splits into two branches, forming a Y-shape.

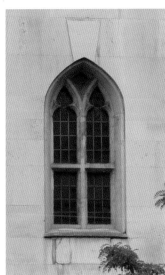

Intersecting or branched ›
A form of tracery in which the *mullions* split into two branches at the springing point, and continue parallel to the curves of the arch.

Curvilinear or flowing ››
A pattern of tracery formed from series of continuously curving and intersecting *bars. See also The Medieval Cathedral, pp. 14, 15.*

Flamboyant ›››
An even more intricate and complex version of *curvilinear or flowing* tracery.

Reticulated ›
A repeating net-like tracery pattern, often of quatrefoils (four-leaved shapes) whose top and bottom *foils* have been elongated into ogees (two S-shaped curves) rather than rounded curves.

Panel or perpendicular ››
A tracery pattern in which the aperture is split into vertical units by the use of repeating *mullions.*

Blind ›››
Any pattern of tracery where there is no aperture and which is instead engaged on a surface in *relief.*

Common Window Forms / 1

The following is a selection of some of the most commonly found window forms and shapes in all periods of architecture.

Cross window
A window composed of one *mullion* and one *transom* in the shape of a cross.

Light
The opening in a window enclosed by one or more panes of glass.

Transom
A horizontal bar or member dividing a window. *See also Street-Facing Buildings, p. 38; Public Buildings, p. 47.*

Mullion
See also Country Houses and Villas, p. 37; Street-Facing Buildings, pp. 38, 44, 45; Public Buildings, p. 47.

Lattice window
A window composed from small square or diamond-shaped panes separated by lead *cames*.

Quarry
A small, square or diamond-shaped piece of glass often used in leaded *lattice windows*.

Cames
The strips of lead used to link window panes to each other in *lattice* or stained-glass windows. They are usually fabricated to be H-shaped in cross section so that they can easily be moulded around panes of glass.

Round-headed window ›
A window in which the *lintel* is arched. *See also Arches, p. 79; Public Buildings, p. 50.*

Pointed window ››
A window in which the *lintel* is a pointed arch. *See also Arches, p. 80.*

Lancet window ›››
Tall, narrow pointed windows, often grouped in threes; named after their resemblance to lancets. *See also The Medieval Cathedral, p. 19.*

 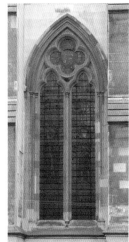 

Oculus/bull's eye window ›
A simple, circular window with no tracery. An oculus also refers to the crowning light at the top of a dome, seen from the interior of the building (the oculus in the Pantheon in Rome is the most famous example). *See also The Renaissance Church, p. 23; Roofs, pp. 157, 158.*

Rose window ››
A circular window delineated with often highly complex tracery which gives it the appearance of a multipetalled rose. *See also The Medieval Cathedral, p. 14.*

Gibbs window ›
A Classical window form whose surround is characterized by repeating *blocked rustication*, often topped by a heavy *keystone*. It is named after the Scottish architect James Gibbs, for whom the window became something of a trademark, though it probably originated in Renaissance Italy. *See also Windows and Doors, p. 103.*

Venetian/Palladian/Serlian window ››
A tri-partite aperture composed of an arched central light flanked by two smaller flat-topped windows. Especially grand examples are articulated with an order and an ornamental *keystone*.

Common Window Forms / 2

Diocletian or thermal window ›
A semicircular window divided into three parts by two vertical *mullions*, the centre light being the larger. It is derived from the Baths of Diocletian in Rome and for that reason is also called a 'thermal' window.

Steel-framed casement window ››
A usually mass-produced casement window whose frame is constructed from steel rather than lead; it is characteristic of early twentieth-century architecture.

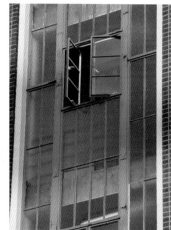

Cabinet window ›
The wooden cabinet-like, traditionally multipaned window found in shopfronts. *See also Street-Facing Buildings, p. 38.*

Shopfront window ››
A window in the street-facing front of a shop, usually large so that merchandise is visible from the outside. *See also The Modern Block, p. 52.*

Ribbon window ›
A series of windows of the same height, separated only by *mullions*, forming a continuous horizontal band or ribbon across a building. Ribbon windows sometimes have concertina frames which allow the lights to be slid along tracks and folded against one another. *See also Concertina folding door, p. 147; Country Houses and Villas, p. 37; Public Buildings, p. 51; The Modern Block, p. 53.*

PVC-framed casement window ››
A mass-produced casement window whose frame is constructed from PVC. It is cheaper to produce than steel casement windows, and PVC has the added advantage that it is not susceptible to rust.

Window Projections and Balconies / 1

Windows are not always set flush with a wall surface, but often project from the wall, in a variety of ways. Projecting windows are sometimes deployed to gain more interior space but are also sometimes used purely for architectural effect. This section also includes some of the projecting elements that are found in conjunction with windows, such as balconies and shutters.

Oriel window ›
A window that projects from one or more upper storeys but does not extend to the ground floor. *See also Country Houses and Villas, p. 34; Street-Facing Buildings, pp. 38, 43.*

Bay window ››
A window that may start on the ground floor and extend up one or more storeys. A variation is the 'bow window' which is curved while a bay window is typically rectangular.

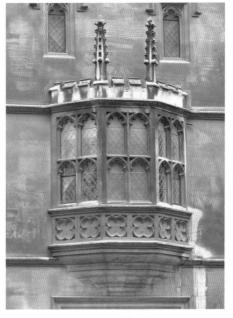

Oversailing window ›
An upper-storey window projecting from the face of a wall. It differs from an *Oriel window* in usually extending across more than one bay.

Trapezoid window ››
An irregular four-sided projection from a wall, containing one or more window lights.

Window Projections and Balconies / 2

Balcony
A platform attached to the outside of a building – cantilevered or supported on brackets – and enclosed on its outer sides by a *railing* or *balustrade*. *See also Street-Facing Buildings, p. 39; The Modern Block, pp. 53, 55.*

Railing
A fence-like structure used to partially enclose a space or platform. The upright members supporting the rail itself are often treated decoratively. *See also Street-Facing Buildings, p. 41.*

Balconette
A stone *balustrade*, or most often cast-iron *railing*, framing the lower section of usually an upper-storey window. *See also Street-Facing Buildings, pp. 41, 42, 43, 44.*

Baluster
A typically stone structure, usually set in a row with others to support a *railing* and form a *balustrade*.

Balustrade
A series of *balusters* that supports a *railing* or *coping*. *See also The Baroque Church, p. 24; Street-Facing Buildings, pp. 39, 44; Public Buildings, p. 47.*

Shutter
A panel, often *louvred*, hinged to the side of a window, which can be closed to keep out light or for security reasons. Shutters can be affixed to the inside or outside of windows. *See also Street-Facing Buildings, pp. 40, 44; Public Buildings, p. 47.*

Louvres
Rows of angled slats placed over a window (often on *shutters*), door or wall surface, designed to allow light and air to circulate but provide a barrier against direct sunlight. *See also High-Rise Buildings, p. 59.*

Roof Lights

Windows are often set into various types of roof to provide daylight to the space below. Roof lights range from small skylights piercing the roofs of houses to large cupolas topping the domes of great cathedrals.

Skylight ›
A window that is parallel to the face of a roof. A small *dome* is sometimes used, especially on a flat roof, to maximize the amount of light entering the space below. *See also Street-Facing Buildings, p. 42.*

Dormer ››
A window that protrudes vertically from the plane of a *pitched roof*. Dormer windows can be included as part of the original design of a building, but are frequently added to existing buildings to create more light and usable space. *See also Street-Facing Buildings, pp. 41, 42, 43; Public Buildings, p. 49.*

Lucarne ›
A type of *dormer* window; the term is usually reserved for the often *louvred, gabled* apertures set into *spires*. *See also The Medieval Cathedral, p. 14; Public Buildings, p. 47.*

Cupola ››
A small *dome*-like structure, usually circular or octagonal in plan, often placed on top of a dome or larger roof and sometimes used as a viewing platform. Cupolas are invariably heavily glazed to admit light into the space below, and for this reason are sometimes known as 'lanterns'. *See also Roofs, p. 157.*

Common Door Forms

The following is a selection of some of the most commonly found door forms and shapes in all periods of architecture.

Single door ›
A door with one *leaf*.

Double door ››
A door composed from two *leaves* hung from opposite sides of the door casement.

Dutch or stable door ›
A single door divided horizontally, usually in the centre, so that the resultant two *leaves* can be opened or closed independently.

Jib door ››
An internal door designed to appear coterminous with the wall surface.

French window ›
A heavily fenestrated double door, usually found in domestic buildings, that opens on to a garden.

Revolving door ››
A door used in spaces with high footfall. It consists of four leaves attached to a central rotating vertical axle. Pushing a leaf causes the door to rotate (revolving doors are sometimes motorized). The design ensures there is no direct interchange between interior and exterior, which is especially useful for regulating interior temperatures.

Sliding door ›
A door set on tracks parallel to the door face. To open, the door is slid along the tracks so that it overlaps with the wall or surface adjacent to the aperture. Sometimes the door slides into the wall.

Concertina folding door ›
A door with a repeating series of *leaves* that can be slid along tracks and folded against one another; typically used for providing openings over a large area.

Up-and-over door ››
A door that can be lifted above the aperture using a counterbalance mechanism; typically used in garages.

Tambour door ›
A door made from a series of conjoined horizontal slats. These are rolled up to open the door.

Self-opening/automatic door ››
A door that requires no user action to open. Instead it is opened mechanically when the user activates infrared, motion or pressure sensors.

Roofs › Types

In so far as buildings are shelters from the elements, by enclosing them from above, roofs are fundamental to all buildings. Roofs may be incorporated into the building structure, continuous with the walls, or stand as almost separate structures in form or materials.

A roof's external faces are very often sloping, to provide a natural mechanism for precipitation to run off clear of the building. However, despite the advantages of sloping roofs, flat roofs are a frequent feature in twentieth- and twenty-first-century architecture. They are often used for aesthetic reasons or to provide more usable space both inside a building, by negating the need for wasteful loft space, and on the outside, by providing a platform for service functions or, in some instances, a space for recreation.

As the variety of roof forms encompassed in this section illustrates, roofs are important not only in a practical sense, but also in terms of the part they can play in various types of architectural display. For example, the spires and domes of churches and cathedrals often function as part of the aesthetic, cultural or even religious ideas embodied by a particular building.

Lean-to roof ›
A single sloped roof built leaning against a vertical wall. (The Dovecote, Naunton, Gloucestershire, UK.)

Pitched or gabled roof ››
A single-ridged roof with two sloping sides and *gables* at the two ends. The term pitched roof is sometimes used to refer to any sloping roof. *See also p. 152.*

Hipped roof ›
Similar to a *pitched roof* but without *gables*. Instead there are sloping roof faces on all four sides. A roof can be 'half-hipped' when two opposing sides are partly hipped and partly gabled. *See also Country Houses and Villas, p. 35.* (Eureka Schoolhouse, Springfield, VT, USA.)

Mansard roof ››
A roof with a double slope, the lower typically being steeper than the higher. Mansard roofs often contain *dormer* windows and are *hipped* at their ends. A typically French design, the term derives from its first proponent, the French architect François Mansart (1598–1666). If a Mansard roof terminates with a flat *gable* instead of hips, it is strictly called a 'gambrel roof'. (Couven Museum, Aachen, Germany.)

Pavilion roof ›
Similar to a *hipped roof* except with a flat face at its apex. (Fontainebleau, France.)

Conical roof ››
A roof in the shape of a cone, usually sitting atop a *tower* or covering a *dome*. *See also The Renaissance Church, p. 22.* (Waterhouse Square, Holborn, London, UK.)

Flat roof ›
A roof whose pitch is horizontal (though a slight incline is often retained to ensure that water runs off). Tar and gravel are traditionally used to seal a flat roof, but more often now *synthetic membranes* are being used. *See also Country Houses and Villas, p. 37; The Modern Block, pp. 52, 53, 54; Concrete, p. 88.* (Ludwig Mies van der Rohe, Neue Nationalgalerie, Berlin, Germany, 1968.)

Saw-tooth roof ››
A roof composed of sloping faces alternating with vertical ones which are often set with windows. Saw-tooth roofs are often used to cover very large spaces where a *pitched roof* would be impractical. (Factory, Sicily, Italy.)

Barrel or cambered roof ›
A roof whose span is in the form of a continuous curve. Barrel roofs are generally semicircular or near semicircular in section, while cambered roof sections have a more gentle curve (like in this example). (Adnams Brewery, Reydon, Suffolk, UK.)

Spire ››
A tapering triangular or conical structure often set atop a *tower* in a church or other medievalized building. *See also p. 154.*

Dome ›
A usually hemispherical structure whose shape derives from the rotation of a vault 360 degrees through its central axis. *See also pp. 157, 158, 159.* (Brunelleschi's Duomo, Florence, Italy.)

Tiling and Roof-Cladding Types

The fundamental practical requirement of a roof is to shelter a building's interior from the elements; thus, it is essential for a cladding material to be water and wind resistant. Tiles, either ceramic or slate, are the most common roof-cladding types. As materials, tiles are particularly suited to this application as they are impervious to water but are also small and individually lightweight, allowing a roof cladding to be built up over time. Ceramic tiles have the added advantage that they can be cast in a variety of shapes to suit the ridges and valleys of a particular roof. For tiles *see also Walls and Surfaces, pp. 110, 111.*

Historically, metals such as lead and copper were used as roof-cladding materials, but this was rare because they were expensive. In twentieth- and twenty-first-century architecture these metals are still sometimes used to clad roofs, while steel is now often used, in the form of large corrugated sheets. Various man-made membranes are also increasingly found cladding roofs, sometimes in concert with 'green roofs' – roofs covered with soil and vegetation.

Hung tiles ›
A very common form of roof cladding, tiles are usually hung from an underlying *timber frame* in overlapping rows – called 'imbrication'. Different-coloured tiles can be used to create a variety of geometrical patterns. *See also Walls and Surfaces, p. 110.*

Hung slate ››
Slate is strictly masonry, but because it can be broken into thin sheets, it is often used in a similar way to *hung tiles*. *See also Walls and Surfaces, p. 110.*

Ridge tiles ›
The tiles which sit over the *ridge* of a roof. In some instances they are adorned with vertically projecting decorative tiles called 'crest tiles'.

Pantiles ››
S-shaped tiles which interlock with adjacent ones, forming a ridged pattern.

Mission or barrel tiles ›
Semicircular or barrel-shaped tiles which are laid in alternating rows of concave and convex arrangements.

Fish scale tiles ››
Flat tiles with curved lower ends. When laid in overlapping rows they resemble the scales of a fish.

Roof felt ›
A fibrous material, usually fibreglass or polyester, infused with bitumen or tar to give it water resistance. It is often laid with a layer of shingles on top or, as here, secured by wooden battens.

Synthetic tiles ››
Tiles made from synthetic materials like fibreglass, plastic or (now very rarely) asbestos.

Synthetic membranes ››
Sheets of synthetic rubber or thermoplastic which are heat-welded together to form a waterproof layer.

Green roof ›
The covering or partial covering of a roof with vegetation (and also growing media and irrigation and drainage systems).

Corrugated steel ››
Sheets of steel corrugated (pressed with a series of alternating peaks and troughs) for rigidity are often used in situations where low cost and speed of construction are necessary. *See also Walls and Surfaces, p. 117.*

Lead ›
Malleable and resistant to corrosion, lead is often used to provide a water-resistant membrane on roofs (and is sometimes used on other parts of buildings). It is usually laid in sheets over wooden battens. *See also Country Houses and Villas, p. 36; Walls and Surfaces, p. 116.*

Copper ››
Like lead, copper is often used to provide a water-resistant membrane on roofs, and is sometimes used on other parts of buildings. When first applied it is a shiny pinky-orange. This quickly corrodes to copper's characteristic green patina, which is resistant to further corrosion. *See also Walls and Surfaces, p. 116.*

Pitched and Gabled Roofs

A single-ridged roof with two sloping sides and *gables* at the two ends. The term pitched roof is sometimes used to refer to any sloping roof. *See also p. 148; The Medieval Cathedral, pp. 15, 18, 19; Country Houses and Villas, p. 35; Street-Facing Buildings, p. 38.*

Gable
The usually triangular part of the wall enclosing the sloping faces of a *pitched roof. See also The Medieval Cathedral, pp. 14, 15; Street-Facing Buildings, pp. 38, 43.*

Ridge
The intersection of two sloping sides at the top of the roof.

Chimney stack
A structure, usually of brick, used to convey smoke from internal fireplaces clear of the building. Where it protrudes above a roof it is often highly decorated. Chimney stacks are usually topped by chimney pots. *See also Country Houses and Villas, p. 35; Street-Facing Buildings, p. 38.*

Coping
The typically projecting and often sloped top course of brick or masonry on a wall, *gable, balustrade* or *pediment*, which helps to carry off water.

Cornice
Strictly, the highest level in a Classical *entablature* which projects over the lower levels; the term is also used, as here, to refer to a continuous horizontal moulding projecting from the face of a wall, especially where it intersects with the roof face. *See also Columns and Piers, p. 70.*

Kneeler
The roughly triangular stone that sits at the foot of the *gable*.

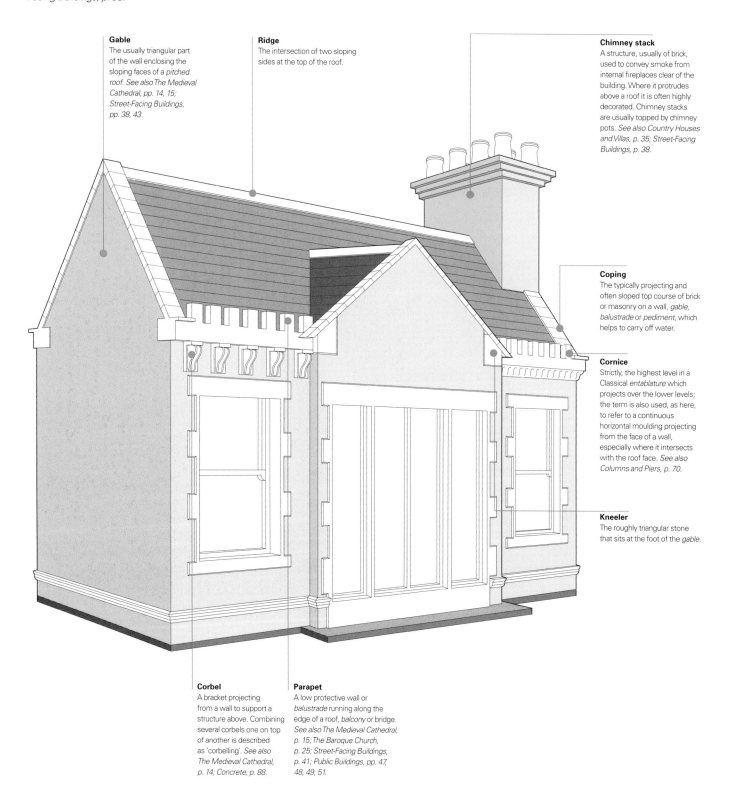

Corbel
A bracket projecting from a wall to support a structure above. Combining several corbels one on top of another is described as 'corbelling'. *See also The Medieval Cathedral, p. 14; Concrete, p. 88.*

Parapet
A low protective wall or *balustrade* running along the edge of a roof, *balcony* or bridge. *See also The Medieval Cathedral, p. 15; The Baroque Church, p. 25; Street-Facing Buildings, p. 41; Public Buildings, pp. 47, 48, 49, 51.*

Pitched and Gabled Roofs › Gable Types

Straight-line gable ›
A gable raised above the roof line but remaining parallel with it.

Crow-stepped gable ››
A gable projecting above the *pitched roof* line in a stepped manner. *See also Country Houses and Villas, p. 34; Street-Facing Buildings, p. 40.*

Side gable ›
A gable on the side of a building, usually perpendicular to the main front. The V-shape where the two *pitched roofs* intersect is called a 'valley'.

Gablet ›
A small gable often used to top a *buttress*. *See also The Medieval Cathedral, p. 15.*

Hipped gable ››
The name given to the gable of a 'half-hipped roof' in which two opposing sides are partly hipped and partly gabled.

Shaped gable ›
A gable in which each side is formed from two or more curves.

Dutch gable ››
A gable in which each side is *curvilinear*; usually topped by a *pediment*.

Spires and Castellations

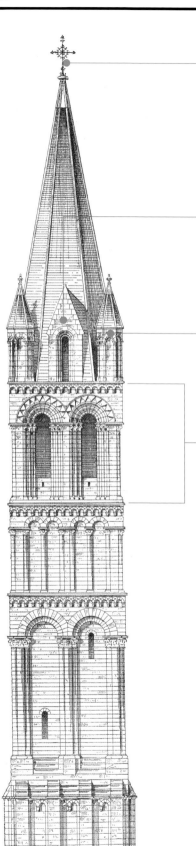

Spire
A tapering triangular or conical structure often set atop a *tower* in a church or other medievalized building. *See also p. 149; The Medieval Cathedral, p. 14.*

Tower
A narrow, tall structure projecting from, or attached to, a building or standing as an independent structure. *See also The Medieval Cathedral, p. 14; Fortified Buildings, p. 31; Country Houses and Villas, p. 34; Public Buildings, pp. 46, 51.*

Finial
The crowning ornament of a *pinnacle, spire* or roof. An ecclesiastical building is usually topped by a cross. *See also The Medieval Cathedral, p. 14; Street-Facing Buildings, p. 43; Public Buildings, pp. 46, 49, 50.*

Lucarne
A type of *dormer* window; the term is usually reserved for the often *louvred*, gabled apertures set into *spires*. *See also the Medieval Cathedral, p. 14; Public Buildings, p. 47; Windows and Doors, p. 145.*

Turret
A small *tower* projecting vertically from the corner wall or roof of a building. *See also Country Houses and Villas, p. 34; Public Buildings, p. 48; p. 156.*

Belfry
The part of the *tower* where the bells are hung. *See also The Medieval Cathedral, p. 14.*

Spires and Castellations › Spire Types / 1

Helm spire ›

An unusual spire formed by four diamond-shaped roof faces which angle inwards, creating *gables* on each of the four sides of the *tower*. (St Mary's Church, Sompting, West Sussex, UK.)

Broach spire ››

An octagonal spire with triangular faces standing on a square base. There are usually half-pyramids or 'broaches' in the corners of the base, which link the base to the four corner faces of the spire that do not coincide with the sides of the *tower*. (St Catherine's Church, Llanfaes, Anglesey, UK.)

Splayed-foot spire ›

Similar to a *broach spire*, except that near the bottom of the spire the four corner faces taper out to a point, with the four side faces splaying out. (St Peter ad Vincula, West Sussex, UK.)

Parapet spire ››

A typically octagonal spire whose triangular faces are set back from the edge of the *tower*. A *parapet* runs around the top of the tower with *turrets* or *pinnacles* set in the four corners. *See also Public Buildings, p. 48.* (Salisbury Cathedral, UK.)

Needle spire ›››

A slender, almost spike-like, spire which sits in the centre of its base. *See also High-Rise Buildings, p. 56.* (Cathedral of St Peter and St Paul, St Petersburg, Russia.)

Open spire ›

A spire characterized by the use of an open network of *tracery* and *flying buttresses*. (Ulm Minster, Germany.)

Crown spire ››

An open spire formed from *flying buttresses* which converge towards the centre, giving the appearance of a crown. (St Dunstan's in the East, London, UK.)

Spires and Castellations › Spire Types / 2

Complex spire ›
A spire composed from a combination of open and enclosed parts, and sometimes different materials. (Neo-Gothic town hall in Liberec, Czech Republic.)

Flèche ››
A small spire usually placed on the *ridge* of a *pitched roof* or at the intersection of the ridges of two perpendicular pitched roofs. *See also Country Houses and Villas, p. 34.* (Notre Dame, Paris, France [now destroyed].)

Tourelle ›
Strictly not a spire, but a small circular *tower* topped by a *conical* roof.

Turret ››
Strictly not a spire, but a small *tower* projecting vertically from the corner wall or roof of a building. *See also p. 154; Country Houses and Villas, p. 34; Public Buildings, p. 48.* (Corn Exchange, Dorchester, UK.)

Crenellations ›
Regularly spaced teeth-like projections from the top of a wall. The projecting flaps are called 'merlons' and the gaps between are 'crenels'. Derived from defensive structures like castles or city walls, they were later used for decorative purposes. *See also Fortified Buildings, pp. 32, 33; Country Houses and Villas, p. 34.* (St Nicholas' Church , Blakeney, Norfolk, UK.)

Machicolations ››
The holes in the floor between adjacent *corbels* supporting a crenelled *parapet*. Machicolations were designed for defensive purposes so that objects and liquids could be dropped on attackers below, but were later used for decorative purposes. *See also Fortified Buildings, p. 32; Country Houses and Villas, p. 34.* (Citadel of the Knights Templar, La Couvertoirade, Larzac, France.)

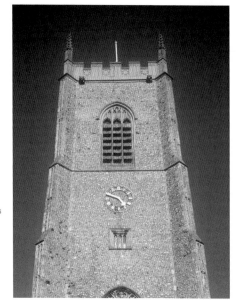

Domes › Exterior

Domes are usually hemispherical structures whose shape derives from the rotation of a vault 360 degrees through its central axis. *See also Country Houses and Villas, p. 35; Public Buildings, p. 50.*

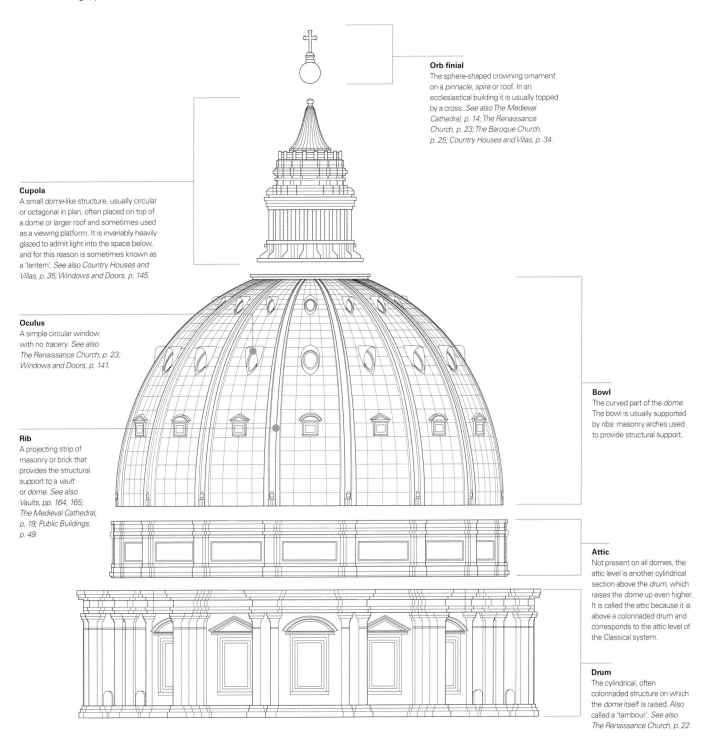

Orb finial
The sphere-shaped crowning ornament on a *pinnacle, spire* or roof. In an ecclesiastical building it is usually topped by a cross. *See also The Medieval Cathedral, p. 14; The Renaissance Church, p. 23; The Baroque Church, p. 25; Country Houses and Villas, p. 34.*

Cupola
A small *dome*-like structure, usually circular or octagonal in plan, often placed on top of a dome or larger roof and sometimes used as a viewing platform. It is invariably heavily glazed to admit light into the space below, and for this reason is sometimes known as a 'lantern'. *See also Country Houses and Villas, p. 35; Windows and Doors, p. 145.*

Oculus
A simple circular window with no *tracery*. *See also The Renaissance Church, p. 23; Windows and Doors, p. 141.*

Rib
A projecting strip of masonry or brick that provides the structural support to a *vault* or *dome*. *See also Vaults, pp. 164, 165; The Medieval Cathedral, p. 19; Public Buildings, p. 49.*

Bowl
The curved part of the *dome*. The bowl is usually supported by *ribs*: masonry arches used to provide structural support.

Attic
Not present on all domes, the attic level is another cylindrical section above the *drum*, which raises the *dome* up even higher. It is called the attic because it is above a colonnaded drum and corresponds to the attic level of the Classical system.

Drum
The cylindrical, often colonnaded structure on which the *dome* itself is raised. Also called a 'tambour'. *See also The Renaissance Church, p. 22.*

Domes › Interior

Tambour gallery
The tambour is the cylindrical wall on which the *dome* itself is raised. Its exterior is often colonnaded while a gallery sometimes runs around its interior. (Dome of St Peter's, Rome, Italy.)

Central oculus
A simple circular window with no *tracery*, here used at the crown of a *dome* to light the interior. *See also p. 157; Windows and Doors, p. 141.*

Coffering
The decoration of a surface with a series of sunken rectangular panels called 'lacunaria'. *See also The Baroque Church, p. 29.*

Pendentive
The curved triangular section formed by the intersection of a *dome* and its *supporting arches*. Here, the pendentive is set with a *roundel* – a circular panel or moulding. *See also The Baroque Church, p. 29; Walls and Surfaces, p. 130.*

Supporting arch
One of four or sometimes eight arches supporting the *dome* above.

Domes › Types

Melon dome ›
A dome in which the structural support is provided by a series of arched *ribs* with the space between infilled, resembling a striped melon. *See also Public Buildings, p. 49.* (Dome of St Peter's, Rome, Italy.)

Saucer dome ››
A dome that has a *rise* much smaller than its *span*, giving it a flatter, upturned-saucer shape. *See also Country Houses and Villas, p. 35.*

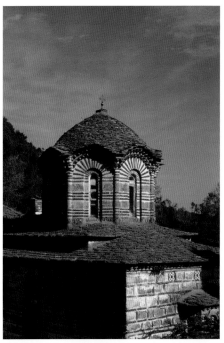

Onion dome ›
A dome with a bulbous, onion-like shape which terminates in a point at its top; in section, similar to an *ogee arch. See also Arches, p. 80.* (Cathedral of the Annunciation, Kremlin, Moscow, Russia.)

Double dome ››
An arrangement where one dome sits inside the other. Double or even triple domes are often used when a dome rises high above a building's roof line and its often decorated underside needs to be easily visible from inside. (US Capitol Building, Washington, DC, USA.)

Geodesic dome ›
A part-spherical or wholly spherical structure composed from a triangulated steel framework. (Buckminster Fuller, United States Pavilion, Expo '67, Montreal, Canada, 1967.)

Lattice dome ››
A modern dome type, formed from a polygonal steel framework usually infilled with glass. (Grimshaw, The Eden Project, Cornwall, UK, 2001.)

Structures › Trusses / 1

The underlying structure supporting a building is, of course, hidden on the exterior and in many building types on the interior as well. However, there are many instances where the interior of the roof structure is revealed and often highly decorated. Ornate hammer-beam ceilings, all manner of rib vaults and the undersides of domes are just a few examples of how the interior roof structure becomes a fundamental part of a building's internal form. This is not confined to traditional building styles, but is a key feature of late twentieth-century High Tech architecture in which the structure becomes the main aesthetic statement, with steel-framed truss roofs often a particularly prominent feature.

A truss roof is a structural framework of one or more triangular units combined with straight members, that can be used to span large distances and support a load. Trusses are most usually constructed from wood or steel beams.

SINGLE-FRAMED ROOF
The simplest kind of truss roof, composed from series of transverse *principal rafters* laid against each other that support a central *ridge beam*.

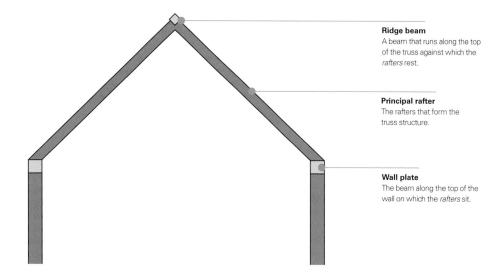

Ridge beam
A beam that runs along the top of the truss against which the *rafters* rest.

Principal rafter
The rafters that form the truss structure.

Wall plate
The beam along the top of the wall on which the *rafters* sit.

DOUBLE-FRAMED ROOF
Similar to a *single-framed roof*, but with longitudinal members added to the structure.

Purlin
A longitudinal beam on top of the *principal rafters* that gives support to the *common rafters* (where applicable) and the roof cladding above.

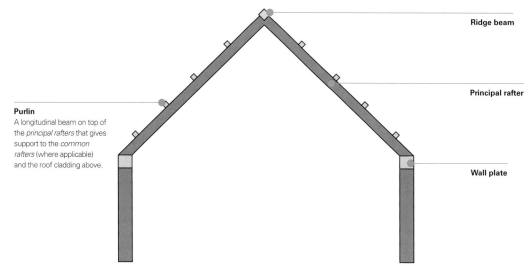

Ridge beam

Principal rafter

Wall plate

WAGON ROOF

A *single-framed* or *double-framed* truss roof to which *collar beams*, *arched braces* and *ashlar braces* have been added.

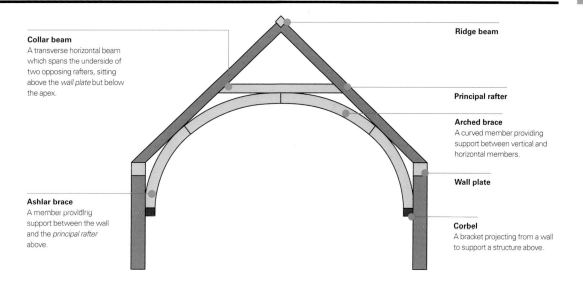

Collar beam
A transverse horizontal beam which spans the underside of two opposing rafters, sitting above the *wall plate* but below the apex.

Ashlar brace
A member providing support between the wall and the *principal rafter* above.

Ridge beam

Principal rafter

Arched brace
A curved member providing support between vertical and horizontal members.

Wall plate

Corbel
A bracket projecting from a wall to support a structure above.

CROWN-POST ROOF

A truss roof in which a crown post – a four-pronged post vaguely reminiscent of a crown – is placed centrally on a *tie beam* to support the *collar beam* and *collar purlin*.

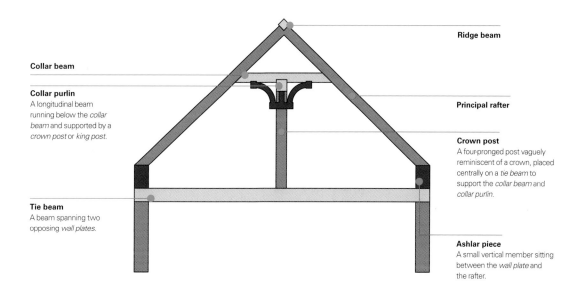

Collar beam

Collar purlin
A longitudinal beam running below the *collar beam* and supported by a *crown post* or *king post*.

Tie beam
A beam spanning two opposing *wall plates*.

Ridge beam

Principal rafter

Crown post
A four-pronged post vaguely reminiscent of a crown, placed centrally on a *tie beam* to support the *collar beam* and *collar purlin*.

Ashlar piece
A small vertical member sitting between the *wall plate* and the rafter.

QUEEN-POST ROOF

A truss roof in which two posts are placed on a *tie beam* to support the *principal rafters* above. The queen posts are held in place laterally by a *collar beam*.

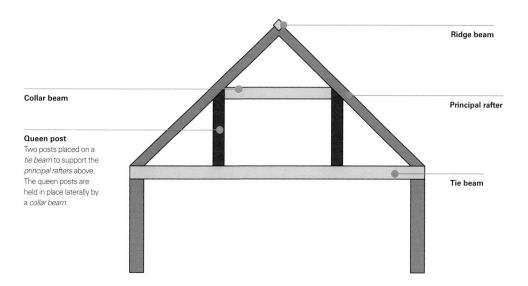

Collar beam

Queen post
Two posts placed on a *tie beam* to support the *principal rafters* above. The queen posts are held in place laterally by a *collar beam*.

Ridge beam

Principal rafter

Tie beam

Structures › Trusses / 2

KING-POST ROOF

A truss roof in which a vertical post is placed in the centre of a *tie beam* to support the *ridge beam*.

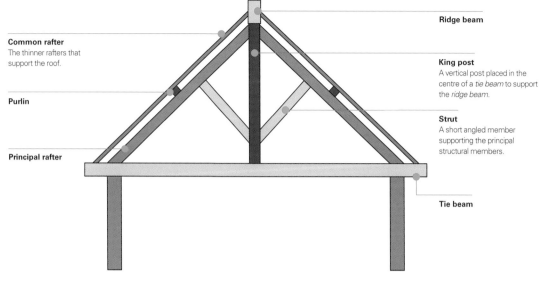

Common rafter
The thinner rafters that support the roof.

Purlin

Principal rafter

Ridge beam

King post
A vertical post placed in the centre of a *tie beam* to support the *ridge beam*.

Strut
A short angled member supporting the principal structural members.

Tie beam

HAMMER-BEAM ROOF

A truss roof where the *tie beams* appear to have been cut, leaving smaller beams projecting horizontally from the wall. Called *hammer beams*, these are usually supported by *arched braces* and carry a *hammer post*.

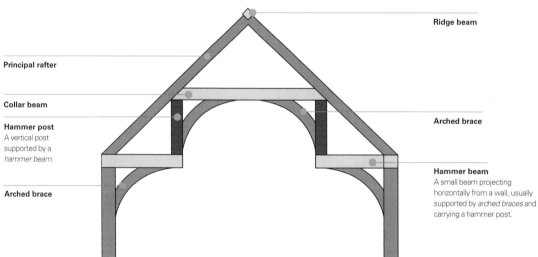

Principal rafter

Collar beam

Hammer post
A vertical post supported by a *hammer beam*.

Arched brace

Ridge beam

Arched brace

Hammer beam
A small beam projecting horizontally from a wall, usually supported by *arched braces* and carrying a hammer post.

Arched truss ›
A truss whose upper and lower chords are composed from multiple members set at an angle to create a curve. (Grimshaw, Waterloo International Terminal, London, UK, 1993.)

Parallel chord truss ›
A truss in which the upper and lower members – called 'chords' – are parallel. The upper and lower chords are most often separated by a triangulated lattice-like structure. (Rogers & Piano, Centre Georges Pompidou, Paris, France, 1977.)

Pratt truss ›
A *parallel chord truss* with both vertical and angled members between the parallel chords, creating a triangulated structure.

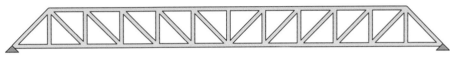

Warren truss ›
A *parallel chord truss* with angled members between the parallel chord, creating a triangulated structure.

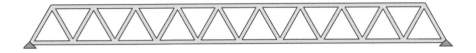

Vierendeel truss ›
A non-triangulated truss with all members horizontal or vertical.

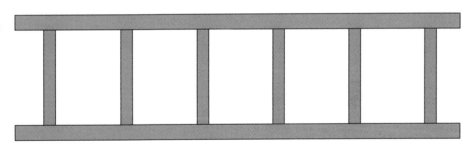

Space frame ›
A three-dimensional truss-like structural framework in which the straight members are arranged in a series of repeating geometrical patterns. Strong but lightweight, space frames are often used to span large distances with few supports. (Populous, Centre Court roof, Wimbledon, London, UK, 2009)

Structures › Vaults

Barrel vault ›

The simplest kind of vault, formed from the extrusion of a single semicircular arch along an axis, creating a semicylindrical form.

Groin vault ››

A vault produced by the perpendicular intersection of two *barrel vaults*. The arched edges between the intersecting vaults are called 'groins' and give the vault its name.

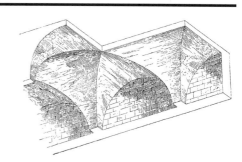

Rib vault

Similar to a *groin vault* except that the groins are replaced by ribs (projecting strips of masonry or brick) which provide the structural framework of the vault and support the infilling or *web*. (Frombork Cathedral, Poland.)

Web

The infilled surface between *ribs*. *See also The Medieval Cathedral, p. 19.*

Wall rib

Decorative longitudinal rib running across the wall surface.

Boss

A projecting ornament marking the intersection of two or more *ribs*.

Transverse rib

The structural rib running across the vault, perpendicular to the wall and defining the bays.

Ridge rib

The decorative longitudinal rib running along the centre of the vault.

Diagonal rib

Structural rib running diagonally across the vault.

Structures › Vaults › Rib Vault Types

Quadripartite vault ›
A vault in which each bay is subdivided into four parts by two *diagonal ribs.* (Durham Cathedral, UK.)

Sexpartite vault ››
A vault in which each bay is subdivided into six parts by two *diagonal ribs* and one *transverse rib.* (Notre Dame, Paris, France.)

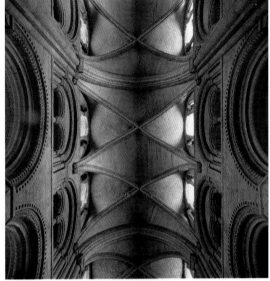

Tierceron vault ›
A vault with additional ribs that emanate from the main supports and abut onto the *transverse ribs* or *ridge rib.* (Exeter Cathedral, UK.)

Lierne vault ››
A vault with additional ribs that do not emanate from the main supports but are placed between adjacent *diagonal* and *transverse ribs.* (Winchester Cathedral, UK.)

Fan vault ›
A vault formed from many ribs of the same size and curve that emanate from the main supports, creating an inverted cone shape with a fan-like pattern. Fan vaults are often highly *traceried* and sometimes decorated with pendants – elements that appear to hang at the conjunctions of adjacent vaults. (Kings College Chapel, Cambridge, UK.)

Stairs and Lifts › Staircase Components

As soon as buildings of more than one storey began to be constructed, a means was needed to provide circulation from one floor to another. Stairs in their various forms have provided the most lasting and durable fulfilment of this requirement, and are now present in almost every building with more than one storey.

Because they are so pivotal to a building's circulation, stairs are often highly decorated or formally dramatic architectural features.

As the examples in this section illustrate, stairs exist in a variety of forms, but their core elements are more or less constant, although not necessarily present in every example.

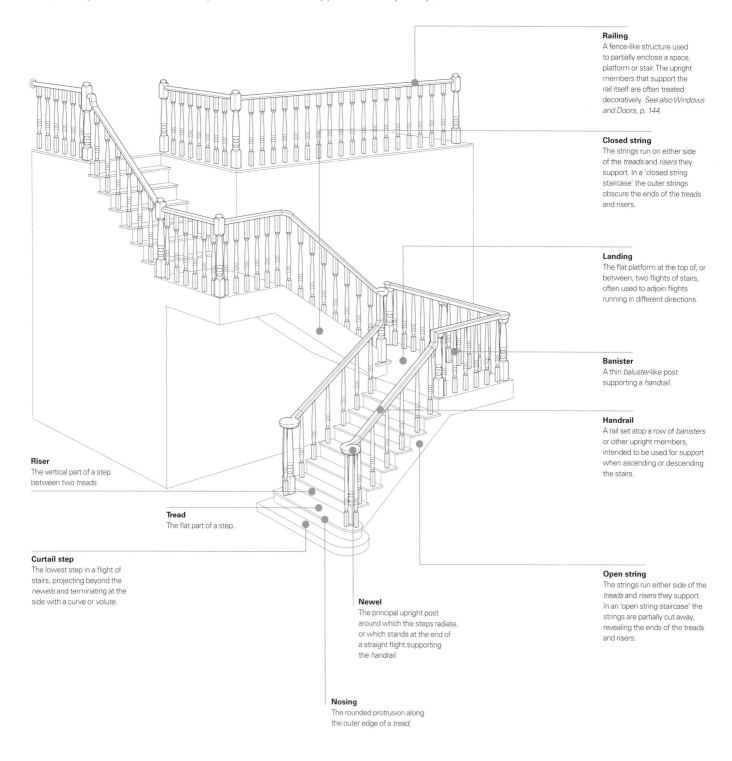

Railing
A fence-like structure used to partially enclose a space, platform or stair. The upright members that support the rail itself are often treated decoratively. *See also Windows and Doors, p. 144.*

Closed string
The strings run on either side of the *treads* and *risers* they support. In a 'closed string staircase' the outer strings obscure the ends of the treads and risers.

Landing
The flat platform at the top of, or between, two flights of stairs, often used to adjoin flights running in different directions.

Banister
A thin *baluster*-like post supporting a *handrail*.

Handrail
A rail set atop a row of *banisters* or other upright members, intended to be used for support when ascending or descending the stairs.

Open string
The strings run either side of the *treads* and *risers* they support. In an 'open string staircase' the strings are partially cut away, revealing the ends of the treads and risers.

Riser
The vertical part of a step between two *treads*.

Tread
The flat part of a step.

Curtail step
The lowest step in a flight of stairs, projecting beyond the *newels* and terminating at the side with a curve or *volute*.

Newel
The principal upright post around which the steps radiate, or which stands at the end of a straight flight supporting the *handrail*.

Nosing
The rounded protrusion along the outer edge of a *tread*.

Staircase Types

Straight ›
A single flight of steps with no turns. When two straight flights run in opposite directions, are linked by a *landing* and sit parallel with no gap between them, it is called a 'dog-leg stair'.

Winder ››
A curved stair or part of a stair in which the *treads* are narrower at one end than at the other.

Open-well ›
A rectangular stair which rises around a central void called a 'well'.

Flying ››
A flight of stone steps built into the wall, each step resting cumulatively on the one immediately below. When a flying stair is semicircular or elliptical in plan it is called a 'geometrical stair'.

Newel ›
A stair that winds around a central *newel*. A 'spiral' stair is one form of newel stair.

Helical ››
A stair, semicircular or elliptical in plan, which winds around a central well and takes the form of a helix. A rare permutation is a 'double-helical stair', formed when two independent stairs wind around the same semicircular or elliptical space.

Cantilevered ›
Any stair in which the steps are cantilevered (supported only at one end).

Open ››
A stair with no *risers*.

Lifts and Escalators

While stairs can provide vertical circulation for a building of a few storeys, they are cumulatively less efficient the higher a building becomes. Moreover, they are unsuitable for disabled and frail persons, and for this reason, lifts are now mandatory in many buildings. Principally, however, the lift's most enduring impact on architecture is that it allowed the construction of high-rise buildings. Without lifts, a building of even six or seven floors would be wholly impractical because of the sheer number of stairs needed to facilitate circulation.

As a form of mechanized circulation, escalators have had an important, though less dramatic, impact on architecture. They are most often found in large public buildings where their ability to move huge volumes of people has facilitated new architectural developments, especially in the field of public transport.

Lift ›
Also known as an 'elevator', a lift is a vertical transportation device, essentially an enclosed platform that is moved up and down by mechanical means: either by a system of pulleys (a 'traction lift') or hydraulic pistons (a 'hydraulic lift'). Lifts are often in a building's central core but are also found, as here, on the exterior.

Escalator ›
A moving staircase formed from a motor-driven chain of steps, usually found inside a building's envelope, but also deployed attached to the exterior. *See also Steel, p. 92.*

Glossary / 1

A

Abacus

In a Classical order, the flat, sometimes moulded, section between the top of the *capital* and bottom of the *architrave. See Columns and Piers, p. 70.*

Abutment

A wall or pier built to withstand an arch's lateral thrust. *See Arches, p. 78.*

Acanthus

A stylized decorative form based on the leaf of an acanthus plant. It is an integral element of *Corinthian* and *Composite* capitals, but is also used as a discrete element or as part of a moulded ensemble. *See Walls and Surfaces, p. 124.*

Acroteria

Sculptures – usually *urns, palmettes* or statues – placed on flat pedestals on top of a *pediment.* If sculpture is placed at the outer angles of a pediment rather than at the apex, they are called 'acroteria angularia'. *See The Classical Temple, p. 9.*

Addorsed

A decorative moulding motif of two figures, usually animals, placed back-to-back. When the figures are facing each other they are said to be 'affronted'. *See Walls and Surfaces, p. 124.*

Adyton

In a Classical temple, a rarely included room at the far end of the *cella* which, if present, is used instead of the cella to hold the cult object. *See the Classical Temple, p. 13.*

Aedicule

An architectural frame set into a wall, deployed to indicate a shrine in a sacred building, draw attention to a particular work of art or provide additional surface variegation. *See Walls and Surfaces, p. 119.*

Agraffe

A carved *keystone. See Walls and Surfaces, p. 124.*

Aisle

In a cathedral or church, the space on either side of the *nave* behind the main *arcades. See The Medieval Cathedral, p. 16.*

Alcove

A typically bowed recession into the surface of a wall. Alcoves differ from *niches* by extending down to the floor. *See Walls and Surfaces, p. 124.*

Altar

The structure or table located in the *sanctuary* at the east end of a cathedral or church, where Communion takes place. In a Protestant church, a table is usually used instead of a fixed altar for the preparation of the Communion. The *high altar* is the principal altar of a cathedral or church, located at the east end. *See The Medieval Cathedral, p. 24.*

Altarpiece

A painting or sculpture set behind the *altar* in a cathedral or church. *See The Medieval Cathedral, p. 21.*

Altar rails

A set of *railings* separating the *sanctuary* from the rest of the cathedral or church. *See The Medieval Cathedral, p. 20.*

Amorphous

An irregularly shaped building that has no easily definable form. *See Contemporary Buildings, p. 65.*

Amortizement

The sloping portion of a *buttress*, designed to shed water. *See Walls and Surfaces, p. 119.*

Amphiprostyle

The term used when a *prostyle* arrangement in a Classical temple is repeated for the *opisthodomos* as well as for the *pronaos. See The Classical Temple, p. 12.*

Ancon

A bracket supporting the *entablature* of a window or door *surround. See Windows and Doors, p. 136.*

Antae

In a Classical temple, the fronts of the two protruding walls of the *cella* that make up the *pronaos* (or the *opisthodomos*), often articulated with a *pilaster* or applied half-column. *See The Classical Temple, p. 12.*

Anthemion

A stylized decorative form based on honeysuckle, the lobes of which point inwards (unlike a *palmette*). *See Walls and Surfaces, p. 125.*

Apophyge

The slightly *concave* moulding at the point where a column *shaft* meets the *capital* or *base. See Columns and Piers, p. 70.*

Applied trim

Supplementary elements applied to the surface of a building or *curtain wall*, often designed to highlight the underlying structural frame. *See The Modern Block, p. 54.*

Apron

An embossed (occasionally recessed) panel immediately below a window or *niche*, often enriched with further decorative elements. *See Windows and Doors, p. 136.*

Apse

The typically semicircular recession from the body of the *chancel* or, indeed, any part of a cathedral or church. *See The Medieval Cathedral, p. 17.*

Arabesque

The term given to intricate decorative mouldings consisting of foliation, scrolls and mythical creatures but omitting human figures. As the term suggests, it derives from Islamic decoration. *See Walls and Surfaces, p. 125.*

Araeostyle

An *intercolumniation* of 3½, or wider, lower column diameters (usually too wide for stone and thus used only in wooden structures). *See The Classical Temple, p. 11.*

Arcade

A repeating series of arches set upon columns or piers. An arcade is termed 'blind' when it is applied to a surface or wall. *See Arches, p. 82.*

Arched brace

In a *truss* roof, a curved member providing support between vertical and horizontal members. *See Roofs, p. 161.*

Arched truss

A truss whose upper and lower chords are composed from multiple members set at an angle to create a curve. *See Roofs, p. 162.*

Architrave

The lowest part of the *entablature* consisting of a large beam resting directly on the *capitals* below. *See Columns and Piers, p. 70.*

Arrow slit

A very narrow window through which an archer could fire. Inside, the wall was often cut away to provide the archer with a wider firing angle. One of the most common forms of arrow slit is the cross, which gives the archer further freedom in the direction and elevation of his arrow. *See Fortified Buildings, p. 32.*

Ashlar

A wall formed from flat-faced oblong blocks of stone laid with very precise joints to create an almost entirely smooth wall surface. *See Walls and Surfaces, p. 102.*

Ashlar brace

In a *truss* roof, a member providing support between the wall and the *principal rafter* above. *See Roofs, p. 161.*

Ashlar piece

In a *truss* roof, a small vertical member sitting between the *wall plate* and the *rafter. See Roofs, p. 161.*

Astragal

A small *convex* moulding, semicircular or three-quarters of a circle in section, often set between two flat planes (*fillets*). *See Walls and Surfaces, p. 122.*

Attic

A room situated just below the roof of a building. In a Classical building, it also denotes a storey above the main *entablature.* On some *domes*, the attic level is another cylindrical section above the *drum*, which raises the dome up even higher. *See Roofs, p. 157.*

Awning or top-hung window

A window hinged along its top, which usually requires a *stay* or friction hinge to stay open. A window hung from its bottom side is called a 'hopper' window. *See Windows and Doors, p. 132.*

B

Bailey

See Outer ward.

Balconette

A stone *balustrade*, or most often cast-iron *railing*, framing the lower section of usually an upper-storey window. *See Windows and Doors, p. 144.*

Balcony

A platform attached to the outside of a building – cantilevered or supported on brackets – and enclosed on its outer sides by a *railing* or *balustrade. See Windows and Doors, p. 144.*

Baldacchino

In a cathedral or church, a free-standing ceremonial *canopy* usually made of wood and often with cloth hangings. *See The Medieval Cathedral, p. 20.*

Ball flower

Roughly spherical ornament of a ball inserted into the bowl of a three-petalled flower visible through its trefoiled opening. *See Walls and Surfaces, p. 125.*

Baluster

A typically stone structure, usually set in a row with others to support a *railing* and forming a *balustrade. See Windows and Doors, p. 144.*

Balustrade

A series of *balusters* that supports a *railing* or *coping. See Windows and Doors, p. 143.*

Banded rustication

A form of rustication in which only the top and bottom joints between blocks are accentuated. *See Walls and Surfaces, p. 103.*

Banding

A thin horizontal stripe or band running around a building or façade. *See High-Rise Buildings, p. 59.*

Banister

A thin *baluster*-like post in a staircase, supporting the *handrail* of a stair. *See Stairs and Lifts, p. 166.*

Bar

In a traceried window, the thin stone rods between the panes of glass that compose the *tracery* pattern. *See Windows and Doors, p. 138.*

Barbican

A further line of defence in front of a castle's *gatehouse*, often designed to enclose attackers who could then be bombarded from above with missiles. Barbican also refers to the fortified outposts lying outside the main defences of a city's walls. *See Fortified Buildings, p. 31.*

Barrel or cambered roof

A roof whose span is in the form of a continuous curve. Barrel roofs are generally semicircular or near semi-circular in section, while cambered roof sections have a more gentle curve. *See Roofs, p. 149.*

Barrel vault

The simplest kind of vault, formed from the extrusion of a single semicircular arch along an axis, creating a semicylindrical form. *See Roofs, p. 164.*

Base

The lowest part of a column standing on a *stylobate*, pedestal or *plinth. See Columns and Piers, p. 70.*

Baseboard

See Skirting.

Basement

The storey below the ground storey. In a Classical building, the basement sits below the *piano nobile* at a level equivalent to that of a *plinth* or pedestal. *See Street-Facing Buildings, p. 43.*

Base-structure

The part on which a building sits or from which it appears to emerge. *See Concrete, p. 88.*

Basket capital

A *capital* with interlaced carving resembling wickerwork, usually found in Byzantine architecture. *See Columns and Piers, p. 77.*

Bas-relief

See Relief.

Bastion

In a castle, a structure or tower projecting from a *curtain wall* to aid defence. *See Fortified Buildings, p. 30.*

Batter

An inclined wall face, sloping towards the top. *See Contemporary Buildings, p. 64.*

Bay-leaf

A decorative element in the form of a bay leaf. It is a common motif in Classical architecture, often present in pulvinated (*convex*) *friezes, festoons* and *garlands. See Walls and Surfaces, p. 125.*

Bay window

A fenestrated projection from a building that may start on the ground floor and extend up one or more storeys. A variation is the bow window which is curved while a bay window is typically rectangular. *See Windows and Doors, p. 143.*

Bead

A narrow *convex* moulding, usually semicircular in section. *See Walls and Surfaces, p. 122.*

Bead-and-reel

A decorative motif consisting of an alternating arrangement of elliptical (or sometimes elongated lozenge-shaped) forms and semicircular discs. *See Walls and Surfaces, p. 125.*

Beak-head

A figurative enrichment composed of a repeating pattern of birds' heads, usually with prominent beaks. *See Walls and Surfaces, p. 125.*

Belfry

The part of a tower where the bells are hung. *See The Medieval Cathedral, p. 14.*

Bell arch

Similar to a *shouldered* arch, a bell arch consists of a curved arch resting on two *corbels. See Arches, p. 81.*

Bevelled or chamfered

A simple moulding, created when a right-angled edge is cut away at an angle. Described as 'hollow' when the chamfer is *concave* rather than flat; 'sunk' when it is recessed; and 'stopped' when it is not carried the whole length of an angle. *See Walls and Surfaces, p. 122.*

Bezant

A coin- or disc-shaped ornament. *See Walls and Surfaces, p. 125.*

Billet

A moulding consisting of regularly spaced rectangular or rounded blocks. *See Walls and Surfaces, p. 125.*

Blind arch

An arch set into a wall or surface but with no opening. For 'blind arcade' see *Arcade. See Arches, p. 82.*

Blind tracery

Any pattern of tracery where there is no aperture, and which is instead engaged on a surface in *relief. See Windows and Doors, p. 139.*

Block capital

The simplest capital form with a gradual change in profile from the round bottom to the square top. This otherwise plain capital type is often decorated in various forms of *relief. See Columns and Piers, p. 76.*

Blocked rustication

Rusticated blocks are separated by evenly spaced gaps or apparent recessions. This form of rustication, especially on a window or door *surround*, was made popular in Britain and beyond by the architect James Gibbs; hence it is sometimes called the 'Gibbs surround'. *See Walls and Surfaces, p. 103.*

Boasted ashlar

An ashlar surface incised with horizontal or diagonal grooves. *See Walls and Surfaces, p. 102.*

Bolection

A bold moulding, either *concave* or *convex*, providing a link between two parallel surfaces in different planes. *See Walls and Surfaces, p. 122.*

Boss

A projecting ornament marking the intersection of two or more *ribs* in a *rib vault. See Roofs, p. 164.*

Bowl

The curved part of a *dome*. The bowl is usually supported by *ribs*: masonry arches used to provide structural support. *See Roofs, p. 157.*

Breaking forward entablature

When an *entablature* projects over the columns or *pilasters* it is said to be 'breaking forward'. *See Street-Facing Buildings, p. 39.*

Brick nog

The use of brick or small blocks of masonry to fill the gaps in a building's timber frame. *See Walls and Surfaces, p. 109.*

Brickwork

A wall produced from rows – called 'courses' – of bricks. *See Walls and Surfaces, p. 105.*

Brise-soleil

A structure attached to the exterior of a *glass-curtain-walled* building (though not exclusively so) that serves to provide shade and reduce solar heat gain. *See Walls and Surfaces, p. 118.*

Broach spire

An octagonal spire with triangular faces standing on a square base. Half-pyramids or 'broaches' in the corners of the square base usually link the base to the four corner faces of the spire that do not coincide with the sides of the *tower. See Roofs, p. 155.*

Broken-based pediment

A pediment whose horizontal base is broken in the centre. *See Windows and Doors, p. 137.*

Bucranium

A decorative motif in the form of a bull's skull, often flanked by *garlands*. It is sometimes found (usually alternating with *paterae*) in the *metopes* in a Doric frieze. *See Walls and Surfaces, p. 126.*

Bull's eye window

See Oculus.

Bush-hammered concrete

Concrete with an exposed aggregate finish which is usually produced with a power-hammer after the concrete has set. *See Walls and Surfaces, p. 112.*

Buttress

A masonry or brick structure providing lateral support to a wall. 'Flying buttresses' are typical in cathedrals and consist of flying half-arches that help to carry down the thrust of the *nave's* high vault or roof. An 'angle buttress' is used at corners, usually of *towers*, and consists of two buttresses set at 90 degrees on the adjoining faces of the two perpendicular walls. When the sides of the buttresses do not meet at the corner they are called 'setback'. A buttress is said to be 'clasping' when

Glossary / 2

two angle buttresses are conjoined into a single buttress enveloping the corner. A 'diagonal buttress' consists of a single buttress set at the corner where two perpendicular walls meet. *See Walls and Surfaces, p. 119.*

C

Cabinet window

The wooden cabinet-like, traditionally multipaned window found in shopfronts. *See Windows and Doors, p. 142.*

Cable

A *convex* moulding whose winding form resembles that of a rope or cable. *See Walls and Surfaces, p. 126.*

Cames

The strips of lead used to link window panes to each other in *lattice windows* or stained-glass windows. They are usually fabricated to be H-shaped in cross section so as to be easily moulded around panes of glass. *See Windows and Doors, p. 140.*

Campaniform capital

An Egyptian bell-shaped capital resembling an open papyrus flower. *See Columns and Piers, p. 77.*

Canopy

A horizontal or slightly pitched projection from a building, providing cover from precipitation or sunlight. *See Walls and Surfaces, p. 118.*

Cant

A wall face angled less than 90 degrees from the façade surface. *See Contemporary Buildings, p. 65.*

Cantilevered

A beam, platform, structure or stair supported at only one end. *See Stairs and Lifts, p. 167.*

Capital

The splayed and decorated upper-most part of the column on which the *entablature* sits. *See Columns and Piers, p. 70.*

Cartouche

A typically oval tablet form surrounded by scrolling and sometimes with a carved inscription. *See Walls and Surfaces, p. 126.*

Caryatid

A heavily draped sculpted female figure that takes the place of a column or pier in supporting an entablature. *See Columns and Piers, p. 68.*

Casement moulding

A *concave* moulding with a deep curved indentation, often found in late medieval door and window casements. *See Walls and Surfaces, p. 122.*

Casement window

A window which is attached to its frame by one or more hinges along one of its sides. *See Windows and Doors, p. 132.*

Cast-in-place concrete

Concrete that is cast cumulatively in vertical layers on-site usually using wooden slats. The impressions left by wooden slats can be kept visible for aesthetic purposes. *See Walls and Surfaces, p. 112.*

Catenary or parabolic arch

An arch whose curve is formed from the inverted shape of an idealized hanging chain supported at each end. *See Arches, p. 79.*

Cauliculus

One of the *acanthus* stalks supporting the *helices* in a *Corinthian capital. See Columns and Piers, p. 74.*

Cavetto

A *concave* moulding, usually a quarter-circle in section. *See Walls and Surfaces, p. 122.*

Cavo-relievo

See Relief.

Ceiling tiles

Made from polystyrene or mineral wool, ceiling tiles are usually lightweight and hung from a metal frame suspended from a ceiling. They are often used to provide sound and heat insulation, and also to hide service pipes and ducts that may lie above the ceiling. *See Walls and Surfaces, p. 111.*

Cella

The central room of a Classical temple usually containing a cult statue. The Parthenon, for example, famously contained a long-lost golden statue of Athena. *See The Classical Temple, p. 13.*

Cellar

A room or space in a building below ground level; typically used for storage.

Cement plaster or render

A form of *lime plaster* to which cement has been added. Mostly impervious to water, cement plasters are frequently used to render exterior surfaces. Modern cement renders sometimes have acrylic additives to further enhance water resistance and provide colour variation. *See Walls and Surfaces, p. 113.*

Chamfered rustication

A form of rustication in which the sides of the blocks are angled, creating V-shaped grooves at the joints. *See Walls and Surfaces, p. 103.*

Chancel

The eastern arm of a cathedral or church, coming off the *crossing* containing the *altar, sanctuary* and often the *choir*. The chancel is sometimes raised on a higher level than the rest of the cathedral or church and separated from it by a screen or *railing. See The Medieval Cathedral, p. 16.*

Chancel screen

See Rood screen.

Chapter house

A separate room or building attached to a cathedral, used to hold meetings. *See The Medieval Cathedral, p. 17.*

Chevet

In a medieval cathedral a *chapel*, usually combined with others, radiating off the *ambulatory. See The Medieval Cathedral, p. 17.*

Chevron

A moulding or decorative motif consisting of a repeating pattern of V-shaped forms, often found in medieval architecture. *See Walls and Surfaces, p. 126.*

Chimney stack

A structure, usually of brick, used to convey smoke from internal fireplaces clear of the building. Where it protrudes above a roof it is often highly decorated. Chimneys stacks are usually topped by chimney pots. *See Roofs, p. 152.*

Choir

The stalled area of a cathedral or church, usually part of the *chancel*, where the clergy and choir – the group of singers affiliated to the cathedral or church – reside during services. *See The Medieval Cathedral, p. 17.*

Ciborium

A canopy, usually supported by four columns, that covers the *altar* in a cathedral or church. *See The Medieval Cathedral, p. 21.*

Cladding

The covering or application of one material over another to protect the underlying layer against the weather or for aesthetic purposes.

Classical orders

An order is the principal component of a Classical building, composed of *base, shaft, capital* and *entablature*. The five Classical orders are the 'Tuscan', 'Doric', 'Ionic', 'Corinthian' and 'Composite', which all vary in size and proportion. The Tuscan, a Roman order, is the plainest and largest. The Doric is found in two distinct varieties: Greek Doric is characterized by its fluted shaft and lack of base; Roman Doric may have a *fluted* or unfluted shaft and also has a base. The Ionic is Greek in origin, but was used extensively by the Romans; it is distinguished by its voluted capital and often fluted shaft. The Corinthian is characterized by the *acanthus* leaves decorating its capital. The Composite is a Roman creation that combines the *volutes* of the Ionic with the acanthus leaves of the Corinthian. *See Columns and Piers, pp. 70–75.*

Clerestory

The upper storey of the *nave, transepts* or *choir* of a cathedral or church, usually with windows that look out over the *aisle* roof. *See The Medieval Cathedral, p. 18.*

Clerestory window

A window piercing the upper storey of the *nave, transepts* or *choir* and looking out over the *aisle* roof in a cathedral or church. In other building types any windows positioned high up on an internal wall are described as clerestory windows. *See The Medieval Cathedral, p. 15.*

Cloister

A covered walk usually surrounding a central courtyard or *garth*. Medieval cloisters are usually *vaulted. See The Medieval Cathedral, p. 16.*

Closed string

See Strings.

Clustered column

See Compound column or pier.

Coat of arms

A heraldic symbolic design representing an individual, family or corporate body.

Coffering

The decoration of a surface with series of sunken rectangular panels called 'lacunaria'. *See Roofs, p. 158.*

Collar beam

In a *truss* roof, a transverse horizontal beam which spans the underside of two opposing rafters, sitting above the *wall plate* but below the apex. *See Roofs, p. 161.*

Collar purlin

In a *truss* roof, a longitudinal beam running below the *collar beam* and supported by a *crown post* or *king post*. *See Roofs, p. 161.*

Colonnade

A repeating series of columns supporting an *entablature*.

Colossal order

A Colossal column or pier extends through more than two storeys. Due to its size, it is rarely used. *See Columns and Piers, p. 69.*

Column

A typically cylindrical upright *shaft* or member composed of *base*, shaft and *capital*.

Common bond

A brick bond type that combines rows of *headers* and *stretchers*; five courses of stretchers alternate with one course of headers. *See Walls and Surfaces, p. 115.*

Common rafter

In a *truss* roof, the thinner rafters that support the roof. *See Roofs, p. 162.*

Complex spire

A spire composed from a combination of open and enclosed parts, and sometimes different materials. *See Roofs, p. 156.*

Composite order

See Classical orders.

Compound arch

An arch formed by two or more arches of diminishing size set concentrically within one another. *See Arches, p. 83.*

Compound column or pier

A column or pier composed of several *shafts*; also described as 'clustered'. *See Columns and Piers, p. 69.*

Concave

A surface or form that recedes in the form of a curve. Opposite of *convex*.

Concave mortaring

Brickwork in which mortar is finished in a recessed arc. *See Walls and Surfaces, p. 106.*

Concentric

A series of shapes of diminishing size but with the same centre, set within one another.

Concertina folding door

A door with a repeating series of *leaves* which can be slid along tracks and folded against one another; typically used for providing openings over a large area. *See Windows and Doors, p. 147.*

Conical roof

A roof in the shape of a cone, usually sitting atop a *tower* or covering a *dome*. *See Roofs, p. 157.*

Console

A double-scrolled bracket. *See Walls and Surfaces, p. 126.*

Convex

A surface or form that curves out like the exterior of a circle or sphere. Opposite of *concave*.

Coping

The typically projecting and often sloped top course of brick or masonry on a *balustrade, gable, pediment* or wall, which helps to carry off water. *See Roofs, p. 152.*

Corbel

A bracket projecting from a wall to support a structure above. When several corbels are combined one on top of each other, it is described as 'corbelling'. *See Roofs, p. 152.*

Corinthian order

See Classical orders.

Corner pavilion

Structures marking the ends of a range, through featuring a discrete architectural arrangement or through an increase in scale. *See Public Buildings, p. 50.*

Cornice

The highest level in a Classical *entablature*, which projects over the lower levels (*see The Classical Temple, p. 9*). The term is also used to refer to a continuous horizontal moulding projecting from the face of a wall, especially where it intersects with the roof face. Or the projecting moulding that tops an aperture *surround*. *See Columns and Piers, p. 70.*

Cornucopia

A decorative element symbolizing plenty, usually a goat's horn overflowing with flowers, corn and fruit. *See Walls and Surfaces, p. 126.*

Corona

The flat vertical face in a Classical *cornice*. *See Columns and Piers, p. 70.*

Corrugated

A surface or structure with a series of alternating peaks and troughs.

Corrugated steel roof

Sheets of steel corrugated for rigidity are often used in situations where low cost and speed of construction are necessary. *See Roofs, p. 151.*

Coupled columns

Two columns placed side by side. When the *capitals* of coupled columns overlap they are called 'geminated' capitals. *See Columns and Piers, p. 69.*

Cove

The *concave* moulding between a wall and ceiling; also sometimes known as a 'bed moulding'. When very large, a coving is viewed as part of the ceiling rather than a moulding – a 'coved ceiling'. *See Walls and Surfaces, p. 120.*

Crenellations

Regularly spaced 'teeth-like' projections from the top of a wall. The projecting flaps are called 'merlons' and the gaps between are 'crenels'. Derived from defensive structures like castles or city walls, they were later used for decorative purposes. *See Roofs, p. 156.*

Crepidoma

The three-stepped foundation level on which a temple or temple front is erected. In a Classical temple it includes the *euthynteria, stereobate* and *stylobate*. *See The Classical Temple, p. 8.*

Crockets

Scroll-like, projecting leaf forms.

Cross window

A window composed of one *mullion* and one *transom* in the shape of a cross. *See Windows and Doors, p. 140.*

Crossette

A corner of a rectangular moulding with small vertical and horizontal flaps or off-sets, often found in window and door *surrounds*. *See Walls and Surfaces, p. 126.*

Crossing

The name given to the space formed by the intersection of the *nave, transept* arms and *chancel* in a church or cathedral. *See The Medieval Cathedral, p. 16.*

Crow-stepped gable

A gable projecting above the *pitched roof* line in a stepped manner. *See Roofs, p. 153.*

Crown post

In a *truss* roof, a four-pronged post vaguely reminiscent of a crown, placed centrally on a *tie beam* to support the *collar beam* and collar purlin. *See Roofs, p. 161.*

Crown-post roof

A *truss* roof in which a crown post is placed centrally on a *tie beam* to support the *collar beam* and collar purlin. *See Roofs, p. 161.*

Crown spire

An open spire formed from *flying buttresses* which converge towards the centre, giving the appearance of a crown. *See Roofs, p. 155.*

Crystalline

Three-dimensional structures consisting of repeating identical or very similarly shaped units. *See Contemporary Buildings, p. 64.*

Cupola

A small dome-like structure, usually circular or octagonal in plan, often placed on top of a *dome* or larger roof and sometimes used as a viewing platform. Cupolas are invariably heavily glazed to admit light into the space below, and for this reason are sometimes known as 'lanterns'. *See Roofs, p. 157.*

Curtail step

The lowest step in a flight of stairs, projecting beyond the *newels* and terminating at the side with a curve or *volute*. *See Stairs and Lifts, p. 166.*

Curtain wall

In castles, a fortified wall enclosing a *bailey* or ward. More generally, a non-load-bearing enclosure or envelope of a building, attached to the structure but standing separate from it. Curtain walls can consist of a variety of materials: brick, masonry, wood, stucco, metal or, most typically in contemporary architecture, glass, which has the benefit of allowing light to penetrate deep into the building. *See Walls and Surfaces, p. 114.*

Curvilinear

A building whose shape is composed from one or more curved surfaces rather than a series of planes. *See Contemporary Buildings, p. 65.*

Curvilinear or flowing tracery

A pattern of tracery formed from series of continuously curving and intersecting bars. *See Windows and Doors, p. 139.*

Cushion capital

A cube-shaped capital with its lower corners rounded off. The resultant semicircular faces are called 'shields'. Its angles may sometimes be incised with narrow grooves called 'tucks'. *See Columns and Piers, p. 76.*

Cusp

In *tracery*, a curved triangular indentation in the arch of a curve or *foil*. *See Windows and Doors, p. 138.*

Cyclostyle

A circular range of columns (without a *naos* or core). *See The Classical Temple, p. 10.*

Cyma recta

A double-curved Classical moulding with the lower curve *convex* and the upper *concave*. *See Walls and Surfaces, p. 122.*

Cyma reversa

A double-curved Classical moulding with the lower curve *concave* and the upper *convex*. *See Walls and Surfaces, p. 122.*

D

Dado

The marked-off region of an interior wall equivalent to the *base* or pedestal level in a *Classical order*. The continuous moulding which often marks the top of the dado level is called a 'dado rail'. *See Walls and Surfaces, p. 121.*

Dagger

A dagger-shaped *tracery* element. *See Windows and Doors, p. 138.*

Decastyle

A temple front composed of ten columns (or *pilasters*). *See The Classical Temple, p. 10.*

Deconstructivist

An appearance characterized by vehemently non-rectilinear forms, and the juxtaposition of divergent and often angular components. *See Contemporary Buildings, p. 65.*

Dentil

A repeating pattern of square or rectangular blocks projecting from the underside of a Classical *cornice*. *See Columns and Piers, p. 73.*

Diagonal braces

Angled members which create a system of triangles to provide additional bracing to a *rectilinear* structure. The addition of diagonal members to a steel-framed structure is known as 'triangulation'. *See Steel, p. 92.*

Diagonal rib

A structural rib running diagonally across a *rib vault*. *See Roofs, p. 164.*

Diamond-faced rustication

A form of rustication in which the faces of the blocks are hewn into regular, repeating patterns of small shallow pyramids. *See Walls and Surfaces, p. 103.*

Diaper

Any decorative pattern in the form of a repeating grid. *See Walls and Surfaces, p. 105.*

Diastyle

An *intercolumniation* of three lower column diameters. *See The Classical Temple, p. 11.*

Diocletian or thermal window

A semicircular window divided into three parts by two vertical *mullions*, the centre *light* being the larger. It is derived from the Baths of Diocletian in Rome and for that reason is also called a 'thermal' window. *See Windows and Doors, p. 142.*

Dipteral

A temple surrounded on all four sides by two rows of columns – a double *peristasis*. *See The Classical Temple, p. 12.*

Discharging arch

An arch built above a *lintel* to help carry the weight either side of the opening. Also called a 'relieving arch'. *See Arches, p. 83.*

Distyle

A temple front composed of two columns (or *pilasters*). *See The Classical Temple, p. 10.*

Dog-leg staircase

A staircase with no central well, composed from two parallel flights of stairs running in opposite directions and linked by a landing. *See Stairs and Lifts, p. 167.*

Dog-tooth

A four-lobed pyramidal shaped form; often found in medieval architecture. *See Walls and Surfaces, p. 127.*

Dome

A usually hemispherical structure whose shape derives from the rotation of a vault 360 degrees through its central axis. *See Roofs, p. 149.*

Door leaf

Generally refers to the flat panel that acts as the barrier of the door itself. *See Windows and Doors, p. 134.*

Door light

Refers to any window cut through the *door leaf*. *See Windows and Doors, p. 134.*

Doric order

See Classical orders.

Dormer

A window which protrudes vertically from the plane of a *pitched roof*. Dormer windows can be included as part of the original design of a building, but are frequently added to existing buildings to create more light and usable space. *See Windows and Doors, p. 145.*

Double dome

An arrangement where one dome sits inside another. Double or even triple domes are often used when a dome rises high above a building's roof line and its often decorated underside needs to be easily visible from inside. *See Roofs, p. 159.*

Double-framed roof

Similar to a *single-framed truss* roof, but with longitudinal members added to the structure. *See Roofs, p. 160.*

Double temple in antis

A Classical temple in antis with the addition of an *opisthodomos*. *See The Classical Temple, p. 12.*

Drawbridge

A movable bridge which can be raised or lowered over a *moat*. Drawbridges were usually made of wood and were often operated with a counterweight system. *See Fortified Buildings, p. 32.*

Drip

A projection on the underside of a moulding or *cornice*, intended to ensure rainwater drips clear from the face of the wall. *See Walls and Surfaces, p. 122.*

Drop

A surface ornament appearing as if suspended from a single point. *See Walls and Surfaces, p. 127.*

Drop arch

An arch squatter in shape than the *equilateral arch*. In a drop arch the centres of each curve are located within the *span*. *See Arches, p. 80.*

Drum

The cylindrical, often colonnaded structure on which a *dome* is raised. Also called a 'tambour'. *See Roofs, p. 157.*

Dry-stone wall

A stone wall constructed from interlocking stones with no mortar. *See Walls and Surfaces, p. 102.*

Dutch gable

A gable in which each side is *curvilinear*, usually topped by a *pediment*. *See Roofs, p. 153.*

Dutch or stable door

A single door divided horizontally, usually in the centre, so that the resultant two *leaves* can be opened or closed independently. *See Windows and Doors, p. 146.*

E

Echinus

The curved moulding supporting the *abacus* in a Doric capital. *See Columns and Piers, p. 70.*

Egg-and-dart

An alternating pattern of egg-shaped and pointed arrow-like elements. *See Walls and Surfaces, p. 127.*

Elevator

See Lift.

Elliptical arch

An arch whose curve is formed from half of an ellipse – a regular oval shape formed from the intersection of a cone by a plane. *See Arches, p. 79.*

Emergency stairs

A staircase running the full length of a building, included to facilitate evacuation during an emergency such as a fire. *See High-Rise Buildings, p. 58.*

Engaged column

A column which is not *free-standing* but built into a wall or surface. *See Columns and Piers, p. 68.*

English bond

A brick bond with alternating courses of *stretchers* and *headers*. *See Walls and Surfaces, p. 115.*

Entablature

The superstructure above the *capital* level composed of *architrave*, *frieze* and *cornice*. *See Columns and Piers, p. 71.*

Equilateral arch

An arch formed from two intersecting curves, the centres of which are at the opposing *imposts*. The chords of each curve are equal to the arch *span*. *See Arches, p. 80.*

Escalator

A moving staircase formed from a motor-driven chain of steps, usually found inside a building's envelope but also deployed attached to the exterior. *See Stairs and Lifts, p. 169.*

Escutcheon plate

The flat, often metal plate which is placed against the *door leaf* to provide a mount for the door handle or knob; escutcheon plates are often decorated. *See Windows and Doors, p. 134.*

Eustyle

An *intercolumniation* of 2¼ lower column diameters. *See The Classical Temple, p. 11.*

Euthynteria

In a Classical temple, the lowest level of the *stereobate* protruding just above the ground level. *See The Classical Temple, p. 8.*

Exposed aggregate

Concrete whose outer surface is removed before it has fully hardened, revealing the aggregate. *See Walls and Surfaces, p. 112.*

Exposed concrete

Concrete that is unclad and left unpainted and exposed on the exterior or interior of a building, for either aesthetic or cost-saving reasons. This use of concrete is also known by its French description – *béton brut* – literally, 'raw concrete'. *See Concrete, p. 88.*

Exposed-frame curtain wall

A type of glass curtain wall. Unlike the *hidden-frame* iteration, here the frame stands proud of the glass surface and may also include some additional trim. Although the frame is highlighted, its only structural function is to attach the glass panes to the supporting frame behind. *See Walls and Surfaces, p. 115.*

External set tiles

Tiles employed on the exterior of buildings principally to provide waterproofing. Because of the relative ease of producing coloured tiles of varying shapes and with decorative details, they are often used to provide various types of surface ornamentation. *See Walls and Surfaces, p. 110.*

Extrados

The outer side of an arch. *See Arches, p. 78.*

F

Fanlight

A semicircular or elongated semicircular window sitting above a door but contained within the overall *surround*, with radiating glazing *bars* in the form of a fan or sunburst. If the *light* above a window is present but not in the form of fan it is usually called a *transom light*. *See Windows and Doors, p. 135.*

Fan vault

A vault formed from many *ribs* of the same size and curve emanating from the main supports, creating an inverted cone shape with a fan-like pattern. Fan vaults are often highly *traceried* and sometimes decorated with pendants – elements which appear at the conjunctions of adjacent vaults. *See Roofs, p. 165.*

Fascia

The flat horizontal divisions in a Classical *architrave*, or in any decorative scheme. *See Walls and Surfaces, p. 122.*

Festoon

A chain of flowers that appears to be suspended in a bow or curve from any number of (usually evenly) spaced points on a surface.

Fillet

A flat band or surface separating two otherwise adjoining mouldings, sometimes standing proud of the surrounding surface. *See Walls and Surfaces, p. 122.* Also the name for the flat strips between the *flutes* in a fluted column.

Finial

The crowning ornament of a *pinnacle*, *spire* or roof. *See Roofs, p. 154.*

Fish-scale tiles

Flat tiles with curved lower ends. When laid in overlapping rows they resemble the scales of a fish. *See Roofs, p. 151.*

Fixed window

A window that does not contain sections which open or close. Windows may be fixed for any number of reasons. Early windows were often fixed because of the difficulty and expense of fashioning opening mechanisms, especially, for example, for intricate *tracery* windows. More recently, windows may be fixed to ensure the efficiency of building-wide environmental and air-conditioning systems, or, in the case of high-rise buildings, as a safety measure. *See Windows and Doors, p. 132.*

Flamboyant tracery

An even more intricate and complex version of *curvilinear or flowing tracery*. *See Windows and Doors, p. 139.*

Flat arch

An arch with horizontal *extrados* and *intrados* created from specially shaped angled *voussoirs*. *See Arches, p. 81.*

Flat-leaf capital

A simple *foliated* capital with broad leaves at each corner. *See Columns and Piers, p. 76.*

Flat roof

A roof whose pitch is horizontal (though a slight incline is often retained to ensure that water runs off). Tar and gravel are traditionally used to seal the roof, but more recently *synthetic membranes* are being used. *See Roofs, p. 149.*

Flèche

A small *spire* usually placed on the *ridge* of a *pitched roof* or at the intersection of the ridges of two perpendicular pitched roofs. *See Roofs, p. 156.*

Flemish bond

A brick bond with alternating *stretchers* and *headers* in the same course. Each stretcher overlaps a quarter of the one below it, while the headers sit aligned with the one two courses below. *See Walls and Surfaces, p. 115.*

Fleuron

A roughly circular floral ornament sometimes found at the top of a *Corinthian* or *Composite capital*. *See Columns and Piers, p. 74.*

Floor tiles

Usually of ceramic or slate, floor tiles can be used throughout a building, but because of their durability and water resistance are most often found in public areas or (especially in domestic settings) in bathrooms and kitchens. *See Walls and Surfaces, p. 111.*

Florentine arch

A semicircular arch whose *extrados* is formed from a curve whose centre sits higher than that of its *intrados*. *See Arches, p. 81.*

Flush mortaring

Brickwork in which the mortar is flat with the adjacent brick faces. *See Walls and Surfaces, p. 106.*

Flushwork

The use of *knapped flint* and dressed stone to create decorative schemes, often in a chequerboard pattern. *See Walls and Surfaces, p. 102.*

Flute

A recessed vertical groove on a column *shaft*. The flat strips between the flutes are called *fillets*. *See Columns and Piers, p. 73.*

Flying stair

A flight of stone steps built into the wall, each step resting cumulatively on the one immediately below. When a flying stair is semicircular or elliptical in plan it is called a 'geometrical stair'. *See Stairs and Lifts, p. 167.*

Flying buttress

See Buttress.

Fly tower

The larger space over a stage in which a theatre's fly system – the series of counterweights and pulleys that allow scenery to be moved on and off stage – operates. *See Public Buildings, p. 51.*

Foil

In *tracery*, the curved space formed between two *cusps*, sometimes in a leaf shape. *See Windows and Doors, p. 138.*

Foliated

General term referring to any ornament incorporating foliage. *See Walls and Surfaces, p. 127.*

Font

A basin, often ornamented, used for holding the baptismal water, often covered by a 'font hood'. Sometimes, the font is located in a 'baptistry' – a building separate from the main body of the church and usually centrally planned around the font. *See The Medieval Cathedral, p. 16.*

Four-centred or depressed arch

An arch made up from four intersecting curves. The centres of the outer two curves sit at *impost* level within the *span* while the centres of the inner two curves similarly sit within the span but below impost level. *See Arches, p. 80.*

Free-standing column

A detached, typically cylindrical upright *shaft* or member. *See Columns and Piers, p. 68.*

French window

Despite its name, actually a heavily fenestrated double door, usually found in domestic buildings and opening on to a garden. *See Windows and Doors, p. 146.*

Fret

A repeating geometrical moulding composed entirely from straight lines. *See Walls and Surfaces, p. 127.*

Glossary / 4

Frieze

The central section of the *entablature* between the *architrave* and *cornice*, often decorated in *relief* (*see The Classical Temple, p. 9*). The term is also used to refer to any continuous horizontal band of relief running along a wall. *See Columns and Piers, p. 70.*

Frogged brick

A commonly found brick with indentations on the top and bottom when laid in the *stretcher* position. The term 'frog' usually refers to the indentation, though it can also refer to the block which makes the indentation in the moulding process. Frogged bricks are lighter than solid bricks and the frogging also provides a great surface area for the mortar to adhere to when laid in courses. *See Walls and Surfaces, p. 117.*

Frosted rustication

A form of rustication in which the faces of the blocks are hewn into stalactite or icicle forms. *See Walls and Surfaces, p. 103.*

G

Gabions

Metal cages filled with dense materials such as stone, but also sand and soil. They are usually used for purely structural purposes especially in civil engineering projects, but can be found as architectural features in many modern buildings. *See Walls and Surfaces, p. 102.*

Gable

The usually triangular part of the wall enclosing the sloping faces of a *pitched or gabled roof*. *See Roofs, p. 152.*

Gablet

A small *gable* often used to top a *buttress*. *See Roofs, p. 153.*

Gallery

In a medieval cathedral, the gallery is an intermediary level standing above the main *arcade* and below the *clerestory*, usually set with shallow arches behind which may lie a gallery space above the *aisle* below. The additional *blind arcade* that is sometimes present at this level is called the 'triforium'. *See The Medieval Cathedral, p. 18.*

Galletting

The insertion of small pieces of stone into *mortar* joints while the mortar is still wet, for decorative purposes. *See Walls and Surfaces, p. 106.*

Gargoyle

A carved or moulded grotesque figure, usually protruding from the top of a wall, designed to carry water away from the wall surface below. *See The Medieval Cathedral, p. 14.*

Garland

A moulded ring or wreath of flowers and foliage. *See Walls and Surfaces, p. 127.*

Garth

A courtyard space surrounded by *cloisters*. *See The Medieval Cathedral, p. 16.*

Gatehouse

A fortified structure or *tower* protecting the gateway into a castle. A potential weak point in the castle's defences, the gatehouse was usually heavily fortified and often included a *drawbridge* and one or more *portcullises*. *See Fortified Buildings, p. 30.*

Gauged arch

An arch of any shape, but usually either round or flat, in which the *voussoirs* have been shaped so as to radiate from a single centre. *See Arches, p. 81.*

Gauged brickwork

Brickwork with very fine joints, often with bricks cut to shape and used in *lintels*. *See Walls and Surfaces, p. 105.*

Geodesic dome

A part-spherical or wholly spherical structure composed from a triangulated steel framework. *See Roofs, p. 159.*

Geometric tracery

A simple tracery type consisting of series of circles often infilled with *foils*. *See Windows and Doors, p. 139.*

Giant column

A column that extends through two (or more) storeys. *See Columns and Piers, p. 69.*

Gibbs window or door surround

A Classical window or door form whose surround is characterized by repeating *blocked rustication*, often topped by a heavy *keystone*. It is named after the Scottish architect James Gibbs, for whom the window became something of a trademark, though it probably originated in Renaissance Italy. *See Windows and Doors, p. 141.*

Glass brick

Originating in the early twentieth century, glass bricks are usually square. Because they are relatively thick, they provide partial obscuration while admitting natural light into and between internal spaces. *See Walls and Surfaces, p. 117.*

Glass curtain wall

See Curtain wall.

Glazed brick

A brick to which a layer of glaze has been applied before firing, to give it a different colour and finish. *See Walls and Surfaces, p. 117.*

Great hall

The ceremonial and administrative centre of a castle, used also for dining and receiving guests and visitors. Halls were richly decorated, often with heraldic ornaments. *See Fortified Buildings, p. 30.*

Greek cross plan

A church plan composed of a central core surrounded by four *transept* arms of equal length. *See The Renaissance Church, p. 26.*

Greek Doric order

See Classical orders.

Green roof

The covering or partial covering of a roof with vegetation (and also including growing media, and irrigation and drainage systems). *See Roofs, p. 151.*

Grisaille

A form of painting whose tonal shades of grey are intended to imitate sculptural *relief*. *See Walls and Surfaces, p. 127.*

Groin vault

A vault produced by the perpendicular intersection of two *barrel vaults*. The arched edges between the intersecting vaults are called 'groins' and give the vault its name. *See Roofs, p. 164.*

Grotesquery

Arabesque-like intricate decorative mouldings including human figures. This type of decoration was inspired by the rediscovery of ancient Roman decorative forms. *See Walls and Surfaces, p. 127.*

Guilloche

A repeating moulding of two or more interleaved curved bands or narrow strips. *See Walls and Surfaces, p. 127.*

Guttae

The small conical projections from the underside of the *regula* in a *Doric entablature*. *See Columns and Piers, p. 71.*

Gypsum plaster

Also known as 'plaster of Paris', gypsum plaster is made by heating gypsum powder, then adding water to form a paste which can be used to cover a surface before the mixture hardens. Gypsum plasters are usually used only for interior surfaces because of their susceptibility to water damage. *See Walls and Surfaces, p. 112.*

H

Hammer beam

In a *truss* roof, a small beam projecting horizontally from a wall, usually supported by *arched braces* and carrying a *hammer post*. *See Roofs, p. 162.*

Hammer-beam roof

A *truss* roof where the *tie beams* appear to have been cut, leaving smaller *hammer beams* projecting horizontally from the wall. These are usually supported by *arched braces* and carry a *hammer post*. *See Roofs, p. 162.*

Hammer post

In a *truss* roof, a vertical post supported by a *hammer beam*. *See Roofs, p. 162.*

Handrail

A rail set atop a row of *banisters* or other upright members, intended to be used for support when ascending or descending a staircase. *See Stairs and Lifts, p. 166.*

Haunch

The curved part of an arch between the *impost* and *keystone*. *See Arches, p. 78.*

Header

A brick laid horizontally with its broad, long face on the bottom but with the short end of the brick exposed on the outer face of the wall. *See Walls and Surfaces, p. 104.*

Header bond

A simple brick bond type in which the bricks are laid with their header face showing. *See Walls and Surfaces, p. 105.*

Helical stair

A stair, semicircular or elliptical in plan, which winds around a central well and takes the form of a helix. A rare permutation is a 'double-helical stair', formed when two independent stairs wind around the same semicircular or elliptical space. *See Stairs and Lifts, p. 167.*

Helix

A small *volute* in a *Corinthian capital. See Columns and Piers, p. 74.*

Helm spire

An unusual spire formed by four diamond-shaped roof faces which angle inwards, creating *gables* on each of the four sides of the *tower. See Roofs, p. 155.*

Herm

See Term.

Herringbone bond

A brick bond type with a zig-zag pattern usually composed from *stretcher* bricks set diagonally. *See Walls and Surfaces, p. 105.*

Hexastyle

A temple front composed of six columns (or *pilasters). See The Classical Temple, p. 10.*

Hidden-frame curtain wall

A type of glass curtain wall where the glass panes are set into a regular steel frame in a way that largely obscures the frame. *See Walls and Surfaces, p. 115.*

High altar

See Altar.

Hipped gable

The name given to the gable of a half-hipped roof in which two opposing sides are partly hipped and partly gabled. *See Roofs, p. 153.*

Hipped roof

Similar to a *pitched roof* but without *gables.* Instead there are sloping roof faces on all four sides. A roof can be half-hipped when two opposing sides are partly hipped and partly gabled. *See Roofs, p. 148.*

Historiated or figured capital

A capital decorated with human or animal figures, often combined with foliage. In some examples the scene is intended to portray a story. *See Columns and Piers, p. 77.*

Hollow brick

A brick with oblong or cylindrical horizontal hollows to reduce the weight of the brick and provide insulation. *See Walls and Surfaces, p. 117.*

Hood mould

A projecting moulding often found in medieval architecture (though not confined to it) that drapes over an aperture. A *rectilinear* hood mould is called a 'label'. *See Windows and Doors, p. 138.*

Horseshoe arch

An arch whose curve is in the form of a horseshoe; it is wider at *haunch* level than at *impost* level. Horseshoe arches are emblematic of Islamic architecture. *See Arches, p. 79.*

Hung slate

Because it can be broken into thin sheets, slate is often used in a similar way to *hung tiles. See Walls and Surfaces, p. 110.*

Hung tiles

Tiles are a common form of roof cladding and are also sometimes used to cover external walls. They are usually hung from an underlying timber or brick frame in overlapping rows – an arrangement called 'imbrication'. Different-coloured tiles can be used to create a variety of geometrical patterns. *See Walls and Surfaces, p. 110.*

Husk

A bell-shaped motif, sometimes found linked in *festoons, garlands* or *drops. See Walls and Surfaces, p. 128.*

I

I-beam

A metal beam, I- or H-shaped in cross section, found in almost all steel-framed structures. *See High-Rise Buildings, p. 57.*

Impost

The typically horizontal band (though it need not be delineated as such) from which the arch springs and on which the *springer voussoir* rests. *See Arches, p. 78.*

Inflexed arch

A pointed arch composed from two *convex* curves rather than the more typical *concave* curves. *See Arches, p. 81.*

Inner ward

A second upper fortified enclosure in a castle, in which the *keep* was often situated. The inner ward was usually inside or adjoining the *outer ward or bailey* and was enclosed by a further *curtain wall* or palisade. *See Fortified Buildings, p. 30.*

Intaglio

See Relief.

Intarsia

The inlaying of strips or different shapes of wood into a surface, forming decorative patterns or figurative scenes. Intarsia also refers to the process of inlaying marble stones in a highly polished decorative arrangement on walls and, especially, floors. *See Walls and Surfaces, p. 128.*

Intercolumniation

The distance between two adjacent columns. *See The Classical Temple, p. 11.*

Interior wall tiles

Usually of ceramic or slate, interior wall tiles are most often used in bathrooms and kitchens to provide waterproofing. *See Walls and Surfaces, p. 111.*

Intersecting or branched tracery

A form of tracery in which the *mullions* split into two branches at the springing point, then continue parallel to the curves of the arch. *See Windows and Doors, p. 139.*

Intrados

A term used specifically to refer to the underside of an arch. In this instance it is synonymous with *soffit,* the more general term for the underside of a structure or surface. *See Arches, p. 78.*

Inverted arch

An upside-down arch often used in foundations. *See Arches, p. 81.*

Ionic order

See Classical orders.

Irregular fenestration

An unevenly spaced arrangement of windows, often of differing sizes. *See High-Rise Buildings, p. 59.*

J

Jamb

The vertical side of a window *surround. See Windows and Doors, p. 132.*

Jib door

An internal door designed to appear coterminous with the wall surface. *See Windows and Doors, p. 146.*

K

Keel

A moulding whose two curves form a pointed edge much like the keel of a ship. *See Walls and Surfaces, p. 122.*

Keystone

The central wedge-shaped block at the top of the arch, locking all the other *voussoirs* into place. *See Arches, p. 78.*

Keep or donjon

A large *tower* at the centre of a castle, sometimes set atop a 'motte' (earth mound), usually enclosed by a ditch. The keep was the most strongly defended part of the castle, where the lord would have resided, and also contained or adjoined the *great hall* and chapel. *See Fortified Buildings, p. 30.*

Keystone mask

A keystone decorated with a sculpted stylized human or animal face. *See Public Buildings, p. 47.*

King post

In a *truss* roof, a vertical post placed in the centre of a *tie beam* to support the *ridge beam. See Roofs, p. 162.*

King-post roof

A *truss* roof in which a vertical post is placed in the centre of the *tie beam* to support the *ridge beam. See Roofs, p. 162.*

Knapped flint

The use of flint stones on a wall face with their cut black faces turned outwards. *See Walls and Surfaces, p. 102.*

Kneeler

The roughly triangular stone that sits at the foot of a *gable. See Roofs, p. 152.*

L

Lady chapel

A subsidiary chapel that usually comes off the *chancel* of a cathedral, dedicated to the Virgin Mary. *See The Medieval Cathedral, p. 17.*

Lancet arch

More slender than the *equilateral arch.* In a lancet arch the centres of each curve are located outside of the *span. See Arches, p. 80.*

Glossary / 5

Lancet window

Tall, narrow pointed windows, often grouped in threes; named after their resemblance to lancets. *See Windows and Doors, p. 141.*

Landing

The flat platform at the top of or between two flights of stairs, often used to adjoin flights running in different directions. *See Stairs and Lifts, p. 166.*

Lantern

See Cupola.

Latch and latch plate

A latch is the catch protruding from a door's outer edge which matches up with a recession on the inside of the door frame, allowing the door to be kept closed. The manipulation of the handle or knob allows the catch to be released and the door to be opened. The latch plate provides a solid surround for the latch, and is usually integral to the latch mechanism rather than the door. *See Windows and Doors, p. 134.*

Lattice dome

A modern dome type, formed from a polygonal steel framework usually infilled with glass. *See Roofs, p. 159.*

Lattice window

A window composed from small square or diamond-shaped panes (*quarries*) separated by lead *cames. See Windows and Doors, p. 140.*

Lean-to roof

A single sloped roof built leaning against a vertical wall. *See Roofs, p. 148.*

Lectern

A stand from which to speak with a sloping front to hold a book or notes. Used in some churches in place of a *pulpit. See The Renaissance Church, p. 28.*

Lierne vault

A vault with additional *ribs* that do not emanate from the main supports but are placed between adjacent diagonal and transverse ribs. *See Roofs, p. 165.*

Lift

Also known as an 'elevator', a lift is a vertical transportation device, essentially an enclosed platform that is moved up and down by mechanical means: either by a system of pulleys (a 'traction lift') or hydraulic pistons (a 'hydraulic lift'). Lifts are often in a building's central core but are also found on the exterior. *See Stairs and Lifts, p. 168.*

Light

The opening in a window enclosed by one or more panes of glass. *See Windows and Doors, p. 132.*

Lime plaster

Historically, one of the most common plasters, lime plaster is formed from sand, lime and water; animal fibres are sometimes used for additional binding. Lime plaster is used for fresco painting. *See Walls and Surfaces, p. 112.*

Lintel

The supporting horizontal member that surmounts a window or door. *See Windows and Doors, p. 132.*

Log cabin

A type of timber building common in North America, constructed from cut logs laid horizontally. The logs have notched ends so they form a strong interlocking arrangement at the corners. Gaps between the logs can be filled with plaster, cement or mud. *See Walls and Surfaces, p. 109.*

Loggia

A covered space, partially enclosed on one or more sides by an *arcade* or *colonnade*. It may form part of a larger building or stand as an independent structure. *See Walls and Surfaces, p. 118.*

Lotus capital

An Egyptian capital in the form of a lotus bud. *See Columns and Piers, p. 77.*

Louvres

Rows of angled slats placed over a window (often on *shutters*), door or wall surface, designed to allow light and air to circulate but provide a barrier against direct sunlight. *See Windows and Doors, p. 144.*

Lucarne

A type of *dormer* window; the term is usually reserved for the often *louvred*, gabled apertures set into *spires. See Windows and Doors, p. 145.*

M

Machicolations

The holes in the floor between adjacent *corbels* supporting a *crenellated* parapet. In fortified buildings machicolations were designed for defence, allowing objects and liquids to be dropped on attackers below, but were later used for decorative purposes. *See Roofs, p. 156.*

Main arcade level

In a church or cathedral, the lowest level of the *nave* interior, set with a series of large arches supported on piers behind

which lie the *aisles. See The Medieval Cathedral, p. 18.*

Mansard roof

A roof with a double slope, the lower slope typically being steeper than the higher one. Mansard roofs often contain *dormer* windows and are *hipped* at their ends. A typically French design, the term derives from its first proponent, the French architect François Mansart (1598– 1666). If a Mansard roof terminates with a flat *gable* instead of hips, it is strictly called a 'gambrel roof'. *See Roofs, p. 148.*

Mask

A decorative motif of an often stylized human or animal face. *See Walls and Surfaces, p. 128.*

Masonry cladding or veneer

The use of masonry purely to face a building rather than to provide structural support. *See Walls and Surfaces, p. 102.*

Mast

A tall, upright post or structure from which other elements can be suspended. *See High-Rise Buildings, p. 58.*

Medallion

A circular or oval decorative plaque, usually adorned with a sculptural or painted figure or scene. *See Walls and Surfaces, p. 128.*

Meeting rail

In a sash window the rails on the two *sashes* that sit adjacent to each other when the window is closed. *See Windows and Doors, p. 133.*

Melon dome

A dome in which the structural support is provided by a series of curved *ribs*, with the space between infilled, resembling a striped melon. *See Roofs, p. 159.*

Metope

The often decorated space between the *triglyphs* in a *Doric* frieze. *See Columns and Piers, p. 71.*

Mezzanine

A storey sitting between two main ones; in a Classical building, the *piano nobile* and *attic.*

Mission or barrel tiles

Semicircular or barrel-shaped tiles that are laid in alternating rows of *concave* and *convex* arrangements. *See Roofs, p. 151.*

Modillion

A *console* often with attached *acanthus* leaf. Usually found projecting from the underside of the *corona* of a *Corinthian* or

Composite cornice, though sometimes also used elsewhere. *See Columns and Piers, p. 74.*

Monumental column

A tall, *free-standing* column erected to commemorate a great military victory or hero. Monumental columns are sometimes topped by a sculpted figure and decorated with *relief* carving. *See Columns and Piers, p. 69.*

Mortar

The paste which, when set, bonds adjacent bricks together in a wall. It is made from a mixture of sand and a binder such as cement or lime, to which water is added. When a mortar joint has been manipulated by a tool before the mortar has set it is said to be 'tooled'. *See Walls and Surfaces, p. 104.*

Moat

A defensive ditch or large trench surrounding a castle for defensive purposes; usually with steep sides and often filled with water. *See Fortified Buildings, p. 31.*

Mosaic

An abstract pattern or figurative scene created by arranging small pieces of coloured tile, glass or stone – called 'tesserae' – on a surface. The tesserae are fixed into position with mortar and grouting. Mosaics are used as both wall and floor decoration. *See Walls and Surfaces, p. 111.*

Mouchette

A drop-shaped *tracery* element. *See Windows and Doors, p. 138.*

Mullion

A vertical bar or member dividing an aperture. *See Windows and Doors, p. 132.*

Multifoiled or cusped arch

An arch composed of several small round or pointed curves, creating recessions called *foils* and triangular protrusions called *cusps. See Arches, p. 81.*

Municipal space

A publicly accessible open area such as a park or ceremonial square.

Muntin

In a *panel door*, muntins are subsidiary vertical members used to further divide the door into smaller panels. In a *sash window*, they are subsidiary glazing rods that separate and hold in place the panes of glass in a sash, creating a grid. *See Windows and Doors, pp. 133, 135.*

Mutule

A projecting block, whose underside is sometimes inclined, sitting below the *corona* in a *Doric cornice. See Columns and Piers, p. 71.*

N

Nail-head

A moulding that consists of a repeating pattern of projecting pyramidal forms, said to resemble the heads of nails. When the pyramid forms are indented into the wall surface it is known as 'hollow-square moulding'. Both are often found in Norman and Romanesque architecture. *See Walls and Surfaces, p. 129.*

Naos

In a Classical temple, the central structure of the temple enclosed by the *peristasis*, usually separated into several compartments. *See The Classical Temple, p. 13.*

Narthex

The westernmost part of a cathedral or church, traditionally not always considered part of the church proper. *See The Medieval Cathedral, p. 16.*

Nave

The main body of a church or cathedral, extending from the west end to the *crossing* or, if *transepts* are absent, to the *chancel. See The Medieval Cathedral, p. 16.*

Neck

In a Classical column, the flat section between the bottom of the *capital* and *astragal* at the top of a *shaft. See Columns and Piers, p. 70.*

Needle spire

A slender, in some instances almost spike-like, spire which sits in the centre of its base. *See Roofs, p. 155.*

Newel

The principal upright post around which the steps in a staircase radiate, or which stands at the end of a straight flight supporting the *handrail. See Stairs and Lifts, p. 166.*

Newel stair

A stair which winds around a central *newel*. A 'spiral stair' is one form of newel stair. *See Stairs and Lifts, p. 167.*

Niche

An arched recess into a wall surface, designed to hold a statue or simply to provide surface variegation. *See Walls and Surfaces, p. 129.*

Nogging

A horizontal piece of timber inserted between two vertical ones to provide structural rigidity. *See Timber, p. 87.*

Nosing

In a stair, the rounded protrusion along the outer edge of a *tread. See Stairs and Lifts, p. 166.*

O

Obelisk

A narrow, tall, roughly rectangular structure tapering upwards with a pyramidal top. Derived from Egyptian architecture, obelisks are used frequently in Classical architecture. *See Columns and Piers, p. 69.*

Octastyle

A temple front composed of eight columns (or *pilasters*). *See The Classical Temple, p. 10.*

Oculus or bull's eye window

A simple circular window with no *tracery*. An oculus also refers to the crowning light seen from the interior at the top of a *dome*; the Pantheon in Rome is the most famous example. *See Windows and Doors, p. 141.*

Ogee arch

A pointed arch, each side of which is composed of a lower *concave* curve intersecting a higher *convex* one. The centres of the outer two concave curves sit at *impost* level within the *span*, or at its centre. The centres of the inner two convex curves stand above the arch *rise. See Arches, p. 80.*

Onion dome

A dome with a bulbous, onion-like shape which terminates in a point at its top; in section, similar to an *ogee arch. See Roofs, p. 159.*

Open pediment

A pediment – triangular or segmental – left open at the top so that the ends do not meet in the centre. *See Windows and Doors, p. 137.*

Open spire

A spire characterized by the use of an open network of *tracery* and *flying buttresses. See Roofs, p. 155.*

Open stair

A stair with no *risers. See Stairs and Lifts, p. 167.*

Open string

See Strings.

Open-well stair

A rectangular stair which rises around a central void called a 'well'. *See Stairs and Lifts, p. 167.*

Opisthodomos

In a Classical temple, the sometimes omitted space similar to the *pronaos*, created at the opposite end of the *cella* but with no through way into it. *See The Classical Temple, p. 13.*

Orb finial

The sphere-shaped crowning ornament of a *pinnacle*, *spire*, or roof. In an ecclesiastical building it is usually topped by a cross. *See Roofs, p. 157.*

Oriel window

A window that projects from one or more upper storeys but does not extend to the ground floor. *See Windows and Doors, p. 143.*

Outer ward

Also called a 'bailey'. The fortified enclosure in a castle where the lord's household resided. It also contained stables, workshops and sometimes barracks. *See Fortified Buildings, p. 30.*

Overdoor

A decorative panel, often set with a painting or bust, placed over a door; sometimes incorporated with the doorcase. *See Walls and Surfaces, p. 129.*

Overhanging jetty

The projection of an upper storey over a lower one in a timber-framed building. *See Walls and Surfaces, p. 109.*

Oversailing window

An upper-storey window projecting from the face of a wall. It differs from an *Oriel window* in usually extending more than one bay. *See Windows and Doors, p. 143.*

Ovoidal window

A window that is roughly oval in shape. *See Street-Facing Buildings, p. 44.*

Ovolo

A *convex* moulding, a quarter-circle in section. *See Walls and Surfaces, p. 123.*

Ovum

An egg-shaped ornamental element found, for example, in an *egg-and-dart* enrichment. *See Walls and Surfaces, p. 129.*

P

Palm capital

An Egyptian capital with splayed leaf forms that resemble the branches of a palm tree. *See Columns and Piers, p. 77.*

Palmette

A decorative motif in the form of a fan-shaped palm leaf, the lobes of which face outwards (unlike an *anthemion*). *See Walls and Surfaces, p. 129.*

Panel

A rectangular recession or projection in a surface. In wood panelling or a *panel door*, panels are boards between the *rails*, *stiles*, *mullions* and *muntins. See Walls and Surfaces, p. 121.*

Panel door

A door constructed from a structural frame of *rails*, *stiles*, *mullions* and sometimes *muntins*, infilled with wooden panels. *See Windows and Doors, p. 135.*

Panel or perpendicular tracery

A tracery pattern in which the aperture is split into vertical units by the use of repeating *mullions. See Windows and Doors, p. 139.*

Pantiles

S-shaped tiles which interlock with adjacent ones, forming a ridged pattern. *See Roofs, p. 150.*

Parallel chord truss

A *truss* in which the upper and lower members – called 'chords' – are parallel. The upper and lower chords are most often separated by a triangulated lattice-like structure. *See Roofs, p. 163.*

Parapet

A low protective wall or *balustrade* running along the edge of a roof, *balcony* or bridge. *See Roofs, p. 152.*

Parapet spire

A typically octagonal spire whose triangular faces are set back from the edge of the *tower*. A parapet runs around the top of the tower with *turrets* or *pinnacles* set in the four corners. *See Roofs, p. 155.*

Pargetting

The decoration of the exterior plaster surfaces of *timber-framed buildings* with embossed or recessed ornamental patterns. *See Walls and Surfaces, p. 113.*

Patera

A circular, dish-like ornament. Paterae are sometimes found (usually alternating with *bucrania*) in the *metopes* in a *Doric frieze*. See *Walls and Surfaces, p. 129*.

Pavilion roof

Similar to a *hipped roof* except with a flat face at its apex. See *Roofs, p. 149*.

Pebble-dash

An exterior rendering of *cement plaster or render* which is then set with pebbles and sometimes small shells. A variation of the procedure sees the pebbles (and shells) added to the render before application to the wall – called 'roughcast'. See *Walls and Surfaces, p. 113*.

Pedestal

The moulded block on which a column or *pilaster* is sometimes raised. See *Street-Facing Buildings, p. 39*.

Pediment

A shallow-pitched triangular *gable* end; a key element of a Classical temple front; also often used to top an aperture, not always triangular. See *Windows and Doors, p. 137*.

Pelta

A decorative motif in the form of an elliptical, circular or crescent-shaped shield. See *Walls and Surfaces, p. 129*.

Pendentive

The curved triangular section formed by the intersection of a *dome* and its supporting arches. See *Roofs, p. 158*.

Perforated brick

A standard brick but with two or three vertical perforations to reduce weight and aid ventilation. See *Walls and Surfaces, p. 117*.

Peripteral

A Classical temple surrounded by colonnades on all four sides. See *The Classical Temple, p. 12*.

Peristasis

In a Classical temple, the single or double row of columns forming an envelope around a temple and providing structural support. Also called 'peristyle'. See *The Classical Temple, p. 12*.

Perron

An exterior set of steps leading to a grand entranceway or portal. See *Country Houses and Villas, p. 35*.

Piano nobile

A Classical building's principal storey. See *Country Houses and Villas, p. 35*.

Pier

An upright (rarely angled) member providing vertical structural support.

Pilaster

A flattened column that projects slightly from the face of a wall. See *Columns and Piers, p. 68*.

Piloti

Pilotis are piers or columns that raise a building above ground level, freeing space for circulation or storage in the space underneath. See *Country Houses and Villas, p. 37*.

Pinnacle

An elongated triangular form, narrowing towards the top, extending into the air. Pinnacles are often decorated with *crockets*. See *The Medieval Cathedral, p. 14*.

Pitched or gabled roof

A single-ridged roof with two sloping sides and gables at the two ends. The term pitched roof is sometimes used to refer to any sloping roof. See *Roofs, p. 148*.

Plate tracery

A basic type of tracery in which the pattern is seemingly incised into, or cut through, a solid layer of stone. See *Windows and Doors, p. 139*.

Plinth

The lowest part of a column *base*. See *Columns and Piers, p. 70*.

Point-loaded/supported glass curtain wall

A type of glass curtain wall where reinforced-glass panes are held in place through point attachments in each corner to the arms of a spider, which is then attached by a bracket to a structural support. See *Walls and Surfaces, p. 115*.

Pointed window

A window in which the *lintel* is a pointed arch. See *Windows and Doors, p. 141*.

Portcullis

A wood or metal latticed gate in the *gatehouse* or *barbican* of a castle, which could be quickly raised and lowered by a pulley system. See *Fortified Buildings, p. 32*.

Portico

A porch extending from the body of a building, usually with a temple front of a *colonnade* topped by a *pediment*. See *Country Houses and Villas, p. 35*.

Post

The vertical side of a door *surround*. See *Windows and Doors, p. 134*.

Pratt truss

A *parallel chord truss* with both vertical and angled members between the parallel chords, creating a triangulated structure. See *Roofs, p. 163*.

Precast concrete

A standardized concrete *panel* or *pier*, cast off-site for quick assembly on-site. See *Walls and Surfaces, p. 112*.

Predella

The step on which the *altar* stands above the rest of the *chancel*. It can also refer to the paintings or sculptures at the bottom of an *altarpiece* or *reredos*. See *The Medieval Cathedral, p. 21*.

Presbytery

In a cathedral or church, the area adjacent to or actually part of the *choir*, where the senior clergy reside during services. See *The Medieval Cathedral, p. 17*.

Principal rafter

In a *truss* roof, the rafters that form the truss structure. See *Roofs, p. 160*.

Projecting window

A window protruding from the surface of a wall. See *Street-Facing Buildings, p. 45*.

Projection

A projection supported solely at one end, with no supporting piers underneath. See *Contemporary Buildings, p. 64*.

Pronaos

In a Classical temple, the porch-like space created at one end of the *naos* by the extending walls of the *cella* with a pair of columns placed between the walls. See *The Classical Temple, p. 13*.

Proscenium arch

An arch surmounting the stage in many theatres, framing the opening between stage and auditorium. See *Arches, p. 83*.

Prostyle

A Classical temple is described as prostyle when the *pronaos* is fronted by *free-standing columns* (usually four or six). See *The Classical Temple, p. 12*.

Pseudodipteral

A Classical temple in which the *pronaos* is articulated by a double row of *free-standing columns*, the sides and rear having a single colonnade (which may be matched by *engaged columns* or

pilasters on the *naos*). See *The Classical Temple, p. 12*.

Pseudoperipteral

A Classical temple whose sides are articulated by *engaged columns* or *pilasters* rather than *free-standing columns*. See *The Classical Temple, p. 12*.

Pulpit

A raised and often ornamented platform from where a sermon is delivered. See *The Medieval Cathedral, p. 20*.

Purlin

In a truss roof, a longitudinal beam on top of the *principal rafters* that gives support to the *common rafters* (where applicable) and the roof cladding above. See *Roofs, p. 162*.

Putto

A figure of a small male child usually unclothed and winged; also sometimes called an 'amorino'. See *Walls and Surfaces, p. 129*.

PVC-framed casement window

A mass-produced casement window whose frame is constructed from PVC. It is cheaper to produce than the steel version, and PVC has the added advantage that it is not susceptible to rust. See *Windows and Doors, p. 142*.

Pycnostyle

An *intercolumniation* of 1½ lower column diameters. See *The Classical Temple, p. 11*.

Q

Quadripartite vault

A vault in which each bay is subdivided into four parts by two *diagonal ribs*. See *Roofs, p. 165*.

Quarry

A small square or diamond-shaped piece of glass, often used with others in leaded *lattice windows*. See *Windows and Doors, p. 140*.

Quarry-faced rustication

A form of rustication in which the faces of stone blocks are treated roughly and look as if they are unfinished. See *Walls and Surfaces, p. 103*.

Queen post

In a *truss* roof, two posts placed on a *tie beam* to support the *principal rafters* above. The posts are held in place laterally by a *collar beam*. See *Roofs, p. 161*.

Queen-post roof

A *truss* roof in which two posts are placed on a *tie beam* to support the *principal rafters* above. The queen posts are held in place laterally by a *collar beam*. See Roofs, p. 161.

Quirked

A moulding with a continuous horizontal V-shaped indention. See Walls and Surfaces, p. 123.

Quoins

The cornerstones of a building. They are often composed of larger *rusticated* blocks and are sometimes in a different material to the one used in the building. See Walls and Surfaces, p. 103.

R

Raffle leaf

A scrolling, serrated leaf-like ornament, often found in Rococo decoration. See Walls and Surfaces, p. 130.

Rail

The horizontal strip or member in *wood panelling* or a *panel door*. See Walls and Surfaces, p. 121.

Railing

A fence-like structure used to partially enclose a space, platform or stair. The upright members that support the rail itself are often treated decoratively. See Windows and Doors, p. 144.

Raked mortaring

Brickwork in which the mortar sits parallel with the brick face but is recessed into the joint. See Walls and Surfaces, p. 106.

Recessed

A feature, say window or balcony, which is set back within the wall surface or building shell.

Rectilinear

A building, façade or window composed only from a series of vertical and horizontal elements. See Contemporary Buildings, p. 64.

Reed

A series of two or more parallel *convex* or projecting mouldings. See Walls and Surfaces, p. 123.

Regula

The small rectangular band just below the *tenia* in a *Doric architrave* from which the *guttae* protrude. See Columns and Piers, p. 71.

Relief

A sculpted surface in which the modelled forms project from – or in some examples are recessed into – the surface plane. Bas-relief or 'basso-relievo' is a low relief with the sculpted scene extending less than half its depth from the relief plane. In high relief or 'alto-relievo' the scene typically extends more than half its depth from the relief plane. 'Mezzo-relievo' is an intermediate relief between high and low relief. In 'cavo-relievo' the scene recedes, rather than projects, from the relief plane; it is also known as 'intaglio' or 'diaglyph'. 'Rilievo stiacciato' is an extremely flat relief, most often found in Italian Renaissance sculpture. See Walls and Surfaces, p. 130.

Reredos

In a cathedral or church, a usually wooden screen placed behind the *high altar*, often decorated with scenes depicting religious iconography or biblical events. See The Medieval Cathedral, p. 21.

Respond

An *engaged column* or *corbel*, usually deployed at the end of an *arcade* against a wall or pier. See Arches, p. 82.

Reticulated tracery

A repeating net-like tracery pattern, often of quatrefoils (four-leaved shapes) whose top and bottom *foils* have been elongated into ogees (two S-shaped curves) rather than rounded curves. See Windows and Doors, p. 139.

Retrochoir

In a cathedral or church, an area behind the *high altar*, sometimes omitted. See The Medieval Cathedral, p. 17.

Return

A 90-degree turn in a moulding. See Walls and Surfaces, p. 123.

Reveal

The inside of the *jamb*, perpendicular to a window frame. If the reveal is not perpendicular it is called a 'splay'. See Windows and Doors, p. 136.

Reverse ogee arch

Similar to an ogee arch, except that the lower two curves are *convex* while the higher two are *concave*. See Arches, p. 80.

Revolving door

A door used in spaces with high footfall. It consists of four leaves attached to a central rotating vertical axle. Pushing a leaf causes the door to rotate (revolving doors are sometimes motorized).

The design ensures there is no direct interchange between interior and exterior, which is especially useful for regulating interior temperatures. See Windows and Doors, p. 146.

Rib

A projecting strip of masonry or brick that provides the structural support to a *vault* or *dome*. See Roofs, p. 157.

Rib vault

Similar to a *groin vault* except that the groins are replaced by *ribs*, which provide the structural framework of the vault and support the infilling or *web*. See Roofs, p. 164.

Ribbon window

A series of windows of the same height, separated only by *mullions* which form a continuous horizontal band or ribbon across a building. Ribbon windows sometimes hold concertina frames, which allow the *lights* to be slid along tracks and folded against one another. See Windows and Doors, p. 142.

Ridge

The intersection of two sloping sides at the top of a *pitched or gabled roof*. See Roofs, p. 152.

Ridge beam

In a *truss* roof, a beam that runs along the top of the truss against which the rafters rest. See Roofs, p. 160.

Ridge tiles

The tiles which sit over the *ridge* of a roof. In some instances they are adorned with vertically projecting decorative tiles called 'crest tiles'. See Roofs, p. 150.

Ridge rib

The decorative longitudinal rib running along the centre of a *rib vault*. See Roofs, p. 164.

Rinceau

A decorative motif in the form of multi-stemmed and intertwining vines and leaves. See Walls and Surfaces, p. 130.

Rise

The height an arch rises from *impost* level to the underside of the *keystone*. See Arches, p. 78.

Riser

In a stair, the vertical part of a step between two *treads*. See Stairs and Lifts, p. 166.

Roll

A simple *convex* moulding, usually semi-circular in section but sometimes more than semicircular. It is usually found in medieval architecture. A variant is 'roll-and-fillet' moulding, which consists of a roll moulding combined with one or two *fillets*. See Walls and Surfaces, p. 122.

Roman Doric order

See Classical orders.

Rood or chancel screen

A screen separating the *choir* from the *crossing* or nave. The rood refers to the wooden sculptural representation of the Crucifixion surmounted on the rood loft above the rood beam. Sometimes a second screen, a 'pulpitum', is used to separate the choir from the crossing or nave, with the rood screen positioned further to the west. See The Medieval Cathedral, p. 20.

Roof felt

A fibrous material, usually fibreglass or polyester, infused with bitumen or tar to give it water resistance. It is often laid with a layer of shingles on top or secured by wooden battens. See Roofs, p. 151.

Roof garden or terrace

A paved garden or terrace situated on the roof of a building. As well as providing a place of recreation, especially useful when space at ground level is at a premium, roof gardens help to regulate the temperature in the spaces below. See The Modern Block, p. 53.

Roof space

Space created between the top of the gallery *arcade* and the underside of the *pitched roof*. See The Medieval Cathedral, p. 18.

Rose window

A circular window delineated with often highly complex tracery that gives it the appearance of a multipetalled rose. See Windows and Doors, p. 141.

Rosette

A circular ornament resembling the form of a rose. See Walls and Surfaces, p. 130.

Roundel

A circular panel or moulding. Roundels can be used as independent motifs, but are often part of a larger decorative scheme. See Walls and Surfaces, p. 130.

Glossary / 7

Round-headed window

A window in which the *lintel* is arched. *See Windows and Doors, p. 141.*

Rowlock header

A brick laid horizontally on its narrow, long side with the short end of the brick exposed on the outer face of the wall. *See Walls and Surfaces, p. 104.*

Rowlock stretcher or shiner

A brick laid horizontally with its long, narrow side on the bottom and the broad, long side exposed on the outer face of the wall. *See Walls and Surfaces, p. 104.*

Rubble masonry

A wall formed from irregularly shaped blocks of masonry, often laid with thick mortar joints. When the gaps between irregularly shaped blocks are filled with rectangular stones of varying heights called snecks, it is called 'snecked rubble masonry'. When similarly sized blocks are grouped together to form horizontal courses of varying heights it is described as 'coursed rubble masonry'. *See Walls and Surfaces, p. 102.*

Running ornament

The name given to a continuous and often intertwining band of ornament. *See Walls and Surfaces, p. 130.*

Rustication

A style of working masonry in which the joints between adjacent blocks of stone are accentuated. In some forms of rustication, the faces of the stone blocks are further delineated in a variety of ways. *See Walls and Surfaces, p. 103.*

S

Sacristy

A room in a cathedral or church used to store the vestments and other objects used in services. May be within the main body of the building or on the side. *See The Medieval Cathedral, p. 17.*

Saddle bar

In a window, the horizontal bars, typically of lead, that support the subsidiary *lights*. *See Windows and Doors, p. 132.*

Sailor

A brick laid vertically but with the broad, long side exposed on the outer face of the wall. *See Walls and Surfaces, p. 104.*

Sanctuary

The part of a *chancel* where the *high altar* is situated; the most sacred part of a cathedral or church. *See The Medieval Cathedral, p. 17.*

Sash window

A window consisting of one or more sashes – glazed wooden frames containing one or more glass panes – which are set into grooves in the *jambs* and slide vertically up and down. A counterweight is usually concealed in the window frame, which is linked to the sash by a cord and pulley system. *See Windows and Doors, p. 133.*

Saucer dome

A dome that has a *rise* much smaller than its *span*, giving it a flatter, upturned-saucer shape. *See Roofs, p. 159.*

Saw-tooth roof

A roof composed of sloping faces alternating with vertical ones which are often set with windows. Saw-tooth roofs are often used to cover very large spaces where a *pitched roof* would be impractical. *See Roofs, p. 149.*

Scallop

A *corrugated* ornament with raised cones between recessed grooves, forming a shell-like pattern. *See Walls and Surfaces, p. 131.*

Scallop capital

A tapering cube-shaped capital, *corrugated* with several raised cones between recessed grooves, forming a shell-like pattern. When the cones do not reach the full height of the capital, they are described as 'slipped'. *See Columns and Piers, p. 77.*

Scotia

The *concave* moulding at the base of a Classical column, between two *tori*. *See Walls and Surfaces, p. 123.*

Scroll

A projecting moulding somewhat like a *roll* moulding but composed from two curves with the upper one projecting further than the lower one. *See Walls and Surfaces, p. 123.*

Scrolled pediment

Similar to an *open pediment* except the ends are turned in on themselves as scrolls. *See Windows and Doors, p. 137.*

Segmental arch

An arch whose curve is one segment of a semicircle whose centre is below *impost* level; its *span* is thus much larger than its *rise*. *See Arches, p. 79.*

Segmental pediment

Similar to a *triangular pediment* except the triangle shape is replaced by a

shallow curve. *See Windows and Doors, p. 137.*

Self-opening or automatic door

A door that requires no user action to open. Instead it is opened mechanically when the user activates infrared, motion or pressure sensors. *See Windows and Doors, p. 147.*

Semicircular arch

An arch whose curve has one centre with the *rise* equal to half the *span*, giving it the form of a semicircle. *See Arches, p. 79.*

Set tiles

Tiles that are fixed directly on to a surface and to each other using a fine mortar or grouting. *See Walls and Surfaces, p. 110.*

Sexpartite vault

A vault in which each bay is subdivided into six parts by two *diagonal ribs* and one *transverse* rib. *See Roofs, p. 165.*

Shaft

The long, narrower section of a column between the *base* and *capital*. *See Columns and Piers, p. 70.*

Shaped gable

A gable in which each side is formed from two or more curves. *See Roofs, p. 153.*

Shopfront window

A window in the street-facing front of a shop, usually large so that merchandise is visible from the outside. *See Windows and Doors, p. 142.*

Shouldered arch

A flat arch supported by two outer arcs, sometimes seen as separate *corbels*. *See Arches, p. 81.*

Shoulders

The two symmetrical lateral projections from the top of an aperture. They are typically small rectangular flaps that form a shoulder, though they can take other more decorated forms. When the shoulders are combined with vertical flaps, the corner motif is called a *crossette*. *See Windows and Doors, p. 136.*

Shutter

A hinged panel, often *louvred*, sitting to the side of a window, which can be closed to keep out the sun or for security reasons. Shutters can be affixed to the inside or outside of windows. *See Windows and Doors, p. 144.*

Side altar

A subsidiary altar, probably with a dedication, located to the side of the main altar. *See The Renaissance Church, p. 26.*

Side gable

A gable on the side of a building, usually perpendicular to the main front. The V-shape where the two *pitched roofs* intersect is called a 'valley'. *See Roofs, p. 153.*

Sidelight

A window to the side of a doorway. *See Windows and Doors, p. 135.*

Sill

The horizontal base of a window *surround. See Windows and Doors, p. 132.*

Single-framed roof

The simplest kind of trussed roof, composed from series of transverse rafters laid against each other that support a central *ridge beam*. *See Roofs, p. 160.*

Skirting

The typically wooden slat, often moulded, affixed to the bottom of an internal wall where it meets the floor. Known as 'baseboard' in the US. *See Walls and Surfaces, p. 120.*

Skylight

A window that is parallel with the face of a roof. Sometimes a small *dome* is used, especially on a flat roof, to maximize the amount of light entering the space below. *See Windows and Doors, p. 145.*

Sliding door

A door set on tracks parallel to the door face. To open, the door is slid along the tracks so that it overlaps with the wall or surface adjacent to the aperture. Sometimes the door slides into the wall. *See Windows and Doors, p. 147.*

Soffit

A general term for the underside of a structure or surface (cf. Intrados). *See Arches, p. 78.*

Soldier

A brick laid vertically with its long, narrow side exposed on the outer face of the wall. *See Walls and Surfaces, p. 104.*

Solomonic column

A helical column with a twisting *shaft*. Said to derive from the Temple of Solomon in Jerusalem, Solomonic columns can be topped by any *capital*.

As they are especially ornate, they are rarely used in architecture but more often found in furniture. See *Columns and Piers, p. 68.*

Space frame

A three-dimensional *truss*-like structural framework in which the straight members are arranged in a series of repeating geometrical patterns. Strong but lightweight, space frames are often used to span large distances with few supports. See *Roofs, p. 163.*

Span

The total distance an arch crosses without additional support. See *Arches, p. 78.*

Spandrel

The roughly triangular space created between the outer side of an arch's curve, a horizontal bounding above (such as a *string course*) and the curve of an adjacent arch or some kind of vertical moulding, column or wall. See *Arches, p. 82.*

Spandrel panel

The usually opaque or semi-opaque part of a *curtain wall* between the head of a glass pane and the bottom of the one immediately above. Spandrel panels often serve to obscure service pipes and cables running between floors. See *Walls and Surfaces, p. 114.*

Spiral staircase

A circular stair winding around a central pole. A type of *newel* stair. See *Stairs and Lifts, p. 167.*

Spire

A tapering triangular or conical structure often set atop a *tower* in a church or other medievalized building. See *Roofs, p. 154.*

Splayed-foot spire

Similar to a *broach spire*, except that near the bottom of the spire the four corner faces taper out to a point, with the four side faces splaying out. See *Roofs, p. 155.*

Springer

In an arch the lowest *voussoir*, situated at the point where the curve of the arch 'springs' from the vertical. See *Arches, p. 78.*

Squinch

An arch constructed across the corner created by the intersection of two perpendicular walls. Squinches are often used to provide additional structural support, especially for a *dome* or *tower*. See *Arches, p. 82.*

Stacked bond

Stretchers stacked on top of each other with the vertical joints aligned. For this reason, it is a relatively weak bonding type so is often used to face a cavity wall or, especially, a steel structure. See *Walls and Surfaces, p. 105.*

Stalls

The rows of seats, usually in the *choir* though also elsewhere in a cathedral or church, typically fixed, with high sides and backs. See *The Medieval Cathedral, p. 20.*

Stanchion bar

The vertical supporting bars, typically of lead, of the subsidiary *lights* in a *fixed window*. See *Windows and Doors, p. 140.*

Stay

A metal rod perforated with several holes to allow for adjustment, used to keep a *casement window* open or closed. See *Windows and Doors, p. 132.*

Steel-framed casement window

A usually mass-produced casement window whose frame is constructed from steel rather than lead; it is characteristic of early twentieth-century architecture. See *Windows and Doors, p. 142.*

Stereobate

In a Classical temple, the first two steps leading up from the *euthynteria* and forming a visible base for the *superstructure*. In non-temple buildings, the term is used to denote the base or foundation level on which a building is erected. See *The Classical Temple, p. 8.*

Stiff-leaf capital

A *foliated* capital, usually with three-lobed leaves whose tops are folded outwards. See *Columns and Piers, p. 76.*

Stile

The vertical strip or member in *wood panelling* or a *panel door*. A subsidiary, usually thinner, vertical strip or member is called a *muntin*. See *Walls and Surfaces, p. 121.*

Stilted arch

An arch whose *springer* is some distance above its *impost level*. See *Arches, p. 81.*

Stop

A termination of a *hood mould* or label at *impost* level. A stop is sometimes marked by a *ball flower* or by the hood moulding being turned away from the aperture. See *Windows and Doors, p. 138.*

Stoup

A small basin filled with holy water, usually placed on the wall near a cathedral or church entrance. Some congregation members, especially in Roman Catholic churches, dip their fingers in the water and make the sign of the cross upon entering and leaving. See *The Medieval Cathedral, p. 20.*

Straight stair

A single flight of steps with no turns. When two straight flights run in opposite directions, are linked by a landing and sit parallel with no gap between them, it is called a 'dog-leg stair'. See *Stairs and Lifts, p. 167.*

Straight-line gable

A gable raised up above the roof line but remaining parallel with it. See *Roofs, p. 153.*

Strainer arch

An arch placed between opposing piers or walls to provide additional lateral support. See *Arches, p. 83.*

Stretcher

A brick laid horizontally with its broad, long face on the bottom and its narrow, long face exposed on the outer face of the wall. See *Walls and Surfaces, p. 104.*

Stretcher bond

The simplest brick bond type, consisting of repeating courses of stretcher bricks overlapping the brick below by half their length. As such, stretcher bond is usually reserved for walls one brick thick, and is often used to face a cavity wall, or timber or steel structures. See *Walls and Surfaces, p. 105.*

Strings

In a stair, the strings run on either side of the *treads* and *risers* which they support. In an 'open string staircase', the strings are partially cut away, revealing the ends of the treads and risers. In a 'closed string staircase', the outer strings obscure the ends of the treads and risers. See *Stairs and Lifts, p. 166.*

String course

A thin, horizontal moulded banding running across a wall. When a string course is continued over a column, it is called a 'shaft ring'. See *Walls and Surfaces, p. 120.*

Struck mortaring

Brickwork in which the mortar is angled so that it slopes inwards from the face of the upper brick. See *Walls and Surfaces, p. 106.*

Strut

In a *truss* roof, a short angled member supporting the principal structural members. See *Roofs, p. 162.*

Stucco

Traditionally, a hard form of *lime plaster* used to render the exterior surfaces of buildings, often to hide an underlying brick structure and provide surface decoration. Modern stuccos are typically forms of *cement plaster*. See *Walls and Surfaces, p. 113.*

Stylobate

In a Classical temple, the topmost step of the *crepidoma* on which the columns stand. The term is also used to refer to any continuous base on which a series of columns stands. See *The Classical Temple, p. 8.*

Sunk panel

A recessed panel in a façade, usually filled with sculptural relief or ornament. See *Walls and Surfaces, p. 121.*

Superstructure

A structure sitting on top of the main body of a building. See *High-Rise Buildings, p. 58.*

Supporting arch

One of four or sometimes eight arches supporting the *dome* above. See *Roofs, p. 158.*

Surround

The general term used to denote the often decorative framing of an aperture. See *Windows and Doors, p. 136.*

Swag

A decorative element, a swag has the form of a cloth that seems to be suspended in a bow or curve from any number of (usually evenly) spaced points on a surface. See *Walls and Surfaces, p. 131.*

Swan-neck pediment

Similar to a *scrolled pediment*, but composed from two opposing flattened S-shape curves. See *Windows and Doors, p. 137.*

Synthetic membrane

Synthetic membranes are used for building envelopes or surface layers. Such materials are usually deployed in tension, and are matched with compression elements such as *masts*. Synthetic membranes are also used in roofs, where synthetic rubber or thermoplastic are heat-welded together to form a waterproof layer. See *Walls and Surfaces, p. 117.*

compression elements such as *masts*. Synthetic membranes are also used in roofs, where synthetic rubber or thermoplastic are heat-welded together to form a waterproof layer. *See Walls and Surfaces, p. 117.*

Synthetic tiles

Tiles made from synthetic materials like fibreglass, plastic or, now very rarely, asbestos. *See Roofs, p. 151.*

Systyle

An *intercolumniation* of two lower column diameters. *See The Classical Temple, p. 11.*

T

Tabernacle

A box or container, often elaborately ornamented, in which the reserved sacrament is stored. *See The Medieval Cathedral, p. 21.*

Tambour

See Drum.

Tambour door

A door made from a series of conjoined horizontal slats which can be rolled up to open the door. *See Windows and Doors, p. 147.*

Tambour gallery

In a dome, a gallery that sometimes runs around the inside of its *drum* or tambour. *See Roofs, p. 158.*

Temple in antis

The simplest temple form. It has no *peristasis*, and the fronts of the protruding walls of the *cella* – called *antae* – and two columns of the *pronaos* provide the frontal emphasis. *See The Classical Temple, p. 12.*

Tenia

The *fillet* at the top of a *Doric architrave* sitting just below the *frieze*. *See Columns and Piers, p. 71.*

Term

A pedestal tapering towards the bottom, topped by a bust of a mythological figure or animal. The name 'term' derives from Terminus, the Roman god of boundaries. A variant is the 'herm' – when the head is a representation of Hermes/Mercury, the Greek/Roman messenger god. *See Walls and Surfaces, p. 128.*

Tester/sounding-board

The board suspended above an *altar* or *pulpit* to help project the voice of the priest or preacher. *See The Medieval Cathedral, p. 20.*

Tetrastyle

A temple front composed of four columns (or *pilasters*). *See The Classical Temple, p. 10.*

Tholos

A circular range of columns surrounding a circular *cella*. *See The Classical Temple, p. 12.*

Three-centred arch

An arch formed from three intersecting curves; the central one has a larger radius than the two on either side, with its centre located below *impost* level. *See Arches, p. 79.*

Three-foiled arch

A three-centred arch with the centre of the central curve standing above *impost* level, creating three distinct arcs or *foils*. *See Arches, p. 81.*

Threshold

The strip, usually of stone and wood, that composes the bottom of the door aperture above which the *door leaf* hangs. *See Windows and Doors, p. 134.*

Tie beam

In a *truss* roof, a beam spanning two opposing *wall plates*. *See Roofs, p. 161.*

Tierceron vault

A vault with additional ribs that emanate from the main supports and abut onto the *transverse ribs* or *ridge rib*. *See Roofs, p. 165.*

Timber cladding

Timber is frequently used as a cladding material in modern architecture. In *weatherboarding* it is almost always laid with the slats horizontal and overlapping. In other forms of timber cladding, slats are laid at any of a whole variety of angles without necessarily overlapping. Timber cladding is most often left stained or untreated rather than painted, to retain the rhythmic effect of colour and grain variation between series of slats. *See Walls and Surfaces, p. 109.*

Timber-framed building

A building whose structural framework is built from timber posts and cross beams (sometimes also with diagonal beams). The spaces in between the framework are usually infilled with brickwork, masonry, plaster, cement or *wattle-and-daub*. When the spacing between studs – the smaller vertical members between larger posts – is very narrow, the timber frame is described as 'close-studded'. The timber frame is sometimes obscured by external timber cladding or, in some instances, tiled or brick walls.

Timber studs

The smaller vertical members between larger posts in a *timber-framed building*. *See Street-Facing Buildings, p. 38.*

Top plate

The horizontal beam on which the rafters sit (equivalent to a *wall plate*). *See Roofs, p. 160.*

Torus

A prominent *convex* moulding, roughly semicircular in section. It is most often found at the *base* of a Classical column. *See Walls and Surfaces, p. 123.*

Tourelle

Strictly not a spire, but a small circular *tower* topped by a *conical roof*. *See Roofs, p. 156.*

Tower

A narrow, tall structure projecting from the *crossing* or west end of a church (*see The Medieval Cathedral, p. 14*). Also, more generally, a narrow, tall structure projecting from or attached to a building or standing as an independent structure. *See Roofs, p. 154.*

Trabeated

A structural system composed from series of vertical posts and horizontal *transfer beams*.

Tracery

Setting thin bars of stonework between panes of glass, creating an ornamental pattern or figurative scene. *See Blind tracery; Curvilinear or flowing tracery; Flamboyant tracery; Geometric tracery; Intersecting or branched tracery; Panel or perpendicular tracery; Plate tracery; Reticulated tracery; Y-tracery.*

Transepts

In a Latin cross plan (with one arm longer than the other three), the transepts bisect the east end of the *nave*. In a Greek cross plan, the transepts refer to the four projections from the cathedral's or church's central core. *See The Medieval Cathedral, p. 16.*

Transfer beam

A horizontal member intended to transfer loads to vertical supports. *See The Modern Block, p. 52.*

Transom

A horizontal bar or member dividing an aperture, or separating panels in a *curtain wall*. *See Windows and Doors, p. 132.*

Transom bar

The bar that runs horizontally above a door, separating it from a *fanlight* or

transom light See Windows and Doors, p. 135.

Transom light

A rectangular window above a door but contained within the overall *surround*. *See Street-Facing Buildings, p. 40.*

Transverse rib

The structural rib running across a *rib vault* perpendicular to the wall and defining the bays. *See Roofs, p. 164.*

Trapezoid window

An irregular four-sided projection from a wall containing one or more window lights. *See Windows and Doors, p. 143.*

Tread

The flat part of a step in a staircase. *See Stairs and Lifts, p. 166.*

Tri-partite portal

A large and often elaborate entranceway composed of three openings. Portals are typically found at the west end of medieval cathedrals and churches, and sometimes also face the *transept arms*. *See The Medieval Cathedral, p. 14.*

Triangular arch

The simplest pointed arch, formed from two diagonal members standing on *imposts* and resting on each other at the apex. *See Arches, p. 80.*

Triglyph

A grooved rectangular block in a *Doric frieze* characterized by its three vertical bars. *See Columns and Piers, p. 71.*

Triumphal arch

An ancient motif of a central archway flanked by two smaller openings. Deployed as a free-standing structure in the Classical world, it was revived in the Renaissance and used as a motif on varieties of structures. *See Arches, p. 83.*

Trompe-l'œil

French for 'trick of the eye', trompe-l'œil is the technique of painting a surface to give the illusion that what is portrayed actually exists in three-dimensional space. *See Walls and Surfaces, p. 131.*

Trumeau

The central *mullion* in an arched window or doorway supporting a *tympanum* above two smaller arches. *See Windows and Doors, p. 138.*

Truss

A structural framework of one or more triangular units combined with straight members that can be used to span large distances and support a load, such as a roof. Trusses are most usually constructed from wood or steel beams. *See Roofs, p. 160.*

Tudor arch

Often regarded as being synonymous with a *four-centred arch*, a Tudor arch strictly denotes an arch formed from two outer curves whose centres sit within the span at *impost* level. The curves are carried on in diagonal straight lines to a central apex. *See Arches, p. 80.*

Turret

Strictly not a spire, but a small *tower* that projects vertically from the corner wall or roof of a building. *See Roofs, p. 156.*

Tuscan order

See Classical orders.

Tympanum

In Classical architecture, the triangular (or segmental) space created by a *pediment*, typically recessed and decorated, often with figurative sculpture (*see The Classical Temple, p. 8*). In medieval architecture, the often decorated infilled space above the *imposts* of an arch supported by two smaller arches. *See The Medieval Cathedral, p. 19.*

U

Undercroft window

In a church or cathedral a window giving light to the crypt. *See The Medieval Cathedral, p. 15.*

Undulating

A building whose shape is composed from intersecting *convex* and *concave* curves creating a wave-like form. *See Contemporary Buildings, p. 65.*

Unequal or rampant arch

An asymmetrical arch whose *imposts* are at different heights. *See Arches, p. 81.*

Unitized glass curtain wall

A type of glass curtain wall where prefabricated panels containing one or more glass panes are attached via a bracket to a structural support. Such panels may also include *spandrel panels* and *louvres*. *See Walls and Surfaces, p. 115.*

Up-and-over door

A door that can be lifted above the aperture using a counterbalance mechanism; typically found in garages. *See Windows and Doors, p. 147.*

Urn finial

The vase-shaped crowning ornament of a *pinnacle*, *spire* or roof. *See Roofs, p. 154.*

V

V-shaped mortaring

Brickwork in which the mortar is finished in a V-shaped recession. *See Walls and Surfaces, p. 106.*

Venetian/Palladian/Serlian window

A tri-partite aperture composed of an arched central *light* flanked by two smaller flat-topped windows. Especially grand examples are articulated with an *order* and ornamental *keystone*. *See Windows and Doors, p. 141.*

Veranda

A partially enclosed gallery-type space, usually attached to the ground level of a house. If located on upper floors it is usually described as a *balcony*. *See Walls and Surfaces, p. 118.*

Vermiculated rustication

A type of rustication in which the faces of the blocks are incised to give the appearance of being, literally, 'worm-eaten'. *See Walls and Surfaces, p. 103.*

Vierendeel truss

A non-triangulated truss with all members horizontal or vertical. *See Roofs, p. 163.*

Viewing platform

An elevated space for sightseeing, often located on a building's roof.

Vitruvian scroll

A repeating pattern of wave-like forms; sometimes called a 'wave-scroll moulding'. *See Walls and Surfaces, p. 131.*

Volute

A scroll in the form of a spiral most often found in *Ionic*, *Corinthian* and *Composite capitals*, but also used in much larger form as an individual element in a façade. *See Columns and Piers, p. 73.*

Voussoir

Wedge-shaped blocks, usually of masonry, from which an arch's curve is formed. (*Keystones* and *springers* are voussoirs). *See Arches, p. 78.*

W

Wagon roof

A *single-framed* or *double-framed* roof to which *collar beams*, *arched braces* and *ashlar braces* have been added. *See Roofs, p. 161.*

Wall plate

In a *truss* roof, the beam along the top of the wall on which the *common rafters* sit. *See Roofs, p. 160.*

Wall rib

A decorative longitudinal rib running across the wall surface in a *rib vault*. *See Roofs, p. 164.*

Warren truss

A *parallel chord truss* with angled members between the parallel chord, creating a triangulated structure. *See Roofs, p. 163.*

Water-leaf

A moulding enriched with a repeating pattern of leaves whose tops are folded like small scrolls, sometimes alternating with darts. *See Walls and Surfaces, p. 131.*

Wattle-and-daub

A primitive construction method in which a lattice of thin wooden strips – the 'wattle' – is literally daubed with a render of mud, soil or clay which is then smoothed off. Wattle-and-daub is most often found infilling timber frames, but in some examples is used to construct entire walls. *See Walls and Surfaces, p. 113.*

Wave

A moulding formed from three curves: a *convex* curve set between two *concave* ones. *See Walls and Surfaces, p. 123.*

Weatherboard

On a door with an exterior face, the weatherboard is a horizontal projecting strip that runs the door's full width and is placed at the bottom of its outside face to deflect rain and wind. *See Windows and Doors, p. 134.*

Weatherboarding

Cladding a building with long, overlapping slats or boards laid horizontally, to protect the interior from the elements or for aesthetic effect. Sometimes the joints between adjacent slats are strengthened by the use of a tongue-and-groove joint. Weatherboarding can be painted, stained or left unfinished. Recently timber weatherboarding has, in some instances, been superseded by the use of plastic though the aesthetic remains similar. *See Walls and Surfaces, p. 109.*

Weathered mortaring

Brickwork in which the mortar is angled so that it slopes inwards from the face of the lower brick.

Weather vane

A movable structure for showing the direction of the wind, typically at the highest point of a building. *See Public Buildings, p. 46.*

Web

The infilled surface between *ribs* in a *rib vault*. *See Roofs, p. 164.*

Winder

A curved stair or part of a stair in which the *treads* are narrower at one end than at the other. *See Stairs and Lifts, p. 167.*

Window lintel

The supporting, usually horizontal, member that surmounts a window. *See Windows and Doors, p. 132.*

Wood panelling

The covering of an interior wall or surface with thin sheets of wood set within a frame of thicker strips, usually running vertically and horizontally. When the wood panelling only goes up as high as the *dado* level it is called 'wainscot'. *See Walls and Surfaces, p. 121.*

Y

Y-tracery

A simple tracery form in which a central *mullion* splits into two branches, forming a Y-shape. *See Windows and Doors, p. 139.*

Index / 1

Index / 3

Acknowledgements

Although this book is in many ways intended to be a departure from the traditional architectural dictionary, it is inevitably indebted to many existing works, unfortunately too numerous to mention separately. I have also accrued debts to several individuals: Alan Powers, for his generosity at the beginning of the project; Kate Goodwin and Ayla Lepine offered considered advice in the early stages; and my brother, Toby Hopkins, was excellent company on several photography trips. Originally published in 2012, *Reading Architecture* was my first book and this new edition is, once again, dedicated to my parents for their continued love, support and encouragement.

Owen Hopkins, 2022

Picture Credits

Dehio/Bezold = G. Dehio & G. Bezold, *Die Kirchliche Baukunst des Abendlandes* (1887–1902)

Viollet = E. Viollet-le-Duc, *Dictionnaire Raisonné de l'Architecture* (1856)

a = above
b = below
c = centre
r = right
l = left

Any line art not listed below was drawn by Gregory Gibbon; any photographs not listed were taken by Owen Hopkins.

6ar, 14, 15 Dehio/Bezold; 6acl, 23 Studio Fotografico Quattrone, Florence; 16–17 Advanced Illustration; 20bl Tom Ricciardi/Dreamstime; 28 Scala, Florence; 40 Jennyt/Shutterstock; 42 Antoine Gyori/AGP/Corbis; 52 Chicago History Museum/Getty Images; 55 STCB, Courtesy Miyagi Prefectural Government, Tourism Division; 56 Bettmann/Corbis; 61a Courtesy Kéré Architecture. Photo: Erik-Jan Ouwerkerk; 62a Courtesy WOHA. Photo: K. Kopter; 66bl © FLC/ADAGP, Paris and DACS, London 2022; 70, 71, 73, 74, 75 from Chambers's *Treatise on Civil Architecture*; 72 drawn by N. Revett for *Ionian Antiquities*; 76al, bl & cr Dehio/Bezold; 76ar, br & cl Viollet; 77al & ar Dehio/Bezold; 77cl Viollet; 84 Iwan Baan; 85b Courtesy Waugh Thistleton Architects. Photo: Will Pryce; 89a © FLC/ADAGP, Paris and DACS, London 2022; 89b Ed Reeve/VIEW; 93a Stephanie Braconnier/Shutterstock; 93b Sankei Archive via Getty Images; 94 Nigel Young/Foster + Partners; 96a Will McClean; 97a & b Giulia Hetherington; 133a, 134 Advanced Illustration; 146cr Imagno/Getty Images; 164al & r Dehio/Bezold

All the following images were supplied by Alamy:

6al David Caton; 6ac Fabrizio Ruggeri; 6acr Russell Kord; 6cr Photo Provider Network; 6bcl Bildarchiv Monheim GmbH; 6bcc Ivan Vdovin; 6bl Kadu Niemeyer/Arcaid; 6bc Building Image; 6br Uwe Kraft/ImageBroker; 6cr Photo Provider Network; 10al B. O'Kane; 10ar David Caton; 20acl Manuel Cohen; 20acr Liam White; 20al David Cantrille; 20ar Brunosphoto; 20bcl ASP Religion; 20bcr F1 online/Bildagentur GmbH; 20br Colin Underhill; 21bl Angelo Hornak; 21br Therin-Weise/Arco Images GmbH; 21cl Dave Jepson; 21cr & 25 B. O'Kane; 29 Angelo Hornak; 32a Steve Frost; 32b Roger Cracknell 01/Classic; 33a Russell Kord; 33b Skyscan Photolibrary; 34 LOOK Die Bildagentur der Fotografen GmbH; 35 Bildarchiv Monheim GmbH; 36 Holmes Garden Photos; 37 Bildarchiv Monheim GmbH © FLC/ADAGP, Paris and DACS, London 2022; 39 Ivan Vdovin; 43 Ellen McKnight; 44 Interfoto; 45 Stock Connection Blue; 46–47 Bildarchiv Monheim GmbH; 48–49 Photo Provider Network; 50 ImageBroker; 51 Tor Eigeland; 53 Matthias Hauser/ImageBroker; 54 Kadu Niemeyer/Arcaid; 57 Philip Scalia; 58 Building Image; 59 Palabra; 60a Peter Cook/VIEW; 60b Hufton+Crow/VIEW; 61b Galit Seligmann; 62b Prisma by Dukas Presseagentur GmbH; 63a Uwe Kraft/ImageBroker; 63b Peter de Kievith; 64a B. O'Kane; 64cl Fabpics; 64cr Duncan Phillips; 64bl Rob Crandall; 64br Douglas Lander; 65al Ruslan S.; 65ar Urban Photography TLV; 65cl Mark Fiennes/Arcaid; 65cr Tony Waltham/Robert Harding Picture Library; 65b Aflo Co. Ltd.; 66al Cephas Picture Library; 66ar Randy Duchaine; 66cl David Cantrille; 66cr Kevin George; 66br Glasshouse Images; 68al Cephas Picture Library; 68ar Felipe Rodriguez; 68cl Alessandro Zanini; 68cr Michael Jenner; 68bl Bill Heinsohn; 68br Miguel Angel Muñoz Pellicer; 69al Nikreates; 69ar Geoffrey Taunton; 69acl Richard Wareham Fotografie; 69acr Randy Duchaine; 69bcl PhotoStock-Israel; 69bcr Bildarchiv Monheim GmbH; 69bl Jon Arnold Images; 69br Ray Roberts © FLC/ADAGP, Paris and DACS, London 2022; 82a Angelo Hornak; 82bl B. O'Kane; 83b Chad Ehlers; 83cl David Cantrille; 83cr Michele Falzone; 85a Boris Baggs/Arcaid Images; 86 Kevin George; 87 Steve Speller; 88 B. O'Kane; 90 AC Manley; 91 S. Ziese/blickwinkel; 92 Renzo Piano © ADAGP, Paris and DACS, London 2022. Photo: Interfoto; 95 Glasshouse Images; 96b aldiami/Herbert Michalke; 98al Marshall Ikonography; 98ar ASP Religion; 98bl Keith Shuttlewood; 98br Lourens Smak; 100a Eric James; 100b Stephen Horsted; 101a Angelo Hornak; 101b Andrew Jankunas; 102acl Paul Cox; 102 acr Marshall Ikonography; 102bcl Joe Doylem; 103ar The Art Archive; 103cl PrimrosePix; 105bcl MS Bretherton; 105bcr Gareth Byrne; 105bl Derek Croucher; 107al Jeff Gynane; 107cl David Cook/Blueshiftstudios; 107bl Roman Milert; 107br Mode Images Ltd; 108al Olaf Doering; 108ar ImageBroker; 108bl Iain Masterton; 108br Paolo Negri; 109al Les Polders; 109ar Pink Sun Media; 109arb Arco Images/ImageBroker; 109c PCL; 109b John Edward Linden/Arcaid; 110al Genevieve Vallee; 110ar DWImages England; 110bl Cosmo Condina; 110br John James; 111al Marshall Ikonography; 111ar Red Cover; 112cr Green Stock Media; 112bl Martin Beddall; 112br Dominic Stichbury; 113a Cubo Images; 113bl Ollivers; 113cl Phil Lane; 113cr Holmes Garden Photos; 114 Alexandros Lavdas; 115al Richard Levine; 116a Renzo Piano © ADAGP, Paris and DACS, London 2022. Photo: Christine Webb Portfolio; 116c Richard Bryant/Arcaid; 116b Ian Badley; 117a Nick Hufton/View Pictures; 117c Photobywayne; 117b Adam Parker; 118al Alex Segre; 118ar & br Ian Dagnall; 119bl Picturesbyrob; 119br Domenico Tondini; 120al Lazyfruit Pictures; 121a Oleksiy Maksymenko; 121bl Adrian Sherratt; 124bl F. Jack Jackson; 125bcr David Lyons; 125br Greenshoots Communications; 126acr David Lyons; 126bcr Independent Picture Service; 128ac, 130ar ImageBroker; 128al Alex Ramsay; 128ar, 130al The National Trust Photolibrary; 128ar Anthony Wordsell; 131cl Ros Drinkwater; 138b Bildarchiv Monheim GmbH; 139ac Fotofacade.com; 139cl ASP Religion; 139c Alexander Shuldiner; 139cr Hale-Sutton Europe; 139bl Jos. Elias-Landmarks series; 139br Suzanne Bosman; 140b & 142bl ImageBroker; 141ar Jim Batty; 141cr Peter Barritt; 142ar Humphrey Evans; 142br Aidan Stock; 143ar Keith Morris; 144a Eclipse; 144b Marc Hill; 145al Martin Bennett; 145ar Keith Morris; 145bl Andy Myatt; 145br Miscellany; 146al Bildarchiv Monheim GmbH; 146ar Alex Segre; 146cl Martin Hughes-Jones; 146bl Geoff du Feu; 147a Built Images; 147cl & 148ar Red Cover; 147cr Michael Willis; 147bl Craig Steven Thrasher; 147br G. Wright; 148al Adrian Sherratt; 148bl Erin Paul Donovan; 148br Bildarchiv Monheim GmbH; 149al Miguel Angel Munoz Pellicer; 149acl ImageBroker; 149acr Lise Dumont; 149 bcl Geogphotos; 149bcr ICP; 149b Banana Pancake; 150al Art Kowalsky; 150ar Greg Balfour Evans; 150bl Chris Howes/Wild Places Photography; 150br E. Petersen; 151al Reimar3; 151ar Image Source; 151acl David Lawrence; 151acr Derek Trask Inv. Ltd.; 151bcl Michael Rose; 151bcr Moonbrush; 153al Mark Boulton; 153ac David Wall; 153ar ICP; 153bcr Bjarki Reyr; 153bl Martin Bond; 153br Jon Arnold Images; 155al Keith Shuttlewood; 155ar Ange; 155cl Travel Ink; 155c Lonely Planet Images; 155cr David Crossland; 155bl WoodyStock; 155br Inspirepix; 156al Vova Pomortzeff; 156ar Paul S. Bartholomew; 156cl Philippe Roy; 156cr Leslie Garland Picture Library; 156bl Faith Matters/Den Reader; 156br Jack Sullivan; 158 Funky Food London/Paul Williams; 159al Stephen Bisgrove; 159ar Diomedia; 159cl Jon Arnold Images; 159cr Phil Degginger; 159bl lcpix_can; 159br Greg Balfour Evans; 163a Renzo Piano © ADAGP, Paris and DACS, London 2022. Photo: Tomobis; 163b David Gee; 164b Maciej Wojtkowiak; 165al Angelo Hornak; 165ar Mike Booth; 165cl Bildarchiv Monheim GmbH; 165cr Robert Stainforth; 165b Holmes Garden Photos; 167al Stephen Dorey ABIPP; 167ar Archimage; 167acl Yadid Levy; 167bcl Stephen Dorey ABIPP; 167bcr Duncan Phillips; 167bl Tom Merton; 167br Michael Ventura; 168 Lourens Smak; 169 David Zanzinger

LAURENCE KING

Published in Great Britain by
Laurence King Student & Professional
An imprint of Quercus Editions Ltd
Carmelite House
50 Victoria Embankment
London EC4Y 0DZ

An Hachette UK company

A CIP catalogue record for this book is available
from the British Library.

TPB ISBN 978-1-52942-034-0
Ebook ISBN 978-1-52942-035-7

10 9 8 7 6 5 4 3 2 1

Commissioning editor: Liz Faber
Design concept: April
Design for this edition: Caroline Guest
Project editor: Gaynor Sermon
Picture research:
    First edition: Peter Kent
    Second edition: Giulia Hetherington

Front cover: Chartres Cathedral, west front, Chartres,
France, mid-twelfth century
Back cover: Centre Georges Pompidou, Paris, France,
1971–77 (Renzo Piano © ADAGP, Paris and DACS,
London 2022. Photo: Interfoto)

Printed and bound in China by Toppan Leefung

Papers used by Quercus are from well-managed forests
and other responsible sources.